Understanding European
Trade Unionism

Understanding European Trade Unionism

Between market, class and society

Richard Hyman

SAGE Publications
London • Thousand Oaks • New Delhi

SAGE Publications Ltd
6 Bonhill Street
London EC2A 4PU

SAGE Publications Inc
2455 Teller Road
Thousand Oaks, California 91320

SAGE Publications India Pvt Ltd
32, M-Block Market
Greater Kailash - I
New Delhi 110 048

British Library Cataloguing in Publication data

A catalogue record for this book
is available from the British Library

ISBN 0 7619 5220 9
ISBN 0 7619 5221 7 (pbk)

Library of Congress Control Number available

Typeset by SIVA Math Setters, Chennai, India
Printed and bound in Great Britain by Athenaeum Press,
Gateshead

*For Rebecca, who has helped me
to a clearer vision*

Contents

Preface

This book has a long and complex genesis. Since the 1980s I have had a teaching and research interest in comparative European industrial relations, and in particular the task of grasping theoretically the distinctive national characteristics and evolution of trade unionism. In the 1990s I tried to focus in particular on the detailed development of unions in Britain and Germany. At the same time I was concerned to analyse the ways in which three contrasting traditions – trade unions as labour market actors, as vehicles of anti-capitalist mobilization and as agents of social integration – were transformed and partially fused in response to changed circumstances and new challenges. To explore the configuration of three 'ideal types' of unionism seemed to require three national cases; and fortuitously a colleague and I, in editing a text on industrial relations in Europe (Ferner and Hyman, 1992), had been forced into the unintended role of 'experts' on Italy.

An invitation to contribute to a conference and subsequent publication on trade union ideologies provided the opportunity to work through some of these themes. The notion of a triangulation between market, class and society was born (Hyman, 1996a). It seemed clear to me that much needed to be developed; the article was in effect a book writ small.

In undertaking this work my concern has been primarily with current issues: how do unions in hard times respond to almost impossible challenges? How far are traditions and inherited assumptions a resource, how far a constraint? To what extent can labour movements escape from their past and redefine their purpose and identity?

To address such questions requires in itself an exercise in historical investigation and analysis. This is by no means an innocent endeavour. It has been said (Plumb, 1969: 17) that 'the past is always a created ideology with a purpose, designed to control individuals, or motivate societies, or inspire classes. Nothing has been so corruptly used as concepts of the past.' This work is not designed as a contribution to corruption. I recognize the truth of the old adage: people make their own history, but they do not make it just as they choose; they make it under circumstances encountered, given and transmitted from the past. The man with the beard had in mind a specific issue: how far people in society could shape their future to their own design. But as Plumb indicates, we also shape our own past (perhaps the better to control our future). Nevertheless, we do not make it just as we choose. 'The historian is engaged in some kind of encounter with an evidence which is not infinitely malleable or subject to arbitrary manipulation' (Thompson, 1978: 222). This is the spirit in which the present study is undertaken.

A work of this kind is never an individual effort. Many people have provided insights which have helped me greatly, and in general I have tried to acknowledge my debts. Others have made valuable suggestions for improvement in my approach, for which I am genuinely grateful. If I have not always followed their ideas it is inevitably partly from obstinacy, even more from doubts as to my own capacity to keep more than three analytical balls in the air at one time, most of all because the time between conception and execution has already been more than enough to try the patience of any publisher.

Plan of the Book

In the introductory chapter I provide a brief exposition of the theme of the whole work: trade union identity, ideology and strategy as outcomes of a tension between orientations which address respectively the labour market, class relations and the constructive role of labour in society. These three elements are examined in turn in the chapters which follow. The approach is in part conceptual and analytical, in part historical and narrative; and the discussion draws on experience not only in the book's three focal countries but on Europe more generally (and occasionally further afield). These chapters are unequal in length. That on the market is the shortest: 'business unionism', the dominant tradition in the USA and Britain, is otherwise exceptional, and arguments presenting unions as primarily or exclusively economic actors are simple in themselves and open to relatively straightforward challenge. The conception of trade unions as class actors requires more extensive treatment, since this has been an important perspective over an extended period in much of Europe. The longest chapter addresses the role of unions as vehicles of social integration, because the issues involved are in many respects extremely complex, because it is necessary to address a particularly wide range of themes and literatures, and because the rhetoric of 'social partnership' has acquired such salience in contemporary Europe.

There follow three chapters which consider the historical development, and current dilemmas, of trade union identity and ideology in three countries, the traditions of which can be seen as involving distinctive configurations of market, class and society. In developing these accounts I cannot refrain from drawing on the economists' notion of 'stylized facts'. This term, as I understand it, denotes propositions which, if they were true, would make an analysis and argument more plausible, but which it would be impolite to confront with awkward counter-evidence of an empirical nature. Historians and sociologists are surely entitled to some analogous licence. In the case of the present work, none of the points I present is (as far as I am aware) untrue; but the accounts I give are necessarily selective. In particular, I focus on what I perceive as dominant tendencies at national level, largely neglecting differences between levels and sectors. While the reader will find plenty of detail, I have nevertheless attempted to develop strong, and certainly challengeable, arguments.

My treatment of these three countries is again unequal. The longest chapter is on Britain: not only because I know it (and its sources) best, but also because of the long historical continuity of its labour movement, and the resulting multifaceted traditions which add special complexity to the story. For the same reasons, the relevant literature (I would suggest with confidence, if not total certainty) is far more extensive than for any other European country. Conversely, my briefer treatment of Germany and Italy might be seen as a reflection of relative ignorance. It could also be argued, more concretely, that their respective labour movements are of more recent origin than the British. Even more importantly, in both cases the fascist caesura, while not totally expunging the influence of earlier development, certainly entails that the trade unionism of the last half-century was in many respects a novel socio-political construct, and it is the developments of this relatively concentrated historical period which deserve primary attention for those concerned to comprehend the present.

The final chapter is also brief, and attempts to draw my arguments together and to suggest some implications for trade union strategy in today's integrating Europe.

1

The Strategic Orientations of Trade Unionism

A *Stylized Introduction*

In the Nordic countries, trade unions and employers' organizations are usually described as the 'labour market parties'. In Britain, it has been traditional to speak of the 'two sides' in industrial relations. In many other European countries, the normal term is the 'social partners'. These differences in vocabulary neatly encapsulate a core concern of this book. In different national contexts and historical periods, trade unions may be seen – by their own members and officials and by outsiders – primarily as economic agencies engaged in collective bargaining over routine terms and conditions of employment; as fighting organizations confronting employers in a struggle between hostile classes;[1] or as components of the fabric of social order. In some times and places, they may be perceived in all these guises simultaneously.

The Eternal Triangle: Market, Class, Society

Trade unions in twentieth-century Europe have displayed a multiplicity of organizational forms and ideological orientations. The pluralism of trade unionisms (Dufour, 1992) is associated with conflicting definitions of the very nature of a union, rival conceptions of the purpose of collective organization, opposing models of strategy and tactics. The dominant identities embraced by particular unions, confederations and national movements – themselves reflecting the specific contexts in which national organizations historically emerged (Crouch, 1993) – have shaped the interests with which they identify, the conceptions of democracy influencing members, activists and leaders, the agenda they pursue, and the type of power resources which they cultivate and apply. The clash between distinctive ideological visions of trade union identity has led in almost every European country to the fragmentation of labour movements.

To simplify the analysis of this complex diversity I identify three ideal types of European trade unionism, each associated with a distinctive ideological orientation. In the first, unions are interest organizations with predominantly labour market functions; in the second, vehicles for raising workers' status in society more generally and hence advancing social justice; in the third, 'schools of war' in a struggle between labour and capital (Hyman, 1994 and 1995).

Trade unions as substantial organizations were products of the industrial revolution, even though in some countries they evolved with no significant disjuncture from pre-capitalist artisanal associations. Indeed the very word *trade* union (which is not translated literally in most European languages) denotes a combination of workers with a common craft or skill. Initially their character and orientations reflected the circumstances of their formation: in most of Europe, brutal resistance by employers to assertions of independence and opposition on the part of the workforce, often accompanied by state repression. Such hostility in turn encouraged in trade unions militant, oppositional, sometimes explicitly anti-capitalist dispositions towards employers; and radical political attitudes which – in circumstances of restricted franchise and autocratic government – were not clearly distinguishable from revolutionary socialism. This, not surprisingly, reinforced the antagonism of unions' opponents.

Yet trade unions survived repression; over decades, indeed generations, survival encouraged and was in turn supported by some form of accommodation. Its features varied between (and often within) countries; but typically the latter half of the nineteenth century saw the more successful unions marginalizing or ritualizing their radicalism, and seeking understandings with employers on the basis of the maxim of 'a fair day's wage for a fair day's work' – a principle whose concrete meaning, Marx complained, was determined by the operation of the (bourgeois) laws of supply and demand.

The clearest instance of this de-radicalization was in Britain, and underlay the Webbs' classic definition of a trade union: 'a continuous association of wage-earners for the purpose of maintaining or improving the conditions of their employment' (1894: 1). Lenin, as is well known, was greatly influenced by the analysis of the Webbs when constructing his 1902 polemic *What is To Be Done?* Left to develop spontaneously, he argued, unions would become preoccupied with the defence of their members' immediate occupational interests. The tendency towards 'pure-and-simple unionism' (*Nur-Gewerkschaftlerei*) – an accommodative and typically sectional economism – could be resisted only through the deliberate intervention of a revolutionary party.

The debates of a century ago became associated with the triple polarization of trade union identities. One model sought to develop unionism as a form of anti-capitalist opposition. This was the goal of a succession of movements of the left: radical social democracy, syndicalism, communism. Despite substantial differences of emphasis – and often bitter internecine conflicts – the common theme of all variants of this model was a priority for militancy and socio-political mobilization. The mission of trade unionism, in this configuration, was to advance class interests.

A second model evolved in part as a rival to the first, in part as a mutation from it: trade unionism as a vehicle for social integration. Its first systematic articulation was at the end of the nineteenth century as an expression of social catholicism, which counterposed a functionalist and organicist vision of society to the socialist conception of class antagonism. On this ideological basis emerged in many countries a division between socialist-oriented unions and anti-socialist confessional rivals. Ironically, however, social-democratic unionism typically assumed many of the orientations of the latter, as social democracy itself shifted – explicitly or implicitly – from the goal of revolutionary transformation to that of evolutionary reform. Already in 1897 the Webbs (who were Fabian socialists) had called for unions to become agencies for the gradual democratization of industry; and across Europe, such a programme was increasingly attractive to union leaders who still proclaimed their socialist credentials but were anxious to legitimate their differences from critics on the left. Concurrently, many christian unionists adopted perspectives which were critical of capitalism, arguing that 'industry ... should have as its aim not private profit, but social needs' (Lorwin, 1929: 587). Despite their organizational confrontation, then, social-democratic and christian-democratic unionisms came to share significant common ideological attributes: a priority for gradual improvement in social welfare and social cohesion, and hence a self-image as representatives of social interests.

A third model, not always clearly demarcated in practice from the second – partly because its ideological foundations have more often been implicit than explicit – is business unionism. Most forcefully articulated in the USA, but with variants in most English-speaking countries, this may be viewed as the self-conscious pursuit of economism. Its central theme is the priority of collective bargaining. Trade unions are primarily organizations for the representation of occupational interests, a function which is subverted if their operation is subordinated to broader socio-political projects: hence they must eschew political entanglements. The clearest articulation of a business union ideology is in Perlman's *Theory of the Labor Movement* (1928), where he condemned the interventions of both revolutionary and reformist socialists as obstacles to the 'maturity of a trade union "mentality"' founded upon workers' need for collective control of employment opportunities. Analogous arguments can be found, however, in the efforts of many continental European trade unions to assert their autonomy from the socialist parties which had engendered them; or in the sometimes tense relationship between British unions and the Labour Party, in which a strict demarcation between 'politics' and 'industrial relations' was often jealously asserted on both sides of the divide. The British notion of 'free collective bargaining' and the German concept of *Tarifautonomie* both imply that there should be at most an arm's-length relationship between the sphere of party politics and that of trade union action.

Traditionally, the ideologically-rooted confrontation of competing models of trade unionism has possessed a self-sustaining dynamic. Each model, embodied in substantial organizations with inherited traditions, principles and modes of operation, has acquired over time a considerable institutional inertia. Yet in many respects, the historically embattled ideologies of trade unionism may be regarded as variants on a single theme: a triple tension at the heart of union identity and purpose. The eternal triangle (see Figure 1.1).

All trade unions face in three directions. As associations of employees, they have a central concern to regulate the wage–labour relationship: the work they perform and the payment they receive. Unions cannot ignore the market. But as

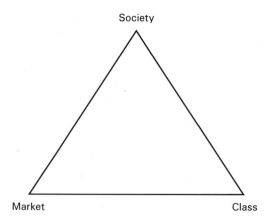

FIGURE 1.1 *The geometry of trade unionism*

organizations of workers, unions embody in addition a conception of collective interests and collective identity which divides workers from employers. Whether or not they endorse an ideology of class division and class opposition, unions cannot escape a role as agencies of class. Yet unions also exist and function within a social framework which they may aspire to change but which constrains their current choices. Survival necessitates coexistence with other institutions and other constellations of interest (even those to which certain unions may proclaim immutable antagonism). Unions are part of society.

In one sense, each point in the eternal triangle connects with a distinctive model of trade unionism. Business unions focus on the market; integrative unions on society; radical-oppositional unions on class. Yet a body resting on a single point is unstable. Pure business unionism has rarely, if ever, existed; even if primary attention is devoted to the labour market, unions cannot altogether neglect the broader social and political context of market relations. This is particularly evident when labour market conditions become adverse, when employers no longer agree to reciprocate in orderly collective bargaining, or when hitherto secure occupational groups find their customary position eroded. Unions as vehicles of social integration sustain a rationale for their existence as autonomous institutions only to the extent that their identities and actions reflect the fact that their members, as subordinate employees, have distinctive economic interests which can clash with those of other sections of society. Those unions which embrace an ideology of class opposition must nevertheless (as indicated above) reach at least a tacit accommodation within the existing social order; and must also reflect the fact that their members normally expect their short-term economic interests to be adequately represented.

Hence in practice, union identities and ideologies are normally located *within* the triangle. All three models typically have some purchase; but in most cases, actually existing unions have tended to incline towards an often contradictory admixture of two of the three ideal types. In other words, they have been oriented to one side of the triangle: between class and market; between market and society;

between society and class. These orientations reflect both material circumstances and ideological traditions. In times of change and challenge for union movements, a reorientation can occur: with the third, hitherto largely neglected, dimension in the geometry of trade unionism perhaps exerting greater influence. This is indeed a major explanation of the dynamic character of trade union identities and ideologies.

In the chapters which follow I explore this evolutionary dynamic, first by examining across a broad spectrum of national experience the ways in which market, class and society have informed trade union identity and practice; then by offering a stylized account of recent developments in three countries: Britain, Germany and Italy. In each case – and in international experience more generally – growing instability in the triangular relationship has generated major challenges for unions, while perhaps also opening new opportunities.

Note

[1] If this seems too strong an interpretation of the term 'two sides' one may refer to the Greek vocabulary of industrial relations; while the term 'social partners' has become popular in some circles, 'the trade unions and their supporters reject or avoid the term, and prefer to use κοινωνικοί ανταγωνιοτές (social antagonists) or κοινωνικοί αντίτταλοι (social adversaries)' (Kravaritou, 1994: 132–3).

2

Trade Unions as Economic Actors

Regulating the Labour Market

In most English-speaking countries, trade unions have traditionally been viewed as organizations the primary purpose of which is to secure economic benefits for their members; in particular, by advancing their 'terms and conditions of employment' through collective bargaining. From such a perspective, broader social and political objectives are of dubious legitimacy, or at best ancillary to unions' economic functions.

In this chapter I discuss the classic analysis of trade union functions presented by Sidney and Beatrice Webb over a century ago, and the doctrine of 'business unionism' which acquired particular force in the USA. In the latter model, industrial relations is perceived as a largely self-contained field of action. Unions succeed best, it is assumed, by their skill and determination in playing the labour market; other forms of union action do not facilitate, and may detract from, unions' economic goals.

Yet it is questionable how far the labour market can be treated as analogous to the general model of commodity markets; and likewise it is misleading to abstract market processes in general from the socio-political environment in which they are located. Accordingly, there is a contradiction at the heart of business unionism: trade unions can intervene effectively in regulating the labour market only to the extent that their aims and actions transcend the purely economic.

The Webbs: Beyond the 'Higgling of the Market'

'A Trade Union, as we understand the term, is a continuous association of wage-earners for the purpose of maintaining or improving the conditions of their employment': so ran the famous opening by Sidney and Beatrice Webb (1894: 1) to their history of British trade unionism.[1] In their subsequent 'scientific analysis' (Webb and Webb, 1897) they presented the core function of unions as counteracting the vulnerability of the individual worker in negotiating a labour contract with an employer who was, in turn, obliged by product market competition to cut wage costs while intensifying the pressure of work. Through the principle of the 'common rule', unions sought above all else to establish minimum standards in employment and hence to insulate the labour market from cut-throat competition.

The Webbs conceived trade unions as agents of a progressive revolution in industrial relations, a transformation from market anarchy and employer despotism to social control and regulation: hence the title of their major interpretative work, *Industrial Democracy*. In their reading, the earliest unions – exclusive societies of skilled craft workers – strove to control the market through the 'device of restriction of numbers'. They fought to defend a specific job territory, excluding outsiders from practising the trade and limiting entry by constraining the number of apprentices. If successful, this ensured an artificial scarcity of their specific category of labour so that the 'higgling of the market' operated in their favour. In the long run, however, the Webbs saw this form of trade unionism as futile, since it gave employers a potent incentive to bypass union regulation and to set up with non-union labour.

Hence their insistence on the superiority of the 'device of the common rule' which defined standard rates of pay, normal working hours and basic health and safety requirements without otherwise interfering with the individual contract between workers and employers. The common rule could itself be determined by any of three routes which they termed the methods of mutual insurance, collective bargaining and legal enactment. The first was the prerogative of unions with generous 'friendly benefits': the common rule was in this case unilaterally defined (usually on the basis of customary standards) and members who were unable to find employment on acceptable terms were supported by an out-of-work 'donation' from union funds. (The Webbs were, of course, writing before the introduction of an insurance-based state system of benefits for sickness, retirement or unemployment.) By its nature, mutual insurance presupposed relatively high union subscriptions and a labour market in which all but a small proportion of members could find work on union conditions; in effect it was a method available only to craft societies, and even for these it was unsuitable in times of market turbulence or rapid technological change.

The method of collective bargaining did not suffer from these limitations. The term, originally invented by Beatrice Webb (then Beatrice Potter) in her 1891 study of the cooperative movement, was not explicitly defined by the Webbs in their analysis[2] but denoted an institutionalized negotiating relationship between trade unions and employers (or their associations). The advantage of this method was that it facilitated adaptation to changed economic circumstances through an agreed compromise; the resulting common rule, being (relatively) acceptable to both sides, was likely to prove more stable than terms unilaterally imposed by either.

Yet collective bargaining also had its limitations. The common rule which it established was only partial, its scope being bounded (more or less) by the coverage of trade union organization. This meant, ironically, that those workers whose individual position in the labour market was weakest were least likely to benefit from the protection of collective regulation. Collective agreements were also potentially precarious: they could not survive a significant shift in the balance of forces between labour and capital, and adjustment to such shifts often involved bitter and protracted conflicts with severe hardship for the workers affected. For the Webbs, then, the logical conclusion was that the role of collective bargaining should be reduced to the regulation of issues of relative detail, while broad general principles should be determined by the 'method of legal enactment'. Statutory regulation of employment might be slow and difficult to achieve, but 'it satisfies more perfectly the Trade Union aspirations of permanence and universality than any other method' (1897: 255).

Business Unionism

While often sensitive to the subtleties of trade union principles and practice, the Webbs showed some considerable naiveté in their belief that legal regulation would increasingly prevail. They failed to recognize the special circumstances which led to extensive legal regulation in certain unionized industries (notably coal and cotton) which they considered prototypical, and seriously underestimated the force of trade union attachment to the notion of 'free collective bargaining'. For most British unions, statutory enactment seemed attractive only in circumstances of economic weakness; in general, it would long be seen as second best to the definition of conditions through agreements which unions themselves negotiated.

This conception of trade union function accorded closely with the American model of 'business unionism', particularly associated with relatively skilled categories of workers occupying a distinctive labour market niche. Such unionism, according to an early analyst of American labour (Hoxie, 1923: 45–6), is:

> ... essentially trade-conscious, rather than class-conscious. ... It aims chiefly at more, here and now, for the organized workers of the craft or industry, in terms mainly of higher wages, shorter hours, and better working conditions, regardless for the most part of the workers outside the particular organic group, and regardless in general of political and social considerations, except in so far as these bear directly upon its own economic ends. It ... accepts as inevitable, if not as just, the existing capitalistic organization and the wage system, as well as existing property rights and the binding force of contract. It regards unionism mainly as a bargaining institution and seeks its ends chiefly through collective bargaining.

This philosophy – that unions existed primarily to enable their members to secure the best attainable wage-work bargain – underlay the formation of the American Federation of Labor (AFL) in the 1880s and was propagated by its president, Samuel Gompers, with the slogan 'pure-and-simple unionism'. In the words of another early AFL leader, Adolph Strasser, 'we have no ultimate ends. We are going on from day to day. We are fighting only for immediate objects' (Gitelman, 1965: 81). As Brody has described it (1991: 284), 'pure-and-simple unionism specified a labor movement pared down to its economic essentials: its goals defined by the concrete job interests of workers; its structure determined by the industrial environment; and its strategy reliant on the exertion of economic power.'

As will be elaborated in the following chapters, those who regarded the labour movement as a vehicle for the pursuit of general working-class interests and for the transformation of society were critical of the model of unions as primarily labour market actors. Lenin, who had read the Webbs' work and was also familiar with developments in American trade unionism, denounced as 'economism' an approach to collective action which operated within a market logic and divided workers according to their various trades and occupations. For much of the European left in the twentieth century, the task of socialists (and social reformers more generally) was to transcend purely economic objectives and imbue trade unionism with social and political aims.

One of the strongest objections to this view was articulated by Selig Perlman (1928). His argument was that American unionism, with its concentration on directly job-related issues, displayed greater maturity than its more politicized European counterparts. Effective trade unionism was a means of collective response to the economic vulnerability described by the Webbs, pursuing workers' aspirations 'for a decent livelihood, for economic security, and for freedom from tyranny on the part of the boss' by securing their common 'job-territory' (1928: 273–4). The pursuit of limited but attainable economic objectives, attuned to workers' direct experiences in the labour market and at work, was for Perlman the only basis for stable trade union organization.

Much academic analysis has shared the conception of trade unions as primarily economic actors. 'The standard view of trade unions is that they are organisations whose purpose is to improve the material welfare of members, principally by raising wages above the competitive wage level' (Booth, 1995: 7, 51). The establishment of collective organization and the conduct of collective negotiations enhance workers' bargaining power, which in turn – according to theoretical and political standpoint – either redresses the imbalance of market power between employer and employee, or constitutes a form of monopoly which distorts the optimal functioning of the labour market. From a conventional economic perspective, unions as economic actors must be seeking to maximize some outcome: but what? In a famous early attempt to answer this question, Dunlop (1944: ch. 3) concluded that a union would seek to achieve the largest possible wage bill (numbers employed times average wages) in the sector of the economy which it organized.[3] Later writers have offered a wide range of variants on this theme (Booth, 1995).

Is there a Labour Market?

'The theory of the determination of wages in a free market is simply a special case of the general theory of value. Wages are the price of labour; and thus, in the absence of control, they are determined, like all prices, by supply and demand' (Hicks, 1933: 1). Yet is labour really a commodity like any other? And indeed, can there be such a thing as a free market?

Is the labour market a market like any other? And if so, what is the commodity that is exchanged in return for the wage or salary? Economists, and also lawyers, have long struggled with these questions. The employment contract is of necessity open-ended. Buy a kilo of potatoes and they become physically your property, while the seller parts company with them for good. But the employer does not buy a worker: that is what distinguishes wage-labour from slavery. Nor, typically, does an employment contract specify an amount of work to be performed: the flow of assignments in any job is to a greater or lesser extent unpredictable.

For this reason, as Marx insisted (drawing on the arguments of Thomas Hodgskin several decades before him), labour as such is not a commodity; what the worker sells is his or her ability to work, or 'labour power'. But here too there is imprecision: no contract can define the amount of energy to be expended, care to be taken, initiative to be displayed. The employer's requirements are rarely predictable in fine detail; managements therefore benefit from retaining a (usually wide) margin of discretion; conversely 'detailed job descriptions are not economic' (Marsden, 1999: 15). In most cases a worker agrees, as part of the employment contract, to be physically present on the employer's premises for a period of time which may or may not be precisely specified; and to comply with the 'reasonable' requirements of management in accordance with 'reasonable' standards of diligence and efficiency.

What counts in law as 'reasonable' (or more often, as unreasonable) has to some extent been indicated by the courts. As Fox has argued (1974: 184), in practice the notional contractual equality of employer and employee has been overlaid by the principle of unilateral disciplinary authority inherent in the feudal relationship between master and servant. However, the legally underwritten authority of the employer is in itself of limited practical effect, for few employing organizations can function without the active commitment and goodwill of the workforce. At the end of the day, moreover, an employer can merely dismiss a recalcitrant employee; no court can order 'specific performance' of work obligations. In reality, then, the content of the employment contract tends to be determined by customary standards of 'a fair day's work' and by the balance of mutual dependence between employer and employee (itself affected by the shifting forces of supply and demand in the external 'labour market', as well as by product market pressures). Under normal conditions, the fine detail of what is performed in exchange for a wage or salary is continuously subject to usually tacit negotiation.

Continuous negotiation is omnipresent for a different reason. Because the employee, unlike the owner of potatoes, cannot permanently alienate his or her 'commodity', any employment contract is in principle terminable. Even a 'permanent' contract is subject to a period of notice on the part of the employee, and usually the employer also. Commons (1924: 285) stated the position starkly: the contract of employment 'is not a contract, it is a continuing implied *renewal* of contracts at every minute and hour. ... The laborer is thus continuously on the labor market – even while he is working at his job he is both producing and bargaining, and the two are inseparable.' In most employments, of course, the default option is to maintain the existing relationship; the 'implied renewal' is rarely a question of conscious decision. Nevertheless, this temporal dimension is another factor underlying the peculiar status of the labour market. Paradoxically, indeed, the more a market logic pervades the employment relationship – the more that either party gives priority to a short-term calculus of costs and benefits, and hence devotes as much energy to bargaining as to producing – the less does this relationship accord with conventional ideas of commodity transactions as precise exchanges and the less likely is it to result in productive efficiency.

One further peculiarity of the employment relationship deserves emphasis. The contract of employment pertains to the worker as an *individual*; yet normally the performance of work, and hence the employment *relationship* more broadly defined, involves the workforce as a *collectivity* – what Marx termed the 'collective labourer'. There is thus a disjuncture between the formal basis of employee obligation, and the reality of productive relations at work (Erbès-Seguin, 1999: 217; Friot, 1999: 207). (This disjuncture is of course one reason for the often counterproductive effects of attempts to apply 'performance-related pay' on an individual basis.)

For all these reasons, labour is a 'fictitious commodity' (Polanyi, 1957). Yet in a different sense, the employment relationship also demonstrates a more general problem underlying purely economic conceptions of market relations. As Durkheim famously insisted (1933: 211–15), not everything in a contract is contractual: 'a contract is not sufficient unto itself, but is possible only thanks to a regulation of the contract which is originally social.' Every market system is necessarily 'embedded' in a structure of social relations: 'the anonymous market of neoclassical models is virtually nonexistent in economic life and ... transactions of all kinds are rife with ... social connections' (Granovetter, 1985: 495).[4]

The point may be made more emphatically: a free market is logically impossible. Historically, markets emerged as merely 'accessories of economic life. As a rule, the economic system was absorbed in the social system.' In all early capitalist societies, production and distribution were tightly regulated by traditional norms and by specific statutory controls: 'regulation and markets, in effect, grew up together' (Polanyi, 1957: 68). The form of this symbiosis, however, varied in particular according to national context; and in consequence, actually existing capitalism assumes many different national configurations with considerable variation in the institutional embeddedness of markets (Crouch and Streeck, 1997).

Partly in consequence, the concept of a market is itself elusive; it 'has taken on so many meanings that the success of any reference to it might be attributed to very loose and partially contradictory definitions which inevitably vary from one culture and language to another' (Boyer, 1996: 96). One aspect of this variation is in degrees of abstraction: a market may simply be a local square or building where goods are bought and sold, but to speak of 'the market' is often to denote a particular interaction of forces of supply and demand (O'Neill, 1998: 3–4). One can see a local market-place, hear the cries of the traders, smell and touch (and perhaps taste) the products on sale; but 'the market' in the more abstract meaning cannot be directly observed by any of the senses. Another difference is in the range of social activity encompassed: 'Markets may be defined narrowly in terms of routinized buying and selling under competitive conditions, or inclusively to embrace not only exchange but the production and consumption of the exchanged goods, and the particular property relations that hold therein' (Sayer, 1995: 98). This broader meaning typically underlies the notion of transition to 'the market' in, for example, the countries of central and eastern Europe.

In his classic analysis of the historical evolution of capitalism, Polanyi made a threefold distinction. In virtually any complex society, *markets* – the purchase and sale, or exchange, of products on the basis of some standardized notion of value – have played some role in economic life. He defined a *market economy*, however, as something far more specific: 'an economic system controlled, regulated and directed by markets alone' (1957: 68). Within a *market society*, such an economic system derived ideological legitimation from the predominance of values exalting individual freedom of contract and the self-interested pursuit of maximum economic returns within competitive markets. As Marx famously described it, in such an environment the 'fetishism of commodities' dominates social relations.

For Polanyi, the creation of a market society was 'entirely unnatural, in the strictly empirical sense of *exceptional*' (1957: 249). The paradigm case was Britain in the late eighteenth and early nineteenth centuries, where the establishment of a regime of economic liberalism reflected an immense *effort* on the part of its protagonists. 'There was nothing natural about *laissez-faire*; free markets could never have come into being merely by allowing things to take their course. ... *Laissez-faire* itself was enforced by the state' (1957: 139). As Gray has more recently put it (1998: 7, 17), *laissez-faire* 'was an artefact of power and statecraft. ... Free markets are creatures of state power, and persist only so long as the state is able to prevent human needs for security and the control of economic risk from finding political expression.'

One may note that the widespread moves in the 1980s and 1990s to re-establish such principles on the basis of ideologies of neo-liberalism have involved efforts in some ways similar in character, and are therefore quite wrongly described as 'deregulation' (Standing, 1997). To take the British example again, the 'withdrawal' of the state from economic regulation actually involved the systematic intervention of government in economic affairs and required an unprecedented increase in the societal pervasiveness of state power. As even more dramatically evidenced in Pinochet's Chile, Chicago-school market liberalism could be imposed only by a massive and brutal explosion of state coercive power. The outcome of intensified market pressures, moreover, has not been to establish an impersonal economic regime but rather to reconfigure the balance of social (and class) forces. 'Deregulation' actually consecrates new rules: intensifying the law of value, with effects which empower some economic actors while disempowering others (the majority).

Thus despite neo-liberal ideology, the state is unavoidably an actor in market economies. 'Far from being an unnecessary interference, the state is a normal feature of real markets, as a precondition of their existence. Markets depend on the state for regulation, protection of property rights, and the currency' (Sayer, 1995: 87). At a different level, as Polanyi expounded in detail, state regulation – in particular of employment relations – has been pursued in most market economies as a means of restricting the scope for a 'free market' in labour. 'The labor market was allowed to retain its main function only on condition that wages and conditions of work, standards and regulations should be such as would safeguard the human character of the alleged commodity, labor' (1957: 177). Unrestricted freedom of contract between employers and workers was generally regarded as unacceptable, whether on humanitarian grounds or from concern at the potential social disruption and disorder which might ensue if competition were to drive standards below a certain threshold. In most actually existing capitalisms, the state has performed an active role in both encouraging the operation of the market and in limiting its capacity to shape the conditions of employment.

Thus in market societies, the wage-labour relation is the product of social and political as well as purely economic forces; or rather, the economic context of employment is itself constituted by social and political structuration. Political economy, as Thompson insisted in his analysis of social protest in the early era of British capitalism, has to come to terms with a 'moral economy' grounded in the powerful hold of 'social norms and obligations' (1971: 79). This same notion of a 'moral economy' has been utilized by Swenson (1989) to explore the dynamics of contemporary trade union wage policy in Germany and Sweden: unions have necessarily articulated specific values which transcend a purely market logic.

Hence markets are subject to at least three potentially conflicting types of determinant: the forces of supply and demand which economists conventionally regard as alone significant; the policy interventions of governments, which are essential at a minimum to guarantee the routine operation of market relations; and the social norms which influence market actors, often in ways which cannot be comprehended in terms of simple material self-interest. In the specific context of industrial relations, this typically involves notions of the 'fairness' of wages in relation to the work involved and to the remuneration of other workers regarded as comparable (Hyman and Brough, 1975).

The Paradoxes of Market-oriented Unionism

If the labour market is only partially a market, and if markets in general can be no more than partially free, what are the implications for business unionism?

First, even committed 'pure-and-simple' unionists have historically shown some ambivalence towards the logic of a market orientation. In times of economic expansion, or when the union could control the supply of scarce skills, playing the market could yield attractive benefits. But in a period of recession, or when changes in technology and work organization allowed employers to put the squeeze on union members, the market logic proved less acceptable, and traditional principles of moral economy based on the ideas of workers' dignity and a living wage were commonly deployed. Famously, Samuel Gompers, when asked what were the objectives of his union, was reported to have answered simply: 'more'. This philosophy reached a dead end if the outcome of market forces was not more but less.

In the USA, the heartland of business unionism, market-oriented strategies yielded diminishing returns in the early twentieth century as labour markets became less favourable (partly because of waves of immigration, partly because of labour- and skill-displacing technologies) and monopolistic employers launched an offensive against trade union job controls. The advocates of a 'pure-and-simple' manipulation of market advantages were forced to reconsider their priorities. Ironically, towards the end of his career Gompers himself was instrumental in securing the inclusion in the Clayton Anti-Trust Act of 1914 of the statement that 'the labor of a human being is not a commodity or an article of commerce'; and as a member of the American delegation at the 1919 Versailles conference, he ensured that the new International Labour Organisation adopted the same principle (O'Higgins, 1997). The corollary seems clear: if labour is not a commodity, unionism cannot be a business.

A second implication has been elaborated, among others, by Flanders (1970: 88) with his distinction between 'market relations' and 'managerial relations'. The logic of this distinction is that trade unionists have an interest not only in the readily definable elements of the employment contract (pay, hours of work, holiday entitlement …) but also in the less tangible aspects of the job, including the processes of discipline and control established by the employer in order to secure and monitor work performance. Accordingly, unions – even those that profess themselves unconcerned with questions of management – cannot escape involvement in such matters if only by virtue of the need to influence the overall wage-work bargain.

Elsewhere, Flanders (1970: 224–5) developed a similar point in his critique of the Webbs. The consequences of what the latter termed the common rule 'extend beyond the securing of material gains to the establishment of *rights* in industry'. In prescribing rules which limit employers' freedom to hire and fire and to set employees to work as they will, collective bargaining is as much a political as an economic process. 'Far from being a change in the method of marketing labour, it has to be regarded as an institution freeing labour from being too much at the mercy of the market.'

Third, regulating the labour market involves political issues in the conventional sense of this term; this follows from the inescapably political structuring of any market economy. The state is not only the ultimate guarantor of contracts, including employment contracts; whether by active intervention or by default, it underwrites a particular (im)balance between different participants in market relations. At a very minimum, unions have to influence the ways in which the state shapes the rules of the game in the labour market, including their own right to exist, to bargain collectively and to mobilize collective action. Beyond this, even trade unions which place overriding priority on their own role as collective bargainers nevertheless take it for granted that the state should regulate at least some substantive aspects of employment contracts – notably, in every country, health and safety – and that part of their own function is to influence such legislation. This was recognized by Lenin when he wrote that even 'economistic' unions saw the need to 'strive to compel the government to pass necessary labour legislation, etc.' (1961: 375).

A fourth factor undermining the possibility of pure business unionism stems from the 'invention' of macroeconomic management in the aftermath of the Keynesian transformation of economic theory and economic policy. After the 1930s, the labour market could no longer be perceived, as was often formerly the case, as an autonomous mechanism; the parameters of supply and demand,

and hence the whole terrain of collective bargaining, were subject to the influence of government intervention. Hence industrial relations and politics could no longer be regarded as separate spheres; the one was conditioned by the other. For this reason too, even business unions could not ignore the state: they had to focus simultaneously on collective negotiations with employers, and on influencing the broader legal and economic framework of collective bargaining.

A fifth challenge to the coherence of a purely market-oriented trade unionism is that the wage or salary – the centrepiece of union action in such economistic conceptions – is itself subject to varying definitions. A century ago, when the philosophy of business unionism was most self-confidently asserted, trade union members were not subject to income tax and could expect few if any social benefits or transfer payments from the state. Today, the nominal wage or salary attached to an employment is only a loose approximation to actual take-home pay, and the latter in turn may not equate to what is generally known (at least in continental Europe) as the 'social wage'. Only if employees display what some analysts have termed a 'money illusion' can trade unions safely focus exclusively on the nominal pay of their members. To the extent that nominal pay, taxation and other deductions, and benefits and services obtained from the state are perceived as interconnected, unions have an obvious interest in influencing all components of the social wage.

Conclusion: Market Unionism and Political Economism

The force of these arguments should be obvious: even trade unions which would prefer to limit their activities to the immediate content of the contracts of employment available to their members are obliged to broaden their concerns to encompass the wider social and political dynamics which structure the labour market. In other words, they are forced to transmute economism into a form of trade union practice which elsewhere (Hyman, 1994) I have called political economism.

To exert effective influence on the market, trade unions must address the state, and in order to assert the relevance of an alternative 'moral economy' they must also participate in civil society. According to their distinctive ideological commitments and strategic orientations, national trade union movements and individual unions may do so enthusiastically or reluctantly. Their choices are also influenced by the specific national context of operation. Thus in countries (which include most of those in western Europe) where the state from was from the outset an overt protagonist in the shaping of a market economy, the political dimension of market intervention was self-evident for most unions. Conversely, in countries where the emergence of capitalism was less dependent on active state initiative, and where the political system made the imposition of alternative forms of regulation difficult to achieve, unions might conclude that there was no practicable option but to play the market as it currently existed. This was certainly Perlman's argument in regard to the USA (1928:196–7): 'American governments are inherently inadequate as instruments of economic reform [and] it is to this situation, more than to anything else, that the stubborn "economism" of the American Federation of Labor must be traced'.

Some unions and national movements, of course, never having regarded business unionism as an adequate *raison d'être*, have from the outset embraced a socio-political orientation as necessary and appropriate. Some of the implications of these alternative starting-points are explored in the following two chapters.

Notes

[1] When they revised the work in 1920 they broadened this definition significantly, referring to 'the conditions of their working lives'.

[2] They commenced the relevant chapter of their book (1897: 173) with the sentence: 'The nature of the Method of Collective Bargaining will be best understood by a series of examples'. For discussions of the meaning which the Webbs gave to the term see Flanders, 1954 and 1970; Fox, 1975.

[3] He discussed a number of possible qualifications to this simple definition.

[4] Jones (1996: 127) has summarized this argument neatly: 'Markets, especially labour markets, do not function because of price-regulated individual transactions by multiple participants. Social institutions are needed which allow such transactions to take place. ... The normative framework which gives particular markets their coherence and their functionality, and tempers the outright exercise of economic power, is best viewed as a form of micro-political regulation, as a social constitution.'

3

Trade Unions and Class Struggle

Contesting the System

Read accounts of trade union history in almost any country and the notion of class struggle is likely to figure prominently. The formation of collective organization commonly involved a fight against repression by the state and brutal resistance by employers. Every labour movement can record its martyrs; and the twin themes of building class unity among workers, and mobilizing against the class antagonist, persist within the iconography of many unions whose present-day situation is far removed from such origins.

In this chapter I present a brief account of the analysis of trade unionism developed by Marx and Engels more than a century ago, and the experience in the twentieth century of those who attempted to develop trade unions as agencies of class struggle according to marxist precepts. I go on to discuss three persistent tensions: between political action and 'economism'; between militancy and accommodation; and between a broad class orientation and narrower sectional concerns. These issues are related in turn to more general debates concerning the concept and theory of class.

'Schools of War'

'That these Unions contribute greatly to nourish the bitter hatred of the workers against the property-holding class need hardly be said,' declared Friedrich Engels after his first encounters with the British labour movement in the 1840s. 'As schools of war,' he continued, the Unions are unexcelled' (MECW, 4: 508, 512).[1] Soon afterwards Karl Marx, in *The Poverty of Philosophy*, declared that labour market competition obliged workers to unite in the face of their employers; and as the scope of their combinations expanded, so 'association takes on a political character' and the interests defended by their unions 'become class interests' (MECW, 6: 211). In the process, trade unionism established an alternative set of principles to the competitive logic of capitalism.

While Marx never offered a fully articulated theoretical analysis of trade unions – much of his writing on the theme was contained in correspondence and in polemic – his fundamental conclusion was that they could not function as purely economic institutions. Partly because he believed that market forces were too strong to allow trade unions to achieve more than limited and temporary success in defending (let alone improving) workers' conditions of employment, he assumed that unions would be obliged to mount an overtly political challenge to the basic principles of the capitalist order. 'The alternative rise and fall of wages, and the continual conflicts between masters and men resulting therefrom, are, in the present organization of industry, the indispensable means of holding up the spirit of the laboring classes, of combining them into one great association against the encroachments of the ruling class. ... In order to rightly appreciate the value of strikes and combinations, we must not allow ourselves to be blinded by the apparent insignificance of their economical results, but hold, above all things, in view their moral and political consequences' (MECW, 12: 169). Time and again Marx insisted, as in 1865 in *Value, Price and Profit* (MECW, 20: 148), that unions were 'fighting with effects, but not with the causes of those effects'; to attain their objectives, as he wrote the following year, they would have 'to act deliberately as organising centres of the working class in the broad interest of its complete emancipation' (MECW, 20: 192).

However, the 'analyses of the revolutionary potential of trade unionism' which Marx produced 'swung back and forth with cycles of class struggle' (Kelly, 1988: 11). At different times, he was forced to qualify all three foundations of his early, optimistic assessment: first, that struggles over wages and hours of work would become increasingly militant and embittered; second, that the compass of collective action would come to unite ever greater numbers of workers; third, that there would be an inevitable transition from economic defence to revolutionary politics. During much of the latter part of the nineteenth century, British trade unionism in particular – which was often considered prototypical of trade unionism in general – seemed to follow a very different course: the militancy of previous decades was moderated, as procedures of collective bargaining became established; the numerous, often tiny unions appeared primarily concerned with the particular occupational or sectoral interests of those they represented rather than the class as a whole; and there was often a reluctance, sometimes formally enjoined by union rulebooks, to entangle with issues considered 'political'.

This was not the whole story, and the complexities of British trade union evolution will be explored in a later chapter. Certainly the eruption of the 'new unionism' at the end of the century, after Marx himself had died, revived Engels' confidence in the anti-capitalist potential of the British labour movement. But the same historical experience informed Lenin's diagnosis of trade union 'economism': left to their own devices, without the active intervention of revolutionaries grouped together in a vanguard political party, unions would inevitably operate within the framework of the capitalist labour market and would shrink from challenging its constraints. In other words, they would be locked into the model of 'pure-and-simple' unionism which Gompers advocated.

The Social-democratic Model

The ideas of Marx were of considerable significance for the early development of socialist parties in continental Europe.[2] This can be seen most clearly in the case of Germany, where large-scale socialist organization was first established – most notably with the formation of the Social-Democratic Workers' Party (*Sozial-demokratische Arbeiterpartei*) in 1869.[3] What would be the relationship between the emergent working-class parties and the trade unions, which in most countries had far weaker roots than in Britain? Marx himself had played a leading role in the creation, in 1864, of the International Workingmen's Association (the 'First International'): a short-lived organization which linked representatives of most main currents of continental socialism with distinctly non-socialist British trade unionists. However, he offered no general prescriptions on 'the principles linking unions with political movements' (Moses, 1990: 110).

One school of thought – which Marx himself explicitly rejected – was propagated by followers of Ferdinand Lassalle, who had founded a workers' party, the *Allgemeiner Deutscher Arbeiterverein* (General German Workers' Association) in 1863, the year before his death. Believing in the existence of an 'iron law of wages', Lassalle considered unions completely ineffectual; if they existed at all they should be subordinated to the party and used as a recruiting agency for members and supporters. After the merger between the Lassalleans and the German social democrats in 1875, these views became one important strand within the rapidly growing European socialist movement. Others, however, adopted a different position, closer to the views of Marx: first, trade unions could yield some practical benefits (even if modest) for their members; second, the very process of combining within unions and struggling against employers would assist in the development of class consciousness; and third, in order to appeal to the widest circle of workers the unions should not be too closely linked to any political party.

In practice this dispute was settled by the evolution of trade unions themselves. German experience was a model for other European countries, for German social democracy was outstanding in its popular appeal, in terms of membership, votes gained at elections and (less dramatically, because of the undemocratic German constitution) parliamentary seats. Under the anti-socialist law of 1878, which remained in force in Germany until 1890, the activities of the party were severely hampered (even though its electoral achievements continued); but despite the government's intentions, the socialist-led trade unions grew rapidly and strike action flourished. The end of illegality was quickly followed by the centralization of the socialist unions under a 'general commission' (*Generalkommission*) headed by Carl Legien, the dominant figure in German trade unionism for the next thirty years.

Increased membership and organizational consolidation led to the pursuit of greater autonomy. 'The catch-phrase describing the unions as "recruiting schools of the party" was adopted by union leaders when they wanted to reassure the party of their loyalty. But it was also obvious that the now quickly developing union movement was trying to lose the image of being merely auxiliary'

(Mommsen, 1985: 374). Increasingly the leaders of the now substantial unions made explicit their reluctance to subordinate the policies of their organizations to the priorities of the party. This was symbolized at the turn of the century when they refused to support May Day demonstrations which might alienate both employers and non-socialist union members, and subsequently by their rejection of the idea of a general strike for political objectives. The party congress in 1906 ratified the separation of powers within the labour movement, accepting the unions' equality of status and urging both party and unions to seek agreement over issues which concerned both (Grebing, 1970: 117; Moses, 1982: 160–1). The separation of 'politics' and 'economics' should not be overstated: Legien and other union leaders remained committed social democrats (Legien himself held a parliamentary seat for many years). However, insistence on the relative autonomy of the political and industrial wings of the movement made it easier for the more conservative leaders of each to head off radicals who called for the fusion of political and industrial militancy (Steenson, 1991: 69).

While controversy over party-union relations arose most starkly in Germany, with local variations the story was repeated elsewhere. Indeed the formation of the Second (Socialist) International after the convening of the International Socialist Congress in Paris in 1889 facilitated the interchange of experience, ideas and strategies among social democrats and trade unionists across Europe.[4] Thus the German pattern was to differing degrees and time-scale replicated in other European countries. The typical scenario was that socialist parties emerged before effective union organization existed (except perhaps in the case of skilled crafts), and socialists took the lead in developing large-scale trade unionism. But once solid unions became established, these soon developed their own dynamic and asserted their own autonomy.

Nevertheless, socialist notions of class interests and class unity did influence the organizational form in which unions evolved. In general, socialists were suspicious of craft-based organization as sectional and divisive (though this was not universally the case: in France, for example, the principles of local and occupational autonomy shaped the approaches of many socialists to trade unionism). The preferred alternative was the industrial union, which brought together all workers in each sector of the economy and enabled a common front against the employers. In addition, establishing a strong central confederation was seen as a way of bringing the whole working class under one umbrella. (For some socialists, indeed, creating 'one big union' was seen as the ideal.) With varying degrees of success, socialist conceptions of class interest thereby shaped the emergence and consolidation of modern trade unionism in much of Europe.

Class and Trade Unionism in the Twentieth Century

In most of western Europe, developments in the past century have reflected the twin logics of the shift in social democracy away from revolutionary objectives, and the growing autonomy (though not complete detachment) of socialist-oriented unions from the 'parent' party.

Nineteenth-century social democracy was a revolutionary doctrine. Common to the various competing tendencies was the assumption that socialists could achieve their goals only through the abolition of capitalism (which might or might not require actual violence). But as socialist parties in many European countries recruited substantial membership and won considerable electoral support, so their actual practice usually turned primarily to the struggle within the existing political institutions for a programme of immediate reforms; overthrowing the system became a long-term, and increasingly rhetorical, goal. When Eduard Bernstein developed his thesis of 'evolutionary socialism' (the title given to the English translation of his book), he was denounced by most continental social democrats; but as Hook (1961: xiv) has suggested, 'Bernstein was doing little more than describing and approving the actual behavior, as distinct from the programmatic declarations, of the German Social Democratic movement and other Western socialist parties'. But Bernstein touched a sensitive nerve, for 'the more effectively reformist the Social Democratic Party was, the more important for its members was the ideology of apocalypse'.

The programmatic commitments to revolution became increasingly hollow, taken seriously only by a left-wing minority in most social-democratic parties. The crunch came with the 1914–18 war, when almost all European socialist parties adopted 'patriotic' positions and in many cases became members of national coalition governments. Revolutionary doctrine then became the preserve of the minority who broke away from official social democracy and subsequently declared themselves as communists.

As long as socialist parties claimed to believe in the possibility – indeed the necessity – of abolishing capitalism in favour of a new social order, there was a logic to the thesis that socialists as trade unionists should work for this greater goal, rather than concentrating on the pursuit of marginal economic improvements within the existing system. Once this ultimate objective was pushed to the distant horizon and finally into oblivion, this logic evaporated. Even though party and unions might still be regarded as wings of a single movement, they were no longer bound together – even rhetorically – by a single over-arching project. If each was concerned only with the pursuit of reforms in the here-and-now, it was hard to dispute the principle that each should determine its own strategy and tactics. Thus the logic of trade union autonomy was strengthened.

The relationship between party and unions was also influenced, in many countries, by the emergence of rival, anti-socialist trade union movements: a development discussed in more detail in the following chapter. The consequences were contradictory. On the one hand, to win the allegiance of the politically unaligned worker it might be prudent to stress unions' pragmatic concern with bread-and-butter issues and downplay their doctrinal affiliations. But on the other, a split between socialist, christian and liberal ideologies might encourage each separate 'labour movement' to highlight its distinctive identity. Hence socialist trade unions might be reinforced in their status as part of a 'family' with its own newspapers, mutual insurance societies, sports and cultural associations, and so on. 'Socialism in both France and Germany before the First World War,' for example, 'became much more than a political creed; it became part and parcel of a whole sub-culture' (Geary, 1981: 92). Thus embedded, trade union leaders (and even more their local activists and representatives) were both sustained but also restrained by a rootedness which was cultural as well as more pragmatically political; there could be no easy recourse to narrow trade union economism.

In effect, the typical outcome was a tension between principle and practice. Social-democratic trade unions in the main retained the language of class, and a conception of common class interests had a considerable influence on aims and methods, in at least three important respects. First, it encouraged a relatively egalitarian approach to wage policy: an approach facilitated by the organizational characteristics noted above, of industrial unionism and strong confederal authority. Second, the rhetoric of class struggle and militant iconography remained important in shaping unions' public identity, the motivation of many of their officials and activists, and the image presented to actual and potential members. Third, the boundary between 'economic' and 'political' action in pursuit of workers' interests was perceived as thin or non-existent; hence, for example, pressure on government to underwrite (at least) minimum standards for all workers was customarily part and parcel of trade union strategy.

Yet counter-tendencies were also important. In the main, unions were most strongly based among relatively skilled workers in higher-paid industries, and could not ignore the distinctive interests of this constituency. Moreover, union membership in most countries was overwhelmingly male, and egalitarian principles rarely extended to gender relations. (Indeed, social-democratic unions, like their catholic counterparts, often supported the notion of the 'family wage' with the corollary that a woman's place was in the home.)[5] Second, the development of institutionalized relations with employers and their associations made professions of class struggle increasingly ritualistic. Third, the logic of trade union autonomy was that a distinct sphere of union action existed, independent of the work of the party; in some countries at least, even social-democratic unions came to see legal enactment as a second-best form of regulation.

Revolutionary Trade Unionism in the Twentieth Century

The evolution of social democracy, and of trade unions associated with social-democratic parties, thus involved movement towards a form of business unionism which was nevertheless distinct from the 'pure-and-simple' unionism proclaimed by the American Federation of Labor. Class solidarity, and the ultimate transition from capitalism to socialism, remained important normative reference points in the self-consciousness of social-democratic trade unionists; even if anti-capitalist aspirations became increasingly detached from day-to-day trade union practice, there was an inherent tension which underlay the stabilization of bargaining relationships and which could, in times of crisis, bring old themes of class conflict to the fore.

This tension was reinforced by the fact that the drift to reformism was often opposed by radical currents either within the social-democratic unions or in rival organizations to their left. One such current, revolutionary syndicalism, involved in key respects a rejection of the social-democratic tradition. It reflected what was, for a time, the dominant tendency within French unionism (*syndicalisme*, of course, simply means trade unionism): emphasising the importance of workers' spontaneous self-activity, local autonomy and independence from political parties. Such independence did not, as was the case with 'non-political' unionism in many countries, imply a rejection of political objectives. Rather, revolutionary syndicalism implied a confidence in the insurrectionary potential of direct industrial action, a hostility to statist conceptions of socialism, and a suspicion that the stratagems and compromises of politicians would betray the revolutionary *élan* of militant trade unionists. 'The party was unnecessary for the emancipation of the proletariat, for this did not depend on the conquest of state powers, either by constitutional means or on the barricades; in fact, the party was a positive hindrance: it misled the workers, wasted their energy in the *cul-de-sac* of parliamentary intrigue and distracted them from the real struggle' (Ridley, 1970: 90–1).

In the early twentieth century, revolutionary syndicalism was an important, even majority tendency in some southern European trade union movements: in Italy and Spain as well as in France. From Spain, syndicalist principles also spread to Latin America. In northern Europe, in the years before the 1914–18 war, syndicalism became the rallying point of a minority of trade union activists who opposed the dominant tendencies within their own organizations: the constraints of centralized discipline, the unions' growing accommodation with employers, and their close links with social-democratic parliamentary politics. In Britain, for example, the syndicalist movement launched by Tom Mann after 1910, though its influence was commonly much exaggerated, certainly helped motivate an upsurge of 'unofficial' trade union militancy. Solidarity, class consciousness nurtured by collective struggle, the revolutionary General Strike: these were the principles counterposed to the new orthodoxies of organizational bureaucracy, cautious collective bargaining and respectable parliamentarism. One may note some parallels with the theory of the mass strike developed in 1905 by Rosa Luxemburg. Though she disagreed with the syndicalist idea of the self-sufficiency of industrial organization and struggle and insisted on the contrary that a revolutionary party was essential, she argued – in contradiction to Lenin[6] – that in favourable circumstances, localized conflicts over 'economic' issues could rapidly become generalized and inspire anti-capitalist political consciousness.

With the outbreak of war in 1914, the influence of syndicalism declined. Despite the internationalism and anti-militarism expressed by pre-war syndicalists, many were transformed into patriots. Those who held true to their former principles in many cases engaged in the more general anti-war campaigns within their national labour movements. The main revolutionary syndicalist tendency to survive embraced anarchism rather than socialism as traditionally understood, hence the more modern term anarcho-syndicalism. For the more orthodox left, the very concept of syndicalism soon became little more than a term of abuse.

But war brought new alignments between trade unionism and class politics. While official trade unions in most belligerent countries agreed an 'industrial truce' for the duration of the war, workers faced unwonted difficulties: the erosion of wages by unprecedented price inflation, long hours of work, speed-up of production, oppressive discipline, challenges to established rules of work organization, the militarization of civil life. The insatiable demand for armaments also brought an influx into the main centres of munitions production of a labour force unfamiliar with the pressures of industrial work and with the urban squalor which enveloped their non-work life.

Hence wartime trade union developments were somewhat paradoxical. European governments which had hitherto regarded unions with suspicion if not downright hostility now came to perceive them as a source of order in industrial relations, while the twin demands of the military recruitment and of war production made labour a scarce resource. In most countries union membership increased rapidly, at the very time that official unions forswore traditional methods of collective pressure. 'The war rallied labour *leaders* to the government and incorporated them into the system. At the same time the savagery and suffering brought about by the war alienated the *rank and file* from the system and opened a wide breach between leaders and "led"' (Kendall, 1975: 98). As the war dragged on without end in sight, eruptions of protest multiplied; and in factory, mine and mill there emerged new, unofficial structures of worker representation: shop stewards' committees in Britain, *Arbeiterräte* in Germany, *consigli* in Italy ...

Typically these emerged spontaneously as means of expressing employees' immediate work-related grievances and seeking to obtain remedies from the employer; but the often thankless task of representing their colleagues was frequently assumed by those with some form of socialist motivation, including pre-war syndicalists. In a number of cases such activists in turn developed a political understanding of the significance of workplace-based trade union organization. Leading theorists of the British movement saw their committees as a means of transcending divisions of skill and function within trade unionism, overcoming the conservative tendencies of full-time officials, and laying the basis for workers' control of the economy and of society (Hinton, 1973).

In Italy, Antonio Gramsci developed a particularly sophisticated analysis at the end of the war, based on the experience of the factory councils in Turin. He denied that there could be a general theory of trade unionism, for the nature of unionism varied according to contingencies of time and place: 'the trade union is not a predetermined phenomenon' (1977: 265). The formal, overarching structures of the union had a necessary purpose in establishing and defending an 'industrial legality' which guaranteed workers some rights within capitalism; conversely, a vigorous system of councils could counteract the bureaucratic and conservative tendencies inherent in official trade unionism and inspire more radical goals and tactics. Ultimately, the collective self-organization constituted by workplace representative structures pointed to the basis of a socialist society: through managing the productive process in their own establishment, workers developed the competence and the ambition to control the economy as a whole. Hence for Gramsci, 'the Factory Council is the model of the proletarian State' (1977: 100).

'Socialists had to adopt a stance on the war' (Geary, 1991: 40); and in most of the countries involved, this resulted in a confrontation between a 'patriotic' majority and an anti-war minority. Occasionally the consequence was organizational fission: as, notably, with the formation of the USPD (Independent Social-Democratic Party) in Germany in 1917 (Miller and Potthoff, 1986: 58–9). Elsewhere, as in

Britain, party unity was facilitated by the existence of a strong 'centrist' tendency which gave qualified support to the war effort but only for limited objectives, and favoured the aim of a negotiated peace (Middlemas, 1980: 25).

Divisions between reformists and revolutionaries, pro- and anti-war factions (the two fault lines not always coinciding precisely) acquired radically new significance after the October revolution in Russia (actually in November 1917 according to the western calendar). The outbreak of war had torn apart the Socialist International; now the Bolsheviks could redefine internationalism in terms of mutual support among revolutionaries around the world. Before 1917 the Russians had possessed only marginal influence within the European left; but as architects of the one enduring European revolution their status was transformed (Geary, 1981: 148). As *successful* revolutionaries, their authority to offer strategic guidance to foreign counterparts (even those with much longer traditions of political activity) was hard to challenge (though many, notably the Germans, did question their key arguments); while to *sustain* the achievements of revolution within an isolated and economically backward country such as Russia, as Lenin himself argued, would be impossible without revolution in western Europe. For such reasons, in January 1919 Lenin issued the call for the formation of a new, Communist International, which held its first congress in Moscow two months later.

The second congress, which opened in April 1920, was a more substantial and more protracted gathering. The mood of revolutionary optimism was still high, and the congress adopted detailed proposals on how revolutionaries should address the trade union struggle. 'The working masses are for revolution, the old trade-union organizations are against it' (Adler, 1983: 175). In addition, the congress adopted the famous '21 Points' defining the conditions to be met by any party seeking admission to the Comintern.

Early expectations that workers across Europe, inspired by social dislocation and economic turmoil as well as by the Russian example, would overthrow the old order were soon dashed. The third congress met in June 1921 in more sombre mood, and developed guidelines for trade union action which assumed a longer haul: a perspective which was even clearer by the time of the fourth congress in December 1922, shortly after the fascist coup in Italy. By the time of the next congress, in 1924, Lenin was dead and Stalin had won the succession. Thereafter the twists and turns of official communist policies owed much to his single-minded efforts to consolidate control, first against Trotsky, then against Bukharin; and perspectives on trade unionism tended towards stereotyped declarations only marginally connected to industrial relations realities.

Even before the Russian call to western supporters, the example of the October revolution had inspired moves to create communist parties in a number of countries. In Germany, notably, the revolutionary Spartacist League which Luxemburg had formed in 1916 took the lead in creating the KPD (*Kommunistische Partei Deutschlands*) in December 1918. Committed (against the arguments of its key leaders) to a policy of anti-parliamentarism and insurrection, the KPD later suffered severely from the abortive uprisings which took place a few months later (in the course of which Luxemburg and Karl Liebknecht were assassinated) and a large left-wing faction broke away. The remainder merged during 1920 with the left of the USPD.

In France and Italy the radicals within the main socialist parties were able to win a majority. In December 1920 the French socialist party (SFIO), having already sent a delegation to Moscow, decided to affiliate to the Comintern and renamed itself PCF (*Parti communiste français*); the anti-communist minority retained the old title. The Italian PSI (*Partito socialista italiana*) applied for membership of the Comintern and accepted the 21 points, but at its Congress in January 1921 refused to expel the 'reformist' minority; at this the 'pure communist' tendency broke away to form the PCI (*Partito comunista italiano*) (Horowitz, 1963: 157–8): a split which may have assisted Mussolini in his seizure of power (Middlemas, 1980: 32).

Among the 21 conditions for membership of the Comintern was the requirement that affiliated parties should 'carry on systematic and persistent Communist activity inside the trade unions'. Communist analysis emphasized both the limitations and the potential of trade unionism. Tendencies towards 'economism' and 'reformism' were inherent in union activity and were reinforced by the policies of most existing leaders, whose surrender to nationalism in 1914 had signalled an increasing willingness to collaborate with employers and bourgeois governments. Nevertheless – particularly in an era of economic disruption and political upheaval – unions could in principle serve a key role in revolutionary class struggle, and it was the task of communist parties to organize their members as disciplined groupings to realise this potential. Communists were to work within the trade unions under the instructions of their party to elect a more militant leadership, win support for more radical demands, encourage direct action by workers and help construct workplace organization which could respond directly to workers' grievances and aspirations. In 1920 Lenin (in the pamphlet *'Left-Wing' Communism, an Infantile Disorder*) warned explicitly against splitting away from 'reactionary' unions rather than fighting from within to reform them.

Yet such a strategy was possible only if internal opposition was tolerated by established union leaders – which could scarcely be taken for granted. Hence for example, in 1921 the anti-communist leadership of the French CGT, threatened by the growing influence of the left, carried out a programme of mass expulsions. Those excluded regrouped to form a new confederation, the CGTU (*Confédération générale du travail unitaire*). This experience indicated some of the tensions inherent in Leninist policy. Most labour movement organizations possess what Drucker (1979) has termed an 'ethos', a set of unwritten rules which include the principles of collective discipline and loyalty to elected leaders. Hence typically, communists who acted as an organized opposition grouping seemed in evident breach of such principles. This challenge to trade union 'ethos' was reinforced by the formation in 1920 of the Red International of Labour Unions (RILU, or Profintern) which vehemently denounced the 'yellow' International Federation of Trade Unions (IFTU) to which most western unions were affiliated (Nicholson, 1986: 69–72). From the outset, it was recognized that determined oppositional activity might inevitably result in a split within trade unionism (Braunthal, 1967: 174–5), though such division was initially viewed as a setback.

The difficulties of acting as a self-proclaimed 'minority movement' – the title explicitly adopted by the oppositional organization established by the British communist party in 1924 – however led some to contemplate more favourably the idea of a break. This was indeed to become official Comintern policy in the 'third period' of 'class against class' enunciated by Stalin in 1928, followed most importantly by the breakaway of the 'revolutionary trade union opposition' (*revolutionäre Gewerkschaftsopposition*) in Germany. Implicit (or sometimes explicit) in this analysis was the belief that unions as such had become increasingly irrelevant to class struggle, or could even be seen as obstacles because of the constraining effect of collective agreements and the conservative role of the 'trade union bureaucracy'; non-unionized workers might be more militant and class-conscious than union members.

This questionable thesis caused disarray within many western communist parties and was tacitly resisted in many countries. Despite Russian denunciations of 'trade union legalism', and the systematic replacement of many sceptical national party leaders by more compliant substitutes, in few countries did the full logic of this position shape communist practice. Britain was perhaps an extreme case, where leading communist trade unionists were deeply imbued with the norms of constitutional behaviour (Hyman, 1987) and certainly 'CP militants shrank from encouraging non-unionism' (Hinton and Hyman, 1975: 49). But the approach that Fishman (1995) has termed 'revolutionary pragmatism' – tempering ideological fervour to the contingencies of time and place – had echoes in other national movements.

After 1934 the formal position was altered once more, with the shift in Comintern line to support for a 'united front' with social democrats in order to resist the rise of fascism. In France this resulted, in 1936, in an amalgamation between the communist CGTU and the much larger CGT (Braunthal, 1967: 429). Further oscillations followed with the outbreak of war in 1939, denounced by the Comintern (following the Stalin-Hitler pact) as 'imperialist' – despite the initial pro-war position of the British and French parties. The line switched yet again in 1941 with the German attack on the Soviet Union; in the countries fighting the Axis powers, communists became ultra-patriotic and denounced any forms of trade union action which risked disrupting war production.

In the post-war era, with the introduction of the Marshall Plan and the onset of the cold war, the virtues of militant trade unionism and the political significance of industrial struggle were once again proclaimed. At international level and within many national movements, the brief moment of unity between socialist and communist (and in some countries, christian) trade union organizations gave way to new ruptures. Particularly in southern Europe, large communist parties with substantial electoral support tended to be associated with large, separate trade unions; where communist parties were weaker, their members and supporters were more likely to form an organized oppositional grouping within the established unions (Courtois, 1991). Nevertheless – and this is a theme explored in more detail in a subsequent chapter – the post-war evolution of communist trade unionism showed interesting affinities with the trends in social-democratic unionism at the turn of the century. Where communist trade unionists were relatively successful in immediate trade union terms – achieving a recognized status for separate union organizations, or winning official positions in non-communist unions – the links between 'politics' and 'economics' often came under strain. In such circumstances, maintaining the subordination of union activity to party discipline tended to prove problematic.

The 'traditional' communist conception linking trade union struggle and revolutionary politics then became primarily the trade-mark of various Trotskyist groupings and parties. In launching the Fourth International in 1938, Trotsky had adapted the Leninist conception of industrial struggle to fit circumstances of a world marked by economic recession, the rise of dictatorship and the threat of war. These features in his view reflected a terminal crisis of capitalism and the sharpening of class antagonism. In this context, he argued, the 'trade union bureaucrats' would increasingly betray the interests of their members; the task of revolutionaries was to challenge existing union leaders and at the same time to encourage the development of independent workplace organization and struggle. In this process, a key instrument would be 'transitional demands': workers' claims (such as cutting working time, without loss of pay, to provide jobs for all) which were objectively unattainable within capitalism but the struggle for which would raise workers' class consciousness.

With varying degrees of (usually short-term) achievement, organizations to the left of the communist parties sought to implement these principles in the post-war decades. In many respects, the problems besetting the militant class-oriented strategies of left-wing trade unionism in previous generations (first social democrats, then communists) recurred. The paradox was that the more successful the initiatives of trade union activists, whatever their politics, the more they were confronted by three interlocking tensions: between socio-political transformation and pragmatic economism; between confrontation and compromise; and between class solidarity and sectionalism.

Theorizing Class: The Implications for Trade Unions

The problem of 'economism', as has been seen, was a major concern of Lenin, and elements of his analysis (though not the label) can be traced back to the writings of Marx and Engels. The implication was that under 'normal' circumstances, most workers would be satisfied for unions to act primarily as vehicles for gaining limited material improvements in the here-and-now. How could this be counteracted? There were two, potentially complementary answers. One, central to Lenin's arguments, was that a disciplined minority of committed revolutionaries could exert decisive influence on the development of collective organization and collective struggle. The other was that 'normal' circumstances did not in fact permit unions to maintain and improve workers' conditions: capitalism made this impossible either through the routine functioning of the law of value, or through the destructive effects of recurrent crises. Under such conditions either workers would spontaneously develop trade union struggle into a challenge to the system, or revolutionaries would at least be able to work with the grain.

In practice, in the twentieth century, experience has given only limited support for these assumptions. With rising productivity, average wages have in the long run increased rather than diminished. Some traditional skills, and the material advantages associated with those who possessed them, have certainly been eroded; but technological innovation has created new scarce skills even as it has destroyed older crafts. There have indeed been phases of crisis; but often this has led workers whose position is threatened, not to radicalization but to a readiness to offer concessions to their employers in an effort to sustain the viability of the firm and hence their own continued employment. The proposition of most twentieth-century radicals, that the compromising tendencies of 'trade union bureaucrats' would be overturned by the militancy of rank-and-file workers, has received only modest and intermittent empirical backing.

Hence a key question both of empirical research and of theoretical analysis is what influences workers, in situations on the one hand of relative economic stability or prosperity, on the other of recession and crisis, to react in ways which either accommodate to the system or else challenge it. And what options thus exist for trade unions, and for radicals who aim to influence trade union policy?

The second tension concerns the relationship between militancy and accommodation. The classic Marxist assumption was that participation in collective struggle strengthened workers' understanding of their common interests with their fellows and their antagonism to employers (and also, in most cases, to the state). Hence strikes and other forms of oppositional action were essential components of anti-capitalist trade union activity. Many left-wing socialists in the early twentieth century objected to the whole notion of collective bargaining with employers, since the resulting agreements would restrict the ability of workers to resist their exploitation by their employers. Later, Trotsky denounced what he saw as 'compromise with the bourgeois-democratic regime' and the subordination of workers' interests to the priorities of the bourgeois state. Here, too, the assumption was that 'trade union bureaucrats' had a vested interest in accommodation with employers and with governments, which set them apart from ordinary workers.

Once again, experience has often indicated that matters are less straightforward. Unions which take every opportunity to fight the employer can expect retaliation; other than in times of social and political turmoil, most workers are unlikely to remain willing to accept for long the costs of such a mode of trade union action, and the outcome is thus likely to be defeat and demoralization. A union negotiator, in Wright Mills' famous phrase (1948: 8–9), acts as a 'manager of discontent': mobilizing workers' grievances and aspirations in order to put pressure on the employer, but then restraining them from disruptive action in order to protect the bargaining relationship. The pressures to combine order with militancy are experienced by workplace activists as well as by national officials, by political radicals as well as by moderates.

A second, more fundamental issue concerns the societal role of trade unionism: are unions unambiguously an oppositional force, or can they legitimately contribute to social stability? Classic marxist analysis in the first decades of the twentieth century assumed that capitalism and the bourgeois-democratic state were unstable, but that their double exhaustion would lead naturally to the transition to socialism. Experience soon showed that there was another alternative: the emergence of fascist or similar authoritarian regimes which destroyed both 'bourgeois' political democracy and the rights of autonomous trade unionism. Revolution could be reactionary, not necessarily emancipatory. If faced with such a risk, were trade unions impelled – in the interests of their constituents and of their own organizational survival – to defend the existing political order, even if this might involve moderating their own objections and actions? This became a crucial dilemma for communists in post-war Italy, for example.

Less dramatically but no less significantly the issue universally arose: was the acceptance of trade unions by their interlocutors – both employers and governments – an achievement which needed protection? As noted above, Gramsci (1977) regarded collective bargaining as a means to establish an 'industrial legality' whereby workers derived rights and protections in their relationship with the employer. Collective bargaining, and union involvement in governmental machinery, both represented at one and the same time an advance and a limitation, since both entailed constraints on unions' freedom of action. How should the costs and benefits be assessed and balanced? To such a question there could never be an unambiguous answer.

To the extent that trade unions are concerned with immediate improvements within capitalism rather than (or as well as) the struggle for socialism, and are under pressure to temper their militancy with a concern for stable relationships with governments and employers, in what sense can they be regarded as class actors? It was seen earlier that Marx himself complained, in 1866, that unions were 'too exclusively bent upon the local and immediate struggles with capital' (MECW, 20: 192) and neglected more general class issues. The paradox of collective organization is that it simultaneously unites and divides workers, since the boundaries of any individual union encompass only a section of the working class. The very term 'trade union' reflects the historical pattern in Britain two centuries ago, when workers in a single trade or craft banded together (often on a purely local basis) to defend their common interests: a defence which might set them against other workers as well as their employers. Modern trade unionism still involves organizational separation of workers on the basis of occupation or sector of employment as well as between nations and, in some countries, according to political or religious identity.

In addition to explicit organizational divisions between different categories of worker, it is important to note that less overt distinctions have always shaped trade union character and action. In most countries, the earliest unions were composed exclusively or predominantly of skilled male workers. As their categories of membership were enlarged, these groups retained a disproportionate influence. With the growth of large-scale mass-production industries, core groups of full-time production workers (typically male, white, with a stable place in the internal labour market) tended to dominate the processes of internal union democracy and normally set the collective bargaining agenda. At the level of national labour movements, priorities were imposed by the big battalions (typically the unions of manual manufacturing workers, notably metal workers). As a corollary, those in lower-skilled jobs with insecure labour market positions – and notably, women and migrant workers or those from ethnic minorities – have in most countries, and for much of the time, been marginalized within trade unionism: their interests not only neglected but rendered almost invisible. Where unions have indeed claimed to represent the general interests of the working class, what they have actually defended and advanced have traditionally been in large measure the particular interests of relatively protected sections. In Britain in the nineteenth century, for example, craft unions possessing in membership a fraction of the labour force with distinctive (relative) advantages were nevertheless widely perceived (and often perceived themselves) as representatives of a general world of labour.

Subsequently, other groups of workers often came to be regarded as representative of the labour movement as a whole even though their interests were distinctive. In many European countries in the first half of the present century, coal-miners assumed the status of archetypal proletarians and helped inspire a particular iconography and discourse of the nature of collective solidarity and collective struggle. The 'mass worker' in engineering production (and above all, on car assembly lines) subsequently constituted the 'model trade unionist' in much of Europe.

It is difficult to deny that the interests of full-time and part-time employees, male and female workers, those with recognized qualifications and those lacking these, manual and white-collar staff, employees in profitable and expanding firms and sectors and victims of economic decline, employed and unemployed, the relatively secure and the absolutely insecure, are not automatically the same. With careful and imaginative strategies they may perhaps be at least partially reconciled; but equally they may provoke damaging conflict. Competitive sectionalism has most commonly been the hallmark of trade union action.

Does this negate the whole idea of class as relevant to the analysis of industrial relations? In part, any answer to this question depends on how class itself is understood and conceptualized. Wright (1997: 44, 51), in his defence of a marxist approach, has noted that this 'has traditionally been constructed most systematically as a highly abstract macro-structural concept' and that a 'problem occurs when we try to move to lower levels of abstraction, since at a relatively concrete, micro-level of analysis there is no longer a simple coincidence of material interests, lived experience and collective capacity'. For this reason, the 'classic' marxist conception has commonly been challenged on at least three grounds: that capitalism does not generate a simple class polarization; that a purely economic model of class formation is inadequate; and that class, 'objectively' defined, is no predictor of collective consciousness or action.

Such challenges often derive from a Weberian theoretical position. While Weber, like Marx, developed an economic theory of class, its character was very different. For Marx, the mainspring of class relations was the system of production; it was the pressure to generate surplus value from workers' productive activity which created a bifurcation of class interests within capitalism. By contrast, Weber analysed class in terms of market position, differentiating between the ownership (or lack) of different types of material property and the possession (or lack) of the qualifications and resources enabling successful participation in markets (including labour markets). Yet the logic of this analysis[7] is that there exists a multiplicity (perhaps indeed a virtual infinity) of classes, since Weber's thesis was that each portfolio of material and qualificational resources (which to some degree surely differentiates every individual) entails a distinctive market situation and hence class location. This destroys any utility of the idea of class as a tool of social analysis, though Weber himself insisted on the key importance of the concept. Some later analysts have indeed responded by insisting that the whole notion of class is incoherent. Others insist that, at the least, one cannot *start* from the assumption of class unity: 'division of labour is not merely a modifier of the grammar of class' (Sayer and Walker, 1992: 29). A different but related argument is that the social embeddedness of markets results in the existence of many different forms of capitalism, with consequential differences in class structure: 'the class situations of individuals and groups and their capacity to pursue collective interests are in part shaped by diverse institutional structurations of capitalism as organized economic activity' (Hall, 1997: 31).

A second major argument of Weber was that class is not the only – and in most historical circumstances, not the primary – axis of social relations. He presented, on an analytical level equivalent to that of class, the notion of social status, 'determined by a specific, positive or negative, social estimation of honor' (1968: 932). While class determined an individual's 'life-chances', status was associated with a particular 'style of life'. Class and status were not coterminous, and Weber made clear his view that the latter was normally the more important in structuring the dynamics of social relations. To some extent as a corollary, he differed vehemently from the argument of Marx that 'in the last analysis' politics was derivative of economic forces – even though he agreed with Marx that economic conflicts often played a key role in political alliances and confrontations. Nevertheless, within Weber's framework it is rather easier than for Marx to account, for example, for the persistent importance in many countries of religious divisions within the working class and hence within trade union movements.

The third issue of key importance is the relationship between class and collective action. Just as Marx argued that only in specific circumstances did a class 'in itself' develop collective self-consciousness and act as a class 'for itself', so Weber insisted (1968: 930): 'every class may be the carrier of any one of the innumerable possible forms of class action, but this is not necessarily so. ... A class does not in itself constitute a group.' In what circumstances, then, do those in common material circumstances come to see themselves as a group with shared interests?

One starting point for an answer is that classes cannot be adequately analysed in isolation. As is well known, classes were originally the categories within which the ancient Romans were enumerated for census purposes; and this purely classificatory conception of class remains important both in sociology and in everyday discourse. Weber's own use of the term 'class situation', and his categorization of 'property' and 'commercial' classes, reflects this approach; yet at the same time he adopted a stronger meaning of 'social class' as a (potentially) collective actor. However, as Giddens notes (1979: 109), how the former connects to the latter is not adequately explained.

In the Marxist tradition, by contrast, classes become coherent categories only through their interrelationships. Touraine (1977b: 117) has insisted that 'to attribute a type of conduct to a class has almost no meaning; to situate it within the relations between classes, on the other hand, is indispensable'. Elsewhere he has written (1977a: 75–6) that whether or not classes in the past had a 'real' existence, today 'classes are not defined by their nature but by their action; hence for the first time we must reject questions of social class and examine only class relations, as Marx began to teach us'. Along similar lines, Thompson famously insisted (1968: 9–11) that in the past as in the present, 'class is a relationship, and not a thing. ... Like any other relationship, it is a fluency which evades analysis if we attempt to stop it dead at any given moment and anatomize its structure.'

One of the most stimulating attempts to explore the implications for trade unionism of class as a relationship was developed by Touraine (1966) in an early work, largely neglected by anglophone writers, on industrial relations.[8] For Touraine, three elements of workers' (class) consciousness can be distinguished analytically: identity, opposition and totality.

The principle of identity represents the categories whereby workers define their individual situation, the groups within which they perceive shared interests. This could be based, for example, on a particular area of employment (such as public administration) or a specific skill or profession. Workers may also identify themselves in much more general terms, for example, as being subject to oppressive management control or as receiving pay which does not fairly reflect their work. However, while the latter orientation may encourage class consciousness, there is no necessary reason why such a type of self-consciousness should prevail; it is no less likely that workers should define their interests in narrow terms, in contradistinction to other groups of employees.

Identity is linked to opposition: the perception of the 'other' – or more strongly, the 'enemy' – helps forge a sense of common identity with those whose situation parallels one's own. But opposition can also be perceived in different forms: for example, in terms of an individual employer, or of capitalists or the rich more generally. Particular workers – Touraine refers specifically to coalminers – may also perceive their situation in opposition to the rest of society, as socially excluded and denigrated.

Whether the reciprocal influence of identity and opposition encourages broad (class) or narrow (sectional) consciousness relates to the principle of totality: locating one's own position within a conception of a 'general interest'. This principle also involves, for Touraine, a view of society as dynamic: a set of relations which have historically evolved and which may be reshaped by deliberate, societal intervention. Underlying his discussion is a perspective on trade union history which is formulated more systematically by Durand (1971). The early phase of capitalist industrialization involved rapid social turbulence and disruption which were evidently societal in scope; this encouraged radical, transformatory projects in early labour movements. As capitalism became accepted as 'normal' and economic relations became more stabilized, collective identities (in particular among skilled workers) became more particularistic and objectives more limited. The subsequent spread of large-scale production based on less-skilled workers was associated with the rise of 'modern' industrial unionism. Here the principle of opposition was often strong, but defensive rather than offensive; earlier socialist visions of an alternative social order had become largely rhetorical. However, with a new phase of economic, social and technological transformation in the late twentieth century, the interconnectedness of different elements of change could once more be perceived, opening possibilities for the principle of totality to inform trade union action once more. The vanguard of such a movement was seen in a 'new working class' of technically qualified employees who bridged the old manual/white-collar divide.[9]

Like all stylized models of social relations, the identity-opposition-totality schema is problematic: some of the difficulties have already been discussed, and some were recognized by Touraine himself. One is that any individual possesses multiple identities; the salience of any of these can vary according to circumstance (Kelly, 1998: 30–1). This is particularly important in the context of trade unionism: 'wage earners, like any social class, and perhaps to a greater extent than other social classes, have multiple and contradictory interests' (Pontusson, 1992: 12). Institutional factors help define perceptions of interests, and hence identities, along specific lines. This influence may be reciprocal and mutually reinforcing: the craft-consciousness of a skilled worker may encourage active membership of a craft union, while the internal life and discourse of the union may underwrite that worker's sense of the centrality and worth of skilled status. The structure of trade unionism and of collective bargaining may – in ways which vary substantially according to national context – foster competition and division through 'coercive comparisons' between different groups of workers, or encourage a broader sense of solidarity (Hyman, 1992). Political or religious identities may likewise condition the ways in which individuals conceive their own status as workers; in many countries, different ideological attachments are of course both cause and consequence of union pluralism. It may well be true that the future prospects of trade unionism as a movement depend on 'its capacity to construct a global project around which can be built alliances to render partially contradictory interests sufficiently convergent' (Freyssinet, 1993: 9); whether, and how, this can be achieved is another matter.

Another key question is the relationship between work and non-work identities. As Giddens has argued (1973: 105), a key issue barely analysed by Marx (or many subsequent writers in the marxist tradition) is 'the processes whereby "economic classes" become "social classes", and whereby in turn the latter are related to other social forms'. There is a stereotype of the traditional proletarian status which emphasizes a common work situation, an integrated and homogeneous local community, and a limited repertoire of shared cultural and social pursuits. Though exaggerated, this stereotype does identify a core of historical reality, particularly in the single-industry manual working-class milieux in which 'modern' mass trade unionism had its strongest roots. By contrast, in contemporary society the spatial location and social organization of work, residence, consumption and sociability have become highly differentiated. Today the typical employee may live a considerable distance from fellow-workers, possess a largely 'privatized' domestic life or a circle of friends unconnected with work, and pursue cultural or recreational interests quite different from those of other employees in the same workplace. This disjuncture between work and community (or indeed the destruction of community in much of its traditional meaning) entails the loss of many of the localized networks which strengthened class identity (Touraine et al., 1987: 102–4).

If working-class identity is at best the contingent and precarious product of 'a series of particularistic loyalties and preferences and a widely differing experience of everyday life' (Eley, 1990: 26), the contours of class opposition are reciprocally contradictory and ambiguous. If differences of gender, ethnicity, politics, religion, language or life-style divide workers they may likewise unite those whose role in production is otherwise a basis for conflict. One evident instance is in societies structured on the basis of 'pillarization' (*verzuiling*) where workers and employers associate collectively according to their particular ideological orientation. Thus, for example, the nature and extent of opposition between catholic trade unions and catholic employers is limited by their common religious affiliation. In a less institutionalized manner, a common ethnic minority background may condition the relationship between workers and their employers (Ram, 1994).

Much more generally, opposition at work is conditioned by the fact that production itself is a collective process within which employers and managers may be viewed as making a necessary contribution. Within an economy based on a bewildering multiplicity of commodities and an elaborate division of labour, managements perform – and are perceived to perform – an indispensable role of planning and coordinating a complex and often baffling productive operation. Yet at the same time the pressures of product market competition mean that managers and employers are agents of discipline, control and disruption to employees' established status through the restructuring of work and (often) the destruction of skills and jobs. Whether workers react in ways which are primarily oppositional or primarily cooperative is typically unpredictable.

Moreover, in many areas of employment it is far from clear who is the 'opponent'. In the public sector – which in many countries employs the majority of trade union members – the employer is not easy to identify. Staff at every level may be united by a common sense of public service, even though this may have altered significantly under the pressure of budgetary constraints, work intensification, job losses and a growing exposure to 'market disciplines' (or indeed full privatization). Even in the private sector, the ownership of companies has become increasingly opaque (often vested in anonymous financial institutions); the managers with whom employees are in direct contact are themselves vulnerable; the company itself may be locked in a struggle for survival with competitors. In harsh economic circumstances, foreign competitors may be the opposition, while workers seek security by constructing a 'productivity coalition' (Windolf, 1989) with their particular employer.

No less problematic is the development of a consciousness of 'totality'. First, it could be argued that the whole logic of trade union action – particularly when institutionalized in collective bargaining with employers or 'political exchange' with governments – encourages a narrow focus on the agenda of negotiation and obstructs attention to the broader structural context. Second, it is by no means self-evident that awareness of this broader context will result in an ambitious goal of transformation: it may lead to the conviction that 'there is no alternative'.

Almost half a century ago some social analysts diagnosed the 'end of ideology'. This assessment was premature: subsequent decades witnessed radical, ideologically driven confrontations in many parts of the world. Today, however, orthodox communism has disintegrated with the fall of the Berlin wall; while orthodox social democracy has atrophied with the eclipse of Keynesianism, the rise of anti-egalitarianism and the triumphalism of free-market liberal ideology. The irony of totalizing consciousness can be seen in the 1990s with the predominance in both academic and more popular discourse of the idea of 'globalization': the encapsulation of an argument that transnational economic forces have become omnipotent, that national politics can involve nothing more than different ways of adapting to external constraints, and *a fortiori* that labour movements can survive only by working with the grain of the existing system (Hirst and Thompson, 1996).

Conclusion: The Necessity and Impossibility of Class Unionism

Why have trade unionists in so many European countries repeatedly defined their activities in class terms? And why is class struggle so often a point of reference for newly emerging labour movements in other continents? Part of the answer must be that class relations are a reality; that exploitation and insecurity are persistent features of the employment relationship. In this sense, whether explicitly or implicitly, trade unions are agencies of class.

Yet conversely, as we have seen, class-based trade unionism is elusive. The 'one big union' rallying workers of every kind within its ranks was never more than a dream; actually existing unions divide at the same time as they unite. And while unions may engage in struggle, they also regulate and normalize the employment relationship.

Class unionism thus constitutes a paradox. As we shall see, unions which define themselves as class actors nevertheless find themselves performing very different roles. Conversely, unions founded on a rejection of the principle of class opposition may nevertheless find themselves echoing the appeals of class radicalism.

Notes

[1] References to the Marx-Engels Collected Works (MECW) are given in the text by volume number rather than date of publication. I do not attempt in this discussion to give a systematic overview of the writings of Marx and Engels; for a brief review which I wrote many years ago see Hyman, 1971; for a more detailed critical assessment of 'classic' marxist writers see Kelly, 1988.

[2] For an analysis of the impact of Marx's ideas in Austria, France, Germany and Italy see Steenson, 1991.

[3] In the nineteenth century, the term 'social-democratic' denoted self-proclaimed revolutionary socialist politics; social democrats endorsed the view expressed by Marx in almost all his writings, that capitalism could not be reformed but must be overthrown – or that it would collapse under the weight of its own contradictions. It was Eduard Bernstein,

at the turn of the century, who first applied elements of Marxist analysis in order to challenge the revolutionary idea (see below); though the idea of reformist socialism had of course a much longer history.

[4] Well into the twentieth century, labour movement internationalism was almost exclusively Eurocentric.

[5] The structures and routines of trade unionism reinforced (and in many countries still do) this bias: 'the world of organised as well as unorganised labour was still the macho world of masculinity, of beer, bar and pub' (Geary, 1991: 28).

[6] Though it should be said that Lenin's own views altered over time from the position set out at the turn of the century in *What is to Be Done?*

[7] It should be noted that Weber, like Marx, never produced a systematic general account of his theory of class. In the case of Marx, Volume 3 of *Capital* concludes, famously, with a chapter on 'Classes' which breaks off after barely a page. Weber's core contribution consists of fragmentary notes, published posthumously.

[8] An exception is the study by Mann (1973), who draws extensively on Touraine's work.

[9] This brief summary inevitably distorts some complex and detailed arguments.

4

Trade Unions in Civil Society

Pursuing Social Dialogue

As was noted in the introduction to this book, in much of Europe trade unions and employers' organizations are routinely described as the 'social partners'. To the native English speaker, until very recently at least, the phrase appeared bizarre. A decade ago, when a colleague and I compiled a text on European industrial relations (Ferner and Hyman, 1992), we carefully edited our contributors' chapters so that the term was replaced by the more mundane 'employers and unions'. For many British militants, the phrase was enough to confirm their prejudices that their continental counterparts were not 'real' trade unionists but were bent on class collaboration. Similar perplexity is caused by the notion of 'social dialogue' which is central to the industrial relations project of the European Union.

Yet words – particularly when they undergo translation – are not always what they seem. We may note, for example, that in many European languages 'social affairs' is the closest available equivalent to 'industrial relations'. The idea of 'social partnership', as the following account demonstrates, has many available meanings, some more 'collaborationist' than others. One relatively prosaic reading is that trade unions are embedded in a host society, have a recognized status within it, and also possess the capacity to shape its development. There are close affinities between this conception and the Webbs' reference, over a century ago (Webb and Webb, 1897: 828) to 'the complete recognition of Trade Unionism as an essential organ of the democratic state'. This, one may note, has made the notion of unions as social partners suspect to many on the right as well as to those on the left.

What does it mean to regard trade unions as embedded in society? The meaning of society is itself imprecise and indeed contested.[1] Sociology is commonly defined as the study (more grandly, the science) of society, but sociologists are far from agreement on what this implies. One leading British sociologist has offered two, significantly different, definitions in a single textbook. One is that 'a society is a group of people who live in a particular territory, are subject to a common system of political authority, and are aware of having a distinct identity from other groups around them'; the other, that '"society" refers to the *system of interrelationships* which connects together the individuals who share a common culture' (Giddens, 1989: 731, 732).[2]

It is clear that trade unionists are subject (even if in some cases reluctantly) to national systems of political authority; and despite Marx's insistence that the workers have no country, trade union practice has often been shaped more by conceptions of national identity and national interests than by ideals of proletarian internationalism. What is also clear – as was argued in the previous chapter – is that unions through their actions, even if oppositional, become enmeshed in systems of interrelationships which at least partially integrate them within their society; and through their achievements, both economic and political, acquire a stake in defending elements of the social order against attack. In the process, while possibly rejecting aspects of the environing culture, they can scarcely escape absorbing many of its core features.

This was indeed a central theme in Thompson's assessment of the British labour movement in the nineteenth century. 'The workers, having failed to overthrow capitalist society, proceeded to warren it from end to end' (1965: 343). What was in one sense a defeat was in another a partial victory (and vice versa). Workers' struggles in crucial respects succeeded in humanizing capitalism; but 'each assertion of working-class influence within the bourgeois-democratic state machinery, simultaneously involved them as partners [that word again!] (even if antagonistic partners) in the running of the machine. Even the indices of working-class strength – the financial reserves of trade unions and co-ops – were secure only within the custodianship of capitalist stability' (343–4).

In this chapter I begin by examining the tradition from which notions of unions as social partners originated: the explicit challenge to socialist doctrines of class struggle. I then sketch the paradoxical assimilation within social-democratic trade unionism of many of the perspectives of its opponents. To this extent, ideological boundaries became blurred even if inherited organizational divisions persisted in many countries. Finally I consider how old notions of 'civil society' have assumed new significance in recent decades, and examine how far trade unions can be identified as actors within the renewal of civil society.

The Anti-socialist Challenge

In much of continental Europe, trade union development was shaped by profound cleavages produced in the eighteenth and nineteenth centuries by the transformation of traditional feudal rural societies into 'modern' industrial and liberal-democratic states. In many countries, this transformation was a traumatic challenge to the economic power and political privileges of the catholic church. Resistance by the church to institutional reform and to the intellectual rationalism which accompanied it provoked a strong anti-clerical orientation within the liberal bourgeoisie as well as in the infant socialist movements: a polarization which to this day remains significant in such countries as France and Italy (Crouch, 1993: 301).

The catholic church in the nineteenth century was a bitter opponent of socialism, which it regarded as a double threat by challenging the existing social order and by encouraging workers to act collectively in pursuit of objectives which they themselves defined. In a number of European countries, socialists reacted in turn by adopting an explicitly anti-religious stance, reinforcing the hostility of the church officialdom (Grebing, 1970: 126–7). Moreover, as Kendall notes (1975: 15), 'to the hierarchy in these years, even the ideology of simple trade unionism was unacceptable'; the church denied that there was any conflict of interest between worker and employer, and insisted that if collective organization were to be formed at all it should combine the two. From the late 1880s, however, there were initiatives by catholics in several European countries to establish their own non-socialist trade unions in response to the unquestionable success of the socialist unions, most notably in Germany, in recruiting mass working-class support (including many catholic workers). Such developments led the pope Leo XIII in 1891 to enunciate a 'new line' (*rerum novarum*).

The new papal decree began with an attack on socialism and an assertion that 'private ownership is according to nature's law'; this right 'must belong to a man in his capacity of head of a family' (1891: 259). The logic was that if the means of production became public property, a man would lose ownership of his own trousers – or his wife. Classes, the argument continued, were not antagonistic but complementary: capital and labour 'should exist in harmony and agreement' (261). However, this implied a reciprocity of obligations: workers should labour loyally for their employers, but employers should respect the dignity of their workers. Pay should be 'enough to support the wage-earner in reasonable and frugal comfort', workloads and hours of work should not be so excessive 'as to stupefy their minds and wear out their bodies' (265–6). Where these standards were not respected, it was the duty of the state to intervene. Collective organization among workers had a role, but mainly to provide mutual support in case of individual need rather than to put pressure on employers. Where unions were controlled by class-conscious socialists, catholics should play no part in them; if necessary they should establish their own separate associations.

In line with these prescriptions, 'christian trade unions' were established in a number of countries, particularly in the southern part of Europe. Often they functioned as friendly societies rather than trade unions in a broader sense. In the few countries where both religions were numerically significant, occasional attempts were made to combine catholics and protestants in single organizations; but such efforts were sometimes proscribed by the catholic hierarchy (as in the Netherlands) or if tolerated (as in Germany) were often accompanied by internal factionalism. Elsewhere, the preference of the catholic church was to establish 'mixed corporations' of employers and employees (Fogarty, 1957: 192). For the most part the religious-based unions had few members, lacked either the will or the resources to undertake effective collective action, and were often viewed by the larger socialist unions as 'yellow' organizations unwilling to challenge the employers. The latter for their part were typically reluctant to have dealings with 'this new interlocutor, moderate but independent' (Reynaud, 1975: 85).

Just as the socialist unions were often elements in an integrated system of working-class organizations, catholicism developed similar structures 'tying the worker into a whole nexus of confessional associations and culture, a product not just of the pulpit but of choral societies, insurance schemes, earthly as well as heavenly, educational associations, trade unions, political parties' (Geary, 1981: 77).

In practice there was a tension between the insistence on a just wage and working conditions consistent with human dignity – the principle that labour was not merely a commodity, properly subject to the blind forces of supply and demand – and the commitment to social peace. This was seen, for example, in the famous London dockers' strike of 1889 (an event which may have helped inspire the pope's pronouncement) when the key leaders were socialists but many of the strikers Irish catholics. Cardinal Manning, who had criticised as unacceptable the dockers' conditions, played an important part in mediating between union and employers. In negotiating this tension, more generally, catholic trade unions (the same was true of the smaller number of protestant unions which followed the initiative of catholics) could adopt a range of positions between supporting demands for improved conditions and resisting efforts to mobilize collectively.

Nevertheless, if catholic unions were to challenge the dominance of the socialists within the growing national trade union movements, it was necessary to demonstrate that they were not mere instruments of the employers. As Cole laconically remarked (1913: 171), 'these Unions were originally intended to be peaceful, and were founded by agreement with the employers; but with time they are being driven by the force of circumstances to take action in the same manner as the "free" [i.e. socialist] Unions. In fact, the catholics and reactionaries who founded them have often got more than they bargained for.' In France, catholic employers proved reluctant to deal at all with the more assertive and independent expressions of catholic unionism (Reynaud, 1975: 85). One should note, however, that a more independent and even militant orientation matched the views of many catholics, in particular those most enthusiastic to establish trade unionism: they were drawn to 'criticisms of *laissez-faire* industrialism and rejection of existing economic institutions. This fervent desire for change made acceptance of these unions by employers, conservative prelates and the state very difficult' (Brose, 1985: 3). Patch (1985: 19) notes that in Germany 'the member unions of the GcG [*Gesamtverband der christlichen Gewerkschaften*, Central Association of Christian Trade Unions] ... learned after 1900 that they must imitate the militant strike tactics of the Free unions if they were to survive'.[3] Eventually the official policy of the catholic church adapted to the new reality: strikes were no longer opposed on principle, and were seen as in some circumstances akin to a 'just war' (Fogarty, 1957: 193).

The more assertive stance in relation to employers went alongside changes in the membership and the leadership of christian unions. Many of the earliest associations were created for white-collar staff rather than manual workers; for example, the first recorded catholic union in France was established in 1887 with the aims of 'uniting catholic salaried employees, giving them moral support, helping them as far as possible to gain employment in catholic firms, organizing meetings and lectures' (Gonin, 1971: 21). But by the turn of the century the profile had changed. In Germany – where the christian unions (like their far larger socialist counterparts) had become the strongest of their kind in Europe – 'the christian unions soon attracted thousands of energetic working-class activists, which distinguished them from the dozens of other organizations founded to wean German workers from Marxism. By 1900 the christian unions were firmly controlled by the blue-collar members and sought primarily to serve their economic interests' (Patch, 1985: 1–2). As this comment also indicates, a more working-class composition was accompanied by greater autonomy in policy and practice (Wallraff, 1975). The first catholic unions were firmly subordinated to the control of the church hierarchy: 'the idea that workers and clerks were incapable of minding their own business died hard' (Fogarty, 1957: 192). But in an interesting parallel to the distancing of socialist unions from party control, the more catholic unions became consolidated the greater their ability to assert relative independence from the church.

The Consolidation of Integrative Trade Unionism

The war of 1914–1918, and the painful process of social and economic reconstruction which followed, brought in some countries a significant reconfiguration of the previously antagonistic relationship between socialist and christian trade unions. First, as was indicated in the previous chapter, in most belligerent nations the socialist parties and their associated trade unions gave at least qualified support to the war effort, and in part as a reward for their patriotism acquired new influence over government. Second, the rise of rank-and-file militancy, the revolutionary upsurge in much of Europe at the end of the war, and the creation of communist parties all helped consolidate social democrats as defenders of the social order; in resisting challenges from the left they were readier to find allies to the right. Third, continuing the process of partial detachment by christian trade unionists from the catholic hierarchy, this period saw the emergence in a number of European countries of a form of 'social catholicism' with anti-capitalist overtones. In combination, these tendencies laid the foundations for a trade union identity as 'social partners' – even though the term itself had not yet been invented.[4]

Perhaps the most notable expression of the consolidation of integrative trade unionism was in Germany. The majority social democrats, who had given their support to the war, joined the government shortly before the armistice; the trade union leadership was consulted and Gustav Bauer, deputy head of the *Generalkommission*, became minister of labour. In the closing days of the war, with Germany on the threshold of revolution, Friedrich Ebert was appointed chancellor.

Given the collapse of the old imperial order and the demoralization of the old ruling class, there was the possibility perhaps of a challenge to capitalism, but at the very least of the establishment of new social and economic rights for the working class. But the government made no attempt to curb the power of the army leaders and indeed encouraged the formation of a quasi-fascist military volunteer force, the *Freikorps* (Moore, 1978: ch. 11). In January 1919 Ebert presided over the repression of the revolutionary upsurge and the murder of Rosa Luxemburg and Karl Liebknecht. In the parliamentary elections of the same month the SPD emerged as by far the largest single party and headed the first government of the Weimar Republic. Restoring order in society and maintaining production in the factories were its priorities. But in March 1920 the Ebert government was forced to flee Berlin by the right-wing Kapp *putsch* – soon defeated after the socialist trade unions, supported by most rival unions, called a successful general strike against the *coup d'état*. However, 'the trade unions, in alliance with other loyal forces, had rescued the democratic republic; that did not stabilise it. In fact their intervention turned out to be a two-edged sword' in that the general strike in defence of the constitution was a display of workers' power which reinvigorated the right (Miller and Potthoff, 1986: 88–90). In the elections of August 1920 the SDP lost support substantially, and was replaced by a right-wing coalition which retained power for most of the decade.

The 'free' (socialist) trade unions had advanced rapidly in the latter part of the war and the period of post-war turbulence, claiming over 8 million members in 1920. By this date their structure had been consolidated with the formation of the *Allgemeiner Deutscher Gewerkschaftsbund* (ADGB). Despite programmatic commitment to the socialization of the economy and the transformation of workers' status, the ADGB leadership shared the same perspectives as their SPD colleagues: the priority of restoring order in industry. This became apparent in the negotiations during 1918 which resulted in an unprecedented agreement between Legien and the employers' leader Stinnes, signed in the days after the end of the war. The agreement established the *Zentralarbeitsgemeinschaft* (ZAG, central community of labour) as a 'common industrial alliance' to facilitate 'the coordination of all economic and intellectual forces and cooperation on all sides' (Moses, 1982: 223). For Legien, this was a means to combat 'unemployment, poverty and misery' (Borsdorf, 1975: 29): the employers agreed (though they failed to deliver) major improvements in employment conditions (Feldman, 1975: 229). Even the employers were surprised at Legien's willingness to collaborate in such a forum (Skrzypczak, 1975: 208–9), which provoked strong left-wing opposition within his own ranks. Thus the ADGB leaders hoped to conclude 'a partnership with their former enemies until the time when German social democracy attained power in Germany' (Feldman, 1975: 230).

The ZAG lingered on until the union withdrew in January 1924. By then it had served its purpose as far as the employers were concerned: helping to stabilize German capitalism in the turbulent post-war era and leaving their own prerogatives largely unrestricted by government.[5] The ADGB for its part was not shaken in its strong commitment to limited and cautious action. 'We in the trade union movement do not require a sun in the firmament but a goal which can be achieved on earth,' declared one of its leaders in 1924. The objective was still 'to discover a practicable and promising path to economic democratization by means of traditional trade union reformism' (Grebing, 1970: 180).

One of the major rank-and-file initiatives in the turbulent years 1918–20 – as in many other European countries – was the creation of unofficial workers' councils (*Arbeiterräte*), often led by revolutionaries. This movement was equally disturbing to the leaders of the SPD and the ADGB, and to forestall the challenge from below they agreed a law of February 1920 which established a more modest structure of works councils (*Betriebsräte*), drawing on earlier German traditions

(Sturmthal, 1964: 53–4). The law required the election of employee representatives (as in the modern German system) in all workplaces with five or more workers, with rights of information and consultation. However, the councils were required to 'support the employer in attaining the objectives of the enterprise' (Grebing, 1970: 156). Just as the ZAG could be seen as a vehicle of partnership between unions and employers at societal level, so the *Betriebsräte* were to apply the same principles within the workplace.

If the socialist trade unions had come to embrace many of the integrative assumptions of their christian counterparts, there was also in some respects a convergence from the other direction. Certainly, the 'red terror' heightened suspicion of the socialists on the part of the GcG, which in November 1918 took the lead in establishing a united front of non-socialist unions; but its leaders were also closely associated with the Stinnes-Legien agreement, which they considered 'a natural step in the course of social evolution long predicted by Christian theorists' (Patch, 1985: 37). War and revolution were seen by some catholics as symptoms of unfettered competitive capitalism; the only solution was to restrict the prerogatives of capital and to foster a more solidaristic social economy (Moses, 1990). The idea of 'christian socialism' was explicitly, if briefly, embraced by some: socialism could be approved as 'the idea of a new, higher, more complete community of life' (Grebing, 1970: 182). While many catholic trade unionists firmly rejected such a view, the official perspectives of their organizations – in contrast to the pre-war position – gave explicit attention to the need for political and economic restructuring at societal level. And despite initial hesitation, they gave their support to the general strike against the Kapp *putsch*.

Thus despite obvious continuing differences, the combination of social and economic crisis with left-wing insurgency brought a common emphasis by socialist and christian trade union leaders on the role of their organizations as vehicles of social integration. 'The leaders of both the Free and christian unions hoped above all to achieve a new, cooperative relationship with employers' (Patch, 1985: 35), saw the ZAG as a first stage towards class conciliation at national level, and envisaged the new works councils as a means of outflanking the radicals at factory level.

Developments in other countries may be treated more summarily. In France, as was seen in the previous chapter, the division within the CGT after 1914 – when a minority supported the war effort – was followed in 1921 by a formal split and the formation of the communist-oriented CGTU. In the process, the leaders of the CGT moderated their former class rhetoric and developed a more explicit defence of reformism. As its secretary Léon Jouhaux insisted, 'we must abandon the politics of the clenched fist and involve ourselves in public affairs. ... We want to be wherever workers' interests are discussed.' 'Trade unionism,' he declared later, 'can develop only within an economically prosperous State' (Reynaud, 1975: 78, 80). This moderating trend was, however, interrupted by the mass struggles of 1936, with widespread strikes and factory occupations which coincided with the 'popular front' elections and resulted in substantial gains for French workers. For the next half century, '1936' remained a potent point of reference for union activists, and helped sustain a 'struggle culture' within the CGT when its counterparts elsewhere in Europe had long redefined their identities (Jefferys, 1997: 135–6).

For their part, the various catholic unions regrouped in 1919 as the *Confédération française des travailleurs chrétiens* (CFTC). Initially its trade union objectives were extremely modest, subordinated to the emphasis on catholic doctrine; and the historically embedded antagonism in France between religion and anti-clericalism stood in the way of any organizational accommodation between CGT and CFTC. Nevertheless, during the inter-war period there was a convergence of policy. 'If the history of the CGT in the 1920s shows how the increasingly distant hope of revolution finally gave way to active reformism, that of the CFTC was exactly the reverse: starting from the most conciliatory of formulae, it gradually hardened its position until this had become close to that of its old rival' (Reynaud, 1975: 87).

In Italy there was no time for such an evolution. Despite internal divisions, the socialist *Confederazione generale del lavoro* (CGL) avoided a major split.[6] Though many of its leaders favoured moderate policies, in particular the participation in national programmes of post-war reconstruction, the eruption of rank-and-file militancy which reached its climax in a wave of strikes and factory occupations in 1919 and 1920 limited their room for manoeuvre; the CGL remained perhaps the most radical majority union in western Europe. As in France, Italian catholic unions regrouped in 1918 to form the *Confederazione italiana del lavoro* (CIL), which declared itself to be 'neither subversive nor servile' (Horowitz, 1963: 121). Militant and moderate trade unions alike fell victim to suppression after the fascist seizure of power in 1922.

Developments in Britain were very different from those in mainland Europe, and also difficult to evaluate; a detailed assessment is attempted in the chapter which follows. It is customary to regard British trade unions as the closest European analogues to American business unions, long committed to a pragmatic role as labour market actors. Hence overt ideological divisions have been more diffuse and less polarized than in other European countries. As indicated previously, union leaders in Britain had from the nineteenth century recognized the need for a political role to influence government policies in their own interests, but few defined themselves primarily as political actors. The socialism which was widely embraced by the 1920s was imprecise and undogmatic (matching the orientation of the Labour Party itself); hence British unions provoked no pressures towards religious separatism, while the communist challenge was far weaker than in other major European countries. Yet conversely it is common to speak of the 'adversarial tradition' in British industrial relations: trade unionists often stressed the conflict of interests between workers and employers, frequently employing the language of class struggle. Adversarialism stood in the way of significant moves towards integrative trade unionism.

Yet a very different reading of this period must be noted. Charles (1973), seeking to justify a catholic interpretation of industrial relations, has challenged the 'conflict theory' underlying conventional accounts. He stresses in particular, first, the Whitley Committee, established in 1916 to investigate 'relations between employers and employed' and which recommended the establishment of a system of Joint Industrial Councils at national sectoral level. Second, he discusses the meetings in 1928–29, popularly known as the Mond-Turner talks, between the TUC and a group of major employers to encourage more cooperative relationships in industry. These and other initiatives, according to Charles (1973: 302–4) helped create 'a positive philosophy of industrial relations' which centred around a 'co-operation norm'.

Despite a contrasting focus and analytical approach, Middlemas (1979) draws conclusions which in some respects are similar. In the period from the 1914–18 war to the end of the 1930s, British governments sought to underwrite social stability and industrial order through encouraging a form of 'corporate bias' which gave both business organizations and trade unions a status as 'governing institutions'. This triangular relationship developed early: 'by 1922 it had become clear that a sufficient number of employers' and union leaders had accepted the need of formal political collaboration with the state. TUC and employers' organizations crossed a threshold which had not even existed before the war, and behaved thereafter in some degree as estates of the realm ...' (1979: 20–1).[7]

Such accounts are at best one-sided readings of contradictory developments. Union leaders, as has been seen, had viewed influence on government as an important objective since the 1860s; significantly, when the TUC was established its governing body was called the Parliamentary Committee. Yet there was a constant oscillation, which continued throughout this later period, between a search for consensual solutions and a more militant and adversarial orientation. Certainly, the failure of the General Strike in 1926 helped destroy illusions that industrial militancy could bring governments to their knees, and encouraged a search for more cautious and methodical intervention in the policy-making process by such leaders as Ernest Bevin and Walter Citrine. But government responses were at best ambivalent and often dismissive. Likewise, the experience of 1926 certainly made many union leaders receptive to more institutionalized cooperation in industrial relations; but the employer participants in the Mond-Turner talks were unrepresentative of British industry more generally, and the initiative foundered (Lowe, 1983).[8] It is impossible to speak convincingly of a paradigm shift in British trade unionism between the wars.

Finally it is necessary to note that an important, but very distinctive, route to integrative trade unionism was followed in Sweden. Here, socialist trade unionism had largely escaped the divisions of other European countries: catholicism had no significant influence and communism was relatively weak. The Socialist Party (*Socialdemokratiska Arbetareparti*, SAP) and the central trade union confederation LO (*Landsorganisationen i Sverige*) had both been established at the very end of the nineteenth century and possessed a close organic interrelationship, cemented by their involvement in common struggles for a democratic franchise. Wartime neutrality insulated the labour movement from many of the tensions occurring elsewhere in Europe. In a predominantly rural society which industrialized late, however, both wings of the movement were relatively weak. Moreover they faced the opposition of a concentrated employer bloc with considerable political influence. Industrial relations in the first decades of the century were marked by an exceptionally high degree of conflict.

The main stimulus to a change in orientation was political. In the 1932 elections the SAP made substantial gains and formed a 'red-green coalition' with the

Agrarian Party. The social democrats were to remain in government without a break until 1976, initiating the development of an extensive welfare state and an increasingly elaborate structure of macroeconomic management (though without significant nationalization). The government also insisted on the need for more cooperative industrial relations in order to encourage industrialization and economic growth, threatening legislation if unions and employers did not themselves establish a lasting truce. This they did, in the 'basic agreement' adopted at Saltsjöbaden in 1938 and followed three years later by a change in the LO constitution which increased its powers over affiliates.

Hence in the 1930s the foundations were laid for an industrial relations system involving peak-level bargaining between LO and its employer counterpart SAF, strong central discipline within both unions and employers' organizations, and a dramatic shift from a high level of conflict to almost uninterrupted industrial peace. This transformation is open to a variety of interpretations. From one perspective (Korpi, 1978 and 1983; Korpi and Shalev, 1979) there was a strategic shift among Swedish trade unionists. Militant struggle with employers was abandoned because it yielded limited results and because a preferable alternative became available: the mobilization of political influence. The latter brought unions enhanced organizational status while institutionalizing full employment (Rothstein, 1990) and shifting income distribution in favour of their members. An opposing assessment (Fulcher, 1988 and 1991) is that Swedish unions succumbed, in effect, to the combined pressures of determined and strongly organized employers and a government which, while in one sense 'friendly', nevertheless gave priority to the requirements of private capital.

For present purposes it is unnecessary to choose between these rival explanations: it is the change itself which is of key significance. The accession to government of their political allies (and there was, and remains, a close overlap of personnel between LO and SAP leadership) 'encouraged a cooperative strategy by the unions. In exchange for social reforms and improved material conditions, the unions declared themselves prepared to show "social responsibility"' (Kjellberg, 1992: 95). Before long, the leaders of the Swedish labour movement would themselves evaluate their industrial relations model as the beneficial outcome of wise strategic choices in the 1930s. In important respects, Swedish developments prefigured post-war patterns elsewhere in Europe.

The Paradox of Social Partnership

The notion of social partnership in many ways encapsulates the tradition which evolved, first as an expression of christian trade unionism but then as a non- (and anti-) communist version of socialist class organization. However, the term itself does not appear to have come into use until after 1945 (and in most European countries, far more recently than that).[9]

The meaning of social partnership is far from obvious: it is an 'elusive and slippery concept' (Metcalf, 1999: 176). The term originated in German, first characterizing the collective actors in industrial relations as *Sozialpartner* and then specifying a broader normative order of *Sozialpartnerschaft*.

Almost certainly, the notion emerged first in Austria (Stourzh, 1986). Here, the interwar confrontation between strongly organized employers and trade unions had been one of the factors precipitating a bloody civil war and paved the way for the Nazi takeover in 1938; while the war brought economic collapse, with national income less than 60 per cent of the level in 1913. 'Both camps were determined to replace class struggle with cooperation. Concerted, consociational policy-making became the guiding principle and the promotion of economic growth and employment became the predominant goals of Austria's social partnership' (Traxler, 1992: 272). The collective organizations on each side saw themselves as important bulwarks of social and economic stability (Tálos, 1993: 18) and helped establish a complex system of wage and price controls ratified through annual peak-level agreements. This sustained institutional relationship in turn encouraged a 'political culture' of social partnership (Fürstenberg, 1985: 31). The newly constituted trade union confederation, the *Österreichischer Gewerkschaftsbund* (ÖGB) – whose leadership was dominated by right-wing social democrats – spoke of 'social partners' in its first report in 1947 (Traxler, 1982: 178, 183). Soon afterwards the ÖGB and one of its employer counterparts expressed their commitment to the principle of *Sozialpartnerschaft* (Franz Traxler, personal communication). This vocabulary did not, however, win a monopoly: more traditional references to 'the collective bargaining parties' (*Kollektivvertragsparteien*) remained in use (Tálos, 1985: 61) and some within the ÖGB preferred the term 'economic partnership' (*Wirtschaftspartnerschaft*) or 'economic and social partnership' (*Wirtschafts- und Sozialpartnerschaft*). There was a certain ambiguity here. For some, social partnership implied that the interests of capital and labour should be viewed as totally harmonious; 'economic partnership' implied a narrower form of collaboration between organizations in other respects opposed. Conversely, 'economic partnership' could be a formula for a more assertive (and potentially conflictual) role for the unions: claiming a legitimate role in shaping the macroeconomic policies of government and the investment policies of companies (Tálos, 1982: 267). Hence one of the ÖGB officials, writing in the 1970s, argued that 'social partnership tends to indicate that the [union and employers'] organizations come together only over employment issues [*sich nur im sozialen Bereich zusammenfinden*]'; whereas 'the Austrian system embraces all areas of economic policy. Therefore to the workers' organizations the term social partnership appears too narrow' (Lachs, 1976: 34–5).

In Germany, the term *Sozialpartner* appeared in the inaugural policy statement of the new chancellor, Konrad Adenauer, to the federal parliament in September 1949, as an affirmation of the principle of 'free collective bargaining': 'the autonomy of the social partners must replace their subordination to the state. ... A reasonable compromise between opposing interests is an essential precondition of national advance, and such a compromise must be achieved by the social partners themselves' (Adenauer, 1975: 162).[10] According to Schmidt (1985: 3–4), in Germany the term 'social partnership' was at first primarily an expression of christian-democratic social philosophy.[11] Before long, however, it was adopted by the more right-wing trade unions (Miller, 1982: 44–5).

The more stereotyped the vocabulary became, the more diffuse was its concrete meaning. Two principles, however, seemed to underlie its application in Germany, both linked to catholic doctrine. First, an explicit element in Adenauer's address, the notion of 'subsidiarity': that the state should not seek to prescribe employment matters but should leave these to be determined by the 'social partners' themselves. In this respect, 'social partnership' seems remarkably akin to the British notion of 'voluntarism'. Second, the concept implied that employers and workers have significant common interests and that their differences are susceptible to peaceful resolution (Gaugler, 1993: 991). Here, however, an argument which was once distinctly anti-socialist had by this time – as already seen – become implicitly, and often indeed explicitly, embraced by social democrats also. The requirement to resolve differences peacefully, and to 'cooperate in good faith' was indeed fundamental to the institutional framework of workplace relationships, often regarded as a key arena of 'social partnership'.

Around the same time the term *sociale partners* came into use in the Netherlands. Here, the background was the establishment of the bipartite Foundation of Labour (*Stichting van de Arbeid*) in 1945 and the tripartite Social and Economic Council (*Sociaal-Economische Raad*) in 1950. The implications of class collaboration were criticized by some left-wing trade unionists; but in general the phrase was uncontroversial. The post-war period was – as in Austria and Germany – marked by a sense of common purpose in rebuilding the economy and the country (*wederopbouw*, or reconstruction) which transcended ideological and social divisions (Peter Leisink, personal communication).

In its strongest sense, 'social partnership' reaffirmed the traditional catholic doctrine of the functional reciprocity of capital and labour, and the need for an orderly and harmonious regulation of their interdependence. Yet this doctrine involved an explicit hierarchical view of this functional interdependence: employers possessed the right to command, workers the duty to obey. 'Social partnership' could, however, be interpreted as entailing a parity of status between the 'partners': 'the notion of 'social partnership' nevertheless implies a notion of "equality" which is different from the traditional catholic social doctrine' (Patrick Pasture, personal communication).

Traditional catholicism can perhaps be identified with Therborn's definition (1992: 36) of one variant of corporatism involving 'an institutionalization of partnership and consensus'; here, an ideological bias against conflict generates strong normative pressures for industrial relations harmony. This may be contrasted with Therborn's second variant, 'an institutionalization, one might perhaps even say ritualization, of conflict'. Here, it is the experience of conflict between strongly organized parties which generates a pragmatic accommodation between the two sides in the interests of mutual survival (though pragmatism may with time acquire ideological reinforcement). This is Marin's interpretation of the Austrian example (1985: 92): 'corporatist co-operation does not imply a common ideology of class harmony. ... Rather, it transforms class conflicts into a permanent war of manoeuvre between interest associations'. Another way of understanding this distinction would be the contrast between 'social partnership' as an ideology of consensus or 'culture of compromise' (Katzenstein, 1984: 10 and 1985: 32) and as a set of institutionalized relationships between opponents whose legal status and/or organizational strength make mutual destruction or mutual accommodation the only options (Thelen, 1991: 126–32; Turner, 1998: 2 and 1999: 508–9).[12]

The pragmatic accommodation of opposing organized interests connected 'social partnership' to conventional industrial relations. In the words of a standard German glossary of personnel management (Tuchtfeldt, 1992: 2081), one meaning of the term is a 'contractual partnership. Social relations in the world of work are regulated by contracts in order to minimize possible conflicts'. In this sense, the concept has a very long pedigree: it can be traced back at least to the work of Sinzheimer in 1916, who wrote of collective agreements as establishing a form of 'social self-determination'. There was a trajectory, as Stourzh has shown (1986: 24) from the language of 'class antagonists' to 'negotiating partners' to 'contractual partners' to 'social partners'.

In its weakest sense, 'social partnership' meant little more than a positive evaluation of pragmatic give-and-take in industrial relations.[13] Yet this positive evaluation – the unapologetic endorsement of the principle of compromise as the central purpose of trade unionism – was in itself significant. To understand the new self-confidence of modest and moderate trade unionism, two key aspects of the post-war context need emphasis.

First, the inter-war years had exposed the fragility of the liberal-democratic order across much of Europe. Increasing class polarization, for previous generations of socialists the precursor of socialism, could be seen instead as the midwife of fascism. Far from challenging the existing order, which might precipitate a similar disaster, the mission of organized labour was now increasingly seen as to defend it. This status as *Ordnungsfaktor* was reinforced after 1948 with the onset of the cold war: as communist trade unionists sought to mobilize against the policies of western European governments, so their rivals tended in the reverse direction. In most of Europe it became increasingly difficult for trade unionists to reject the politics of the communist bloc but to sustain a militant oppositional role domestically. Another consequence was that the ideological differences between socialist and christian trade unionists became far less significant than in the past, given the new geo-political significance of their common anti-communism.

Second, in many European countries the old political and industrial elites had been discredited by their support for fascism or collaboration with the Nazi occupiers, while labour movements had gained in stature through their role in wartime resistance. The resistance struggle itself had often – notably, perhaps, in the Netherlands – inspired an ideology of national unity which carried over into the process of post-war reconstruction. The new era saw the widespread implementation of policies of macroeconomic management normally identified with the British economist Keynes, though there were other progenitors too. For many socialists, whether or not included in government (as in many countries they now were) this was an expression of their traditional ideal of a planned economy. Planning was moreover often accompanied by extensive nationalization[14] and a state welfare regime.

In such a context – viewed by some as a half-way stage to socialism – the question arose: must trade unions discover a new role? One line of argument was that, in a planned economy, the planning process must extend to wage determination. If 'free collective bargaining' was to survive, it must at least be adapted to the new macroeconomic regime through a coordinated process (either bipartite, through central agreements with employers' organizations, or tripartite, with direct government involvement) accommodating wage movements to overall economic circumstances.

A different, but often complementary argument was that the new circumstances offered unions a far wider portfolio of options than in the past. Rather than merely negotiating with employers (individually or collectively) over the terms of the immediate employment relationship, they could help shape the broader 'social wage'. Restraint in the traditional arena of collective wage bargaining could be a trade-off for influence over fiscal policy (important at a time when an increasing proportion of union members had become significantly affected by income taxes for the first time), enhanced welfare provision and favourable labour market policies, for example. Enhanced rights for trade union organization, in some countries associated with a formal consultative role in the formulation and implementation of public social and economic policy, could itself be linked (as both cause and effect) to the moderation of goals and methods. The strategic switch made by the Swedish unions in the 1930s now seemed an attractive option in Europe more generally.

This provided the basis for developments which in the 1960s and 1970s were often termed 'corporatist' (or 'neo-corporatist'): the close involvement of trade union confederations in bargaining with their employer counterparts (and often, directly or indirectly, with governments) in which restraint in wage negotiations was traded against compensating concessions, more or less substantial, to their advantage.[15] For critics on the left, the benefits were definitely *less* substantial than the sacrifices. Other assessments were less negative: for example, Regini (1984: 129) suggested that the attraction to unions was that peak-level concertation (a term which soon became preferred by many authors to 'corporatism') could create 'the possibility of modifying market outcomes to labour's advantage'. In yet another rendering, such peak-level concertation constituted a form of 'political exchange' (Baglioni, 1987; Pizzorno, 1978) in which the arena of collective bargaining shifted from the industrial to the political level. Also involved was a shift in the methods and resources of unions themselves: from the mobilization of economic pressure to the organization of political influence.

By the late 1980s it was becoming unfashionable to write of concertation, for a variety of reasons. First, in many European countries there had been a political shift to the right, with governments now firmly rejecting the unions' economic and social policy agenda and perhaps objecting in principle to 'corporatist' deals. Second, the capacity of individual national governments to pursue policies which bucked the general trend of an increasingly integrated international economy seemed to be declining. Third, many employers and their organizations proved less willing than previously to perceive their own role as 'social partners'. Fourth, in most countries the unions had lost membership (in some cases drastically) and their mobilizing capacity had been eroded; it no longer seemed necessary for employers and governments to buy their compliance.

Yet by the end of the century, analysts were diagnosing a return of concertation (Regini, 1997). The 'new social pacts' negotiated at peak level in various European countries displayed many different forms (Fajertag and Pochet, 1997). A common source, however, was the perceived weakness of many national governments. The neo-liberal policies adopted, albeit to very different degrees, from the early 1980s had achieved at best limited success; and economic stagnation and high unemployment threatened the legitimacy of the established political class. In many countries, involving trade unions as co-managers of crisis came to appear an attractive option for governments and employers. The same was the case, it should be added, at the level of the European Union, where the discourse of social partnership had become firmly embedded since the 1970s.[16]

Yet more than ever, hard times expose the problematic character of this discourse. 'Social partnership' could be justified in positive terms if it entailed union collaboration in the construction of a new and better social order: the optimistic vision of the first post-war decades. If it had come to mean sharing responsibility for the dismantling of many of the previous gains – acting as 'mediators of transnational economic pressures' (Mahnkopf and Altvater, 1995) the rationale could only be the pessimistic one that this was the 'least-worst option'. Such a role could further undermine trade unions' legitimacy both as economic representatives and as political mediators. The identity as 'social partners' was initially intimately linked – at least in many European countries – to the credibility of social-democratic advance. This credibility became eroded as the vocabulary of social partnership extended. The trend possessed particular poignancy and irony, since the last decades of the twentieth century saw a growing social-democratic domination of trade union movements in western Europe.

Trade Unions and Society: A Social-democratic Hegemony?

Paradoxically, the era when the integrative model of trade unionism came to predominate in western Europe also saw the eclipse of the specifically christian union organizations which had first been the bearers of its underlying principles. In Germany, former ideological divisions were transcended with the post-war reconstruction of the labour movement in a single confederation (the·*Deutscher Gewerkschaftsbund*, DGB) within which a minority of christian democrats coexisted, sometimes uneasily, with a social-democrat majority.[17]

A similar process occurred in Austria, where a unitary confederation with strong centralized control was established after the war. Despite the particularly close overlapping of the ÖGB leadership and that of the Social-democratic Party (SPÖ), all political and confessional tendencies were united in the new confederation, which uniquely in western Europe encompassed the whole of organized labour. A distinct catholic 'fraction' was created in the early 1950s, with semi-official status.[18]

In Italy, likewise, a unitary confederation (the *Confederazione generale italiana del lavoro*, CGIL) was established in 1944, with the communists as the largest political tendency; but with the onset of the cold war most catholics and many socialists broke away. Partly with American assistance, two new confederations were established, the *Confederazione italiana dei sindacati lavoratori* (CISL) and the *Unione italiana del lavoro* (UIL) (Bedani, 1995; Romero, 1992). While CISL was dominated by catholics, in turn closely linked to the christian-democratic party, it was however never formally based on religious ideology, claiming to be open to 'all those trade union forces which follow the same objectives of independence and democracy' (Horowitz, 1963: 222). Over time, moreover, it became increasingly detached from its original political-ideological identity, and many of its activists and officials were socialists.

A similar 'deconfessionalization' occurred in France. Here, at the end of the war the catholic CFTC refused to unite with socialists and communists in a single union;[19] but there were serious internal divisions between those anxious to emphasize a religious identity and those with a more humanistic orientation (Mouriaux, 1983: 190–92). In 1964 a large majority voted to abandon any religious identification and to change the name to *Confédération française démocratique du travail* (CFDT); a small minority maintained the former title and principles (Gonin, 1971; Groux and Mouriaux, 1989). For a period at least, the CFDT embraced a radical socialist programme, including demands for workers' control of production (*autogestion*).

In the Netherlands, where the traditional division of society into socialist, catholic and protestant 'pillars' was mirrored in an ideologically divided trade union movement, a merger process between the socialists and catholics (the two largest trade union 'pillars') took place during the 1970s.[20] For several decades, Belgium has been the only European country in which a substantial trade union with an explicit religious identity has survived (Pasture, 1994). The dwindling significance of the old rivalry between christian and socialist trade union movements was signalled in 1974 when the European Trade Union Confederation (ETUC), created the previous year by European affiliates of the mainly social-democratic International Confederation of Free Trade Unions (ICFTU), accepted into membership the main catholic and ex-catholic unions.[21]

The eclipse of distinctive christian unionism was followed by what might be termed the social-democratization of communist unionism. As was noted in the previous chapter, in those (mainly southern) European countries where communist unions attracted substantial membership,[22] they faced the same tensions evident in social-democratic unions in the first decades of the century: between party control and autonomy, and between ultimate revolutionary aims and everyday reformist practice.

Three main developments help explain the outcome of these tensions. First was the impact on western communists of the suppression of the reform movements in Hungary in 1956 and Czechoslovakia in 1968, often shattering former uncritical loyalty to Moscow. Second, the stabilization of post-war capitalism and of the post-war polities of western Europe put in question former models of revolutionary transformation, encouraging the emergence of a 'Eurocommunism' which looked to a more gradual and incremental process of constructing aspirations for and confidence in a new social order. Third, the creation of the European Community posed serious dilemmas: whether simply to denounce the 'Europe of the capitalists and monopolists', or to engage critically but constructively in efforts to shape the direction of European integration. All these developments divided communist parties and their associated unions; the collapse of the Soviet bloc after 1989 provided the *coup de grâce*.

The process began in Italy, with the largest communist party in western Europe (the PCI) attracting for some time roughly a third of the popular vote, and with the associated CGIL confederation by far the largest trade union. Three important developments in the 1970s marked the transformation. First, the upsurge in collective organization and militancy at the end of the 1960s brought a close collaboration between the three main union confederations (for a time, fusion seemed possible) and it was agreed that their leaderships should loosen their ties to their associated political parties. Second, the PCI – already more critical of Moscow than most of its western counterparts – made a bid to move into the political mainstream and seek a 'historic compromise' with other progressive forces. This change was inspired in part by the threat of right-wing political violence and a fear of a fascist coup. Third, political disorder and economic crisis encouraged governments to involve the unions in a process of political exchange, to which CGIL – despite intermittent strains – gave explicit or implicit support.

The shift of CGIL from many of its political traditions – a process to be explored in detail in a later chapter – involved, in effect, the adoption of many of the policies and perspectives formerly associated with its ideological rivals. In other words, it adapted to the dominant social-democratic orientation of western European trade unionism. This change of character was recognized in 1974 when the newly established ETUC accepted CGIL as a member – though only after the latter had ended its membership of the Moscow-dominated World Federation of Trade Unions (WFTU).

The Italian example was soon followed in Spain. Under the Franco regime the clandestine communist party (PCE) had coordinated shop-floor workers' commissions as the main trade union opposition to the official fascist structures. Soon after Franco's death in 1975 the commissions became the basis of a national trade union, the *Comisiones Obreras* (CC.OO.), with a commitment to workplace activism and militancy. When a series of national social pacts was agreed by its newly-formed social-democratic rival, the UGT, the CC.OO. at first held aloof; but after the threat of a right-wing military coup in 1981 it too became a signatory (Martínez Lucio, 1992: 503–5). The growing conversion of CC.OO. to the principle of political exchange, and – to some degree – to a more moderate industrial strategy, was also in line with the Eurocommunist orientation of the PCE leadership itself. In effect, a process of social-democratization occurred in Spain also, and CC.OO. too was eventually deemed suitable for ETUC membership.[23]

For a long time the main exception to this process was in France, where the communist party (PCF) maintained a rigid commitment to traditional orthodoxies and stamped on internal dissidence. Though the CGT was in theory independent of the party and indeed always elected a non-communist minority to its leadership, in practice it followed closely the policies of the PCF. In the 1990s, however, with the end of doctrinal leadership (and financial subventions) from the east, and with electoral support for the PCF severely reduced, it was necessary to develop new political orientations; after a change of leadership the PCF began a painful process of redefining its objectives. The CGT itself, suffering a sustained and severe decline in membership, was forced to seek new directions. In December 1995 it withdrew from WFTU (by now a hollow shell, with the collapse or re-orientation of most of the state-controlled unions of the former Soviet bloc) and adopted a new set of statutes. These came close to eliminating the old appeals to anti-capitalist class struggle, and affirmed a commitment to the ideals of 'liberty, equality, justice, laicity, fraternity and solidarity'. There was little here to distinguish the CGT from it main rivals. Its ideological accommodation with the social-democratic centre was rewarded in 1999 when it too was admitted to the ETUC.

The Rediscovery of Civil Society

The previous discussion referred rather loosely to the hegemony of social-democratic trade unionism; necessarily so, for in the past half century when this has become the dominant organizational form of west European unionism its meaning and orientation have become increasingly diffuse.[24]

In the most general terms, social-democratic trade unionism may be defined as a synthesis between pragmatic collective bargaining and a politics of state-directed social reform and economic management. At its core was an approach which I have previously termed 'political economism' (Hyman, 1994: 113–15). Political aspirations unconnected to the material interests of unions' actual or potential constituents tended to become largely ceremonial and rhetorical; union representatives were increasingly preoccupied with the collective bargaining agenda, at least insofar as employers were prepared to negotiate with *them*. Yet in contrast to narrow business unionism, it was recognized that industrial relations was not a self-contained field of action: success in collective bargaining was shaped by the macroeconomic context and by the legislative regulation of individual and collective employment rights, while the social wage broadly defined reflected the whole matrix of social policy.

It was a necessary condition of the success of political economism that the economic environment was more favourable in this formative period than at any time before or since. Despite the challenges (in most European countries) of repairing massive wartime destruction, the first post-war decades were in the main a period of substantial economic growth and (at least by comparison with the interwar era) of tight labour markets. There was scope for regular improvements in workers' standards of living and in other terms of the employment contract. For a generation of union members and their representatives, increased real wages and other gains became the expected outcome of each bargaining round. From the late 1960s, moreover – often as a result of rank-and-file pressure on more conservative leaderships – union demands and achievements in collective bargaining embraced qualitatively new issues: control of working conditions, humanization of production, reversing the extreme division of labour, providing opportunities for career development. To an important extent, trade unions gained an opportunity to reshape the collective bargaining agenda rather than merely responding to employers' priorities. Political economism seemed a new and *progressive* basis for interest representation: an approach most clearly linked to the social-democratic tradition, but one which could also be claimed as consistent with both christian and communist models of trade unionism. In particular, a favourable economic environment meant that unions could satisfy the material self-interest of their immediate members (who in most union movements, irrespective of ideological orientation, comprised relatively advantaged sections of the working class) while addressing broader issues of social solidarity. The context was also one in which political exchange could readily produce positive-sum outcomes.

The matrix for the formative period of 'social partnership', and for the various Keynesian-influenced systems of post-war macroeconomic management, was the regulatory capacity of the nation-state. As Rogers has argued (1995: 370), the scope for pressure on the state to deliver material benefits of general application itself encouraged 'the political project of uniting across differences'. It is indeed true that in most European economies the pivotal importance of the export sector ensured that industrial relations policies were consistent with international competitiveness. Nevertheless the national state, and the parties to collective bargaining, could address the labour market as a more or less closed system.

This context altered radically in the last quarter of the twentieth century. Economic expansion in most developed economies slowed, turning into stagnation and recession. International product market competition intensified, partly because of the emergence of new industrial economies, partly through the rise as key economic actors of multinational corporations (MNCs) which could not easily be cast as 'social partners' in any specific national system. 'Globalization' became the new buzzword, and helped legitimize the accompanying slogan of 'deregulation'.[25] The new economic orthodoxy rejected Keynesian demand management, in its extreme form insisting that governments could and should have little or no influence over employment, in more moderate versions laying primary or exclusive stress on supply-side measures which typically involved weakening or eliminating standardized patterns of regulation in favour of labour market 'flexibility'.[26]

By the end of the century, most European social-democratic parties had come to endorse such analyses, dismissing much of their traditional politics of state regulation as akin to the bureaucratic centralism of 'state socialism' which had collapsed with the Berlin wall.[27] Unions remained welcome as interlocutors largely insofar as they endorsed policies of retrenchment and restraint. At the same time, at company level the requirements of competitiveness (often against overseas establishments of the same enterprise) frequently left no evident alternative to one form or another of concession bargaining. Social-democratic trade unionism, predicated on direct institutionalized bargaining (or partnership) with governments and employers, seemed no longer capable of delivering positive results.

It is in this context that the concept of civil society has become of evident relevance for European trade unions. With a diminished capacity to mobilize traditional forms of economic and political pressure – partly because of the condition of the labour market, partly because of the shift in employment away from sectors and occupations where strike action could exert a rapid persuasive impact, partly because the whole practice of 'social partnership' had implied the obsolescence of old methods of militant action – unions were ill placed to respond to a far less sympathetic environment. There was a need to develop alternative means to exert influence and to mobilize, if not collective action, at least collective opinion. Civil society was increasingly seen as an arena of trade union engagement.

What is the meaning of civil society? As with most concepts with strong political significance, the notion is imprecise and contested: 'riddled with contradictions' (Hann, 1996: 1) and with 'weak or incomplete sociological moorings' (Hall, 1995: 3). There is much debate, on both left and right, over the analytical utility and practical implications of the term: many consider that it would be best abandoned. From my perspective it can provide an important basis for analysis of the societal role of trade unions, but only if many of the deficiencies of prevalent definitions are avoided.

It is clear that the import of 'civil society' has varied substantially over time. For Aristotle, it mainly implied an idealization of political life in the Greek-city state as founded on a community of active citizens. By the time of the revival of the concept in the seventeenth and eighteenth centuries, the core problem was how the apparatus of government, or the actions of those wielding state power, connected to social life more generally. At least three different approaches can be identified. The first saw no necessary separation between state and civil society; the latter was the arena of social relationships which could nurture active citizens whose participation in political life ensured that government reflected the popular will. A second perceived civil society as an arena of conflict and competition, which would prove socially destructive without the existence of a relatively autonomous state which could impose law and order.[28] A third, by contrast, saw the state as a potentially repressive instrument – 'power corrupts' – which could be constrained only by the counterbalancing effect of a vigorous civil society comprising a network of voluntary associations.[29]

This third conception has dominated the modern revival of interest in civil society. This occurred in the context of the practical and theoretical critique of authoritarian state regimes – primarily in eastern Europe but also in southern European and Latin American dictatorships, for example – and the struggle to consolidate a new, liberal-democratic order. The argument was that these societies were totalitarian in the sense that the government (or the ruling party) exercised control over all areas of social relations: economic, cultural and recreational as well as more overtly political. The development of civil society as an autonomous sphere of social life was often deliberately suppressed as a potential threat to the regime. By contrast, the construction and stabilization of a post-authoritarian order required the cultivation of a sphere of voluntary social relationships.[30]

In itself, this is a plausible interpretation of the past and prescription for the future. The devil is in the detail: how does the analysis of the balance between citizens and state power connect to the understanding of other types of power relationship within society? More specifically, where does economic power fit in?

For some writers, this is simply neglected: for example, Hall (1995: 15) writes that 'civil society must depend upon the ability to escape any particular cage'; but nowhere does he consider whether the relationship between employers and workers, or oligopolistic companies and consumers, might constitute a highly constricting cage. Likewise, Gellner (1995: 32–3) insists that it is inadequate to conceive civil society simply as 'that set of diverse non-governmental institutions, which is strong enough to counterbalance the state, and ... prevent the state from dominating and atomizing the rest of society'. But his rationale is that non-state authority can itself be oppressive;[31] it is possible 'to escape the tyranny of kings, but only at the cost of falling under the tyranny of cousins'. Other possible tyrannies are not discussed: in particular, the tyranny of blind market forces or of calculative corporate strategists.

But often the very definition of civil society endorses subordination to economic compulsion as a desirable alternative to political subjection. For example, Pérez-Díaz (1995: 81) prescribes as the 'institutional core' of civil society 'a government which is limited and accountable ...; a market economy ...; an array of free, voluntary associations ...; and a sphere of free public debate'. Along similar lines, Giner (1995: 304) specifies that 'any mature civil society exhibits at least five prominent dimensions: individualism, privacy, market, pluralism and class'. These authors summarize the starting point of most modern exponents of civil society: a preference for individualism over collective interest representation, an ideological commitment to 'free' markets. In this company, Giner is indeed relatively heterodox in recognizing that class division is a logical outcome of a structure of social relations in which inequality of economic power is a prized characteristic. But Walzer also (1995: 153, 165), having defined civil society as a 'space of uncoerced human association', goes on to note that economic inequality 'commonly translates into domination and radical deprivation [through] a socially mediated process'. His doubts are untypical. Most writers on civil society perceive economic coercion as far less problematic than political; 'for these theorists a market economy continues to form an essential element of the freely associative life which underpins democratic political institutions' (Beetham, 1997: 76).

Such a perspective is not new. Marx argued that civil society, in the mid-nineteenth century, was shaped by capitalist priorities;[32] and Gramsci, in the 1920s, wrote how political philosophy was dominated by the free marketeers of his time. The logic of the dominant contemporary conceptions of civil society is that it is an unqualified good to escape from the frying pan of state domination to the fire of the authoritarianism of market forces and corporate capital. Yet as O'Neill (1998: 70) insists, most conceptions of civil society are predicated on the existence of autonomous individuals with the capacity to make significant choices; whereas this capacity is systematically suppressed where the disciplines of unfettered markets are allowed full play. 'The logic of capitalist private property and the market often conflicts with plurality and free association. ... The resources for meaning, authority, and social integration are undermined ... by the expansion of an increasingly illiberal corporate economy' (Cohen and Arato, 1992: xiii, 24).

There are, however, alternative interpretations of civil society: as a countervailing potential not only to the state but also to economic domination.[33] Keane (1988: 14) makes the point pithily: 'I certainly don't wish to restrict the definition of civil society to the stiff-necked terms of neo-conservatism, as if civil society could only ever be synonymous with a non-state, legally guaranteed sphere dominated by capitalist corporations and patriarchal families'. Here too, Gramsci is relevant: as Nielsen notes (1995: 43) he 'reconceptualized civil society into a tri-partite conception in which civil society is juxtaposed not only against the state, taken as a coercive governmental apparatus, but, strikingly, against the economy and the private sphere of the family as well'. Altvater develops this perspective (1995: 152): in addition to state regulation of market forces, civil society provides the potential for a 'third hand' which 'comprises all non-market networks for diversified quality production, such as public goods, which have to be produced by society and societal agents, since they cannot be supplied simply by the market mechanism or as the intended output of state actions'. This indicates the poten-tial role of civil society as a means – at least potentially, in congruence with more explicit and systematic state action – of subjecting market forces to conscious social control. This function is not least important in the context of the labour market. It is also one where social consensus is scarcely likely to underlie col-lective regulation within civil society.

This indicates a further aspect of Gramsci's analysis of civil society: that this is characteristically a terrain of contestation and struggle. For Gramsci (as indeed for Marx), ideological domination within any society tended to reflect material domination; but such hegemony was not irresistible. Any challenge to prevailing power structures, however, was likely to prove successful only as the culmination of a process (perhaps protracted) of instilling an alternative set of values and an alternative vision of societal order: 'actively building a counter-hegemony' (Cox, 1987: 70–4). To make the benign vision of civil society a reality would require 'social struggles and public policy initiatives that enabled citizens, acting together in "sociable" public spheres, to strive for equal power, and so maximize their capa-city to play an active part in civil society' (Keane, 1988: 14). This evidently implies a very different focus on civil society than that prevailing in the literature: 'a more *inclusive* usage of civil society, in which it is not defined *negatively*, in opposition to the state, but *positively* in the context of the ideas and practices through which cooperation and trust are established in social life' (Hann, 1996: 22). This is consistent with Beck's recent call (2000: 11) for a 'society of citizens who stand up for people's rights' (a rough approximation of the untranslatable *zivilcouragierte Gesellschaft*).

It should be clear that such a conception of civil society has implications for the societal role of trade unions. The network of labour market regulation established in part through trade union action could well be comprehended in the terms just quoted. Indeed, the early forms of 'common rule' identified by the Webbs rested to a large degree on the commitment to a set of shared beliefs and values on the part of the members of a particular occupational community. The *normative* foundation of their commitment to irreducible standards of pay and working conditions sustained their willingness, if necessary through considerable personal sacrifice, to uphold this 'common rule'. However, the development of 'modern' industrial relations has typically involved a double-edged process of consolidation. Underwriting labour market regulation through government action – the Webbs' favoured method, 'legal enactment' – or through analogous processes of codification within the 'internal state' (Burawoy, 1979: ch. 7) of the modern corporation gave stability to the rules established. Yet at the same time, the 'juridification' of labour market regulation detached the process from its original normative foundations; and in changed circumstances made the common rule vulnerable to counter-attack. This, in essence, is the story of industrial relations in most of the developed world in recent decades. To counter this challenge, trade unions need to discover, rediscover or refocus their role as protagonists in civil society.

Social Institution or Social Movement?

'Modern civil society is created through forms of self-constitution and self-mobilization' (Cohen and Arato, 1992: ix). Of course material circumstances – including the structural imbalance in the distribution of political and economic resources – set limits to creativity in civil society. Nevertheless, such limits normally contain some scope for collective initiative which can in turn produce structural change. The nature of this potential, and the dynamics whereby it can be successfully realized, are the subject matter of a growing literature on social movements and have generated an increasingly sophisticated set of theoretical arguments.

Social movements are not easily defined: they are 'amorphous entities which resist neat classification' (Byrne, 1997: 11). For Byrne they may be identified as 'networks of interaction' held together less by formal organization than by commitment to a set of values which they seek to communicate in the community as a whole, and which may challenge key aspects of the existing order (1997: 13–20). In Tarrow's terms, they engage in 'contentious politics', and over time develop 'learned conventions of contention ... which help them to overcome the deficits in resources and communication typically found among the poor and disorganized' (1998: 20). Their main instrument is ideological; 'they rely more on cultural impact than on articulated connections with the political system' (Shaw, 1994: 655).[34] Moreover, to convince others of the justice of their demands, social movements must first convince their own immediate constituents: there is a need for 'conscious strategic efforts by groups of people to fashion shared understandings of the world and of themselves that legitimate and motivate collective action' (McAdam et al., 1996: 6).

Such analysis has obvious relevance to trade unionism.[35] Almost universally, unions emerged as social movements challenging key principles of the prevailing social and economic order. Their ability to exert influence over the conditions of work and social existence required that first they forged a sense of collective capacity on the part of their own constituency: collective identity and hence external effectiveness rested on a sustained process of internal dialogue (Offe and Wiesenthal, 1985). And as a closely related point, trade unionism 'cannot accumulate social power outside of an active relation to social issues, and it cannot effectively wield industrial power unless it is socially powerful' (Hardman, 1928: 111).

Yet since Michels it has been common to analyse trade union development in terms of a contradiction between ideals and organizational interests. For Herberg

(1968: 238), writing in the 1940s, trade unions were caught in a dualism between acting as 'a businesslike service organization, operating a variety of agencies under a complicated system of industrial relations' and as 'an expression and vehicle of the historical movement of the submerged laboring masses for social recognition and democratic self-determination'. Over time, in his view, the former had become increasingly dominant. Similarly, Flanders (1970: 15–16) insisted that 'trade unions have always had two faces, sword of justice and vested interest'.[36] It was the conception of social purpose which 'generates loyalties and induces sacrifices among its own members, and ... these are important foundations of its strength and vitality'. Yet as the 'rules and conventions' of industrial relations had accumulated, products of the unions' own successes, so the 'spirit of idealism' had become submerged. The corollary, as Offe and Wiesenthal (1985) have suggested, was the consolidation of a bureaucratic mode of representation eventually resulting in an erosion of unions' legitimacy and mobilizing capacity; paradoxically, then, organizational consolidation could generate organizational weakness.

In the past decade or more, most European trade union movements have grappled with this contradiction. To differing degrees, and in different ways, most have made efforts to recapture the role of a social movement and to engage as actors in civil society. There remain, however, three clear dilemmas.

The first is the relationship between external and internal influence. In principle there is an evident reciprocity involved: only to the extent that unions can move their own members and supporters to action are they likely to exert much force in their external relationships; but their demonstrated ability to make an impact in the wider world is likely to influence their constituents' 'willingness to act'. In some contexts, where unions enjoy success, this reciprocity can create a virtuous circle; but when efficacy wanes, the outcome can well be a vicious circle of declining relevance. To break out of such vicious circles, unions are compelled to go back to their roots – while redefining their ideals and objectives in the light of contemporary circumstances and their constituents' contemporary aspirations. This requires an often painful mutual interaction among actual and potential trade unionists.

Second, if unions are to redefine their role as actors in civil society, there is a tension between a status as 'social partners' involved in institutionalized dialogue with those wielding economic and political power, and an effort to shape beliefs and values in the wider society. Many European trade unions have increasingly seen a need to act in a campaigning role; but this is to embrace, however awkwardly, a form of 'contentious politics' which is not calculated to win the sympathy and support of the powerful.

Third, to the extent that unions do choose to campaign for popular support and influence, how do they relate to other social movements? The movement/ organization dialectic which underlies the history of trade unionism is also evident in the case of social movements more generally. Those which become relatively effective tend to acquire a more or less accepted status as 'non- governmental organizations' (NGOs). They occupy a terrain which trade unions, having abandoned in the past, cannot easily repossess. Yet in many countries (and also at international level), unions have proved reluctant to collaborate with such bodies and have often attempted to present themselves as aspiring monopolists in the representation of civil society. Such efforts have rarely proved wholly successful; but are unions able to act as partners in engaging with civil society? Tarrow (1998: 134–5) has argued that 'coalitions of organizations' can exert influence far greater than the sum of their parts; but in the main, only when unions have been forced to come to terms with the decline in their autonomous influence have they contemplated broader alliances of this kind. And for such alliances to acquire a stable basis, labour movements themselves have to expand their horizons; in the words of Waterman (1998: 2) 'adding to the lay trinity [liberty, equality, fraternity] the values of diversity, peace and ecological care'.

Conclusion

This chapter has followed a circuitous path. At the outset, it was seen how conceptions of trade unions as integral actors within society were used to challenge social-democratic (and also communist) notions of unions as agents of class struggle. Yet there ensued a double dialectic: christian unions which had first articulated the philosophy of integrative unionism were forced to recognize the reality of conflicting interests between workers and employers, a conflict which despite goodwill on their own part might require militant action if workers' legitimate interests were to be protected; social democrats (and later, communists) gave increasing attention to their new role as defenders of social order and economic stability, either abandoning the politics of class struggle or creating a widening gap between political rhetoric and everyday practice.

In the Europe which emerged after 1945, this ideological synthesis was expressed in the notion of social partnership. Yet this concept was always ambiguous. It could denote anything between total incorporation into the prevailing socio-economic order, and pragmatic collective bargaining. In most senses, it implied a long-term positive-sum bargaining relationship, in which cooperative participation in expanding productivity yielded the potential for sustained gains from economic growth, full employment and enhanced social welfare. This material basis for collaboration was however challenged by the harsher economic circumstances which afflicted western Europe from the 1970s onwards. While in many countries hard times inspired closer 'neo-corporatist' relations as a means of damage limitation, this made it far more difficult for unions to win assent among their own constituents, resulting in many cases in an erosion of their own legitimacy. Loss of legitimacy helped make attacks on established regulatory regimes an attractive option for employers and governments.

In this context, unions in many countries have been obliged to consider new strategic options (or to rediscover old ones). Engagement with civil society, and a role as a social movement, have been central to the redefinition of trade union identities. How such redefinition has occurred has differed considerably from country to country, as the following chapters will indicate. Yet we may conclude with a paradox, which rounds off our thematic discussion of market, class and society. Those who pioneered the conception of unions as actors within, rather than against, existing society were typically innocent of economic analysis. Yet the triumph of the social partnership model half a century ago depended strongly on economic foundations; as these foundations have been undermined, so unions have had to seek instruments of market regulation which transcend the consensual. And as the clash of economic interests has returned to centre stage, so the logic of class has acquired new resonance.[37] The triangle is complete. Some of the complexities of this geometry will be revisited in the final chapter.

Notes

[1] Margaret Thatcher, a former British prime minister, notoriously remarked that 'there is no such thing as society'. In most European countries, such an assertion would probably be taken as evidence of insanity.

[2] Giddens (1989: 31) defines culture as consisting 'of the *values* the members of a given group follow, the *norms* they follow, and the *material goods* they create'.

[3] The 'Mainz theses' adopted by the GcG in 1899 insisted that 'workers and employers have common interests. ... Without both capital and labour power, no production' but finally noted that 'the strike should be employed only as a last resort and when promising success' (Schneider, 1989: 415). This acceptance, however grudging, of the legitimacy of strikes in some circumstances was reaffirmed at the 1900 GcG congress (Otto, 1975: 55). See also Schneider, 1985.

[4] Though it is widely assumed to date back at least to the interwar period, I have not discovered any example before the 1940s. See below.

[5] Limmer (1966: 55) views the ZAG agreement as a valuable tactical manoeuvre by the employers which helped reduce pressure for nationalization of key industries.

[6] Though pro-war trade unionists formed the *Unione italiana del lavoro* (UIL) in 1918.

[7] Middlemas adds (1979: 21) that 'because their association with the state remained vulnerable to revolt from below, they took care to veil it as far as possible'.

[8] A fascinating analysis of the potential transformation of the public role of British trade unionism was written by the head of the TUC Research and Economic Department, and secretary to the Mond-Turner conferences, W. Milne-Bailey. He emphasised (1934: 89, 144) that in many countries trade unions had gained a 'public character' which was yet to be fully recognized in Britain, but that even here they had 'become closely associated with the functioning of the state'. The functions, and the philosophy, of unions had evolved gradually and perhaps imperceptibly; and in a world where economic planning was becoming increasingly important their core activity could evolve further: 'there is no reason why Trade Unions ... should not make themselves increasingly responsible for the entire function of labour supply and regulation. ... They will remain autonomous institutions ... but with functions which link them to the State in a consultative and constructive way' (373, 379). This semi-corporatist vision was not to be realized in Britain, then or subsequently; Milne-Bailey himself died shortly afterwards.

[9] For advice and information on the origins of the concept I am grateful to Michael Fichter, Peter Leisink, Patrick Pasture and Franz Traxler.

[10] I have not discovered an earlier usage in Germany. Krips (1958: 114) states that 'this concept came into use around 1950'.

[11] The term appeared in the resolutions adopted by 1950 Essen congress of the christian-democratic 'social committees' (the trade union section of the CDU) (Homann, 1955: 145).

[12] Alternatively, there could be a distinction between 'real social partnership' embedded in a mutually accepted ideology and/or established institutions and a 'fictitious' form in which the notion is employed manipulatively or unthinkingly (as is probably the case in contemporary 'Euro-speak').

[13] In the words of the Austrian president of the ETUC, Fritz Verzetnisch, 'for me social partnership means the readiness to discuss things together' (Hammerschmied et al., 1997: 30).

[14] In such contrasting cases as France and Austria, notably, the 'commanding heights' of the economy were taken into public ownership.

[15] The literature on this theme rapidly became enormous. For one collection reviewing the issues involved see Goldthorpe, 1984; and for a more disenchanted assessment see Panitch, 1980.

[16] Though not, it should be added, in the English language, where 'management and labour' or 'the two sides of industry' remained the normal forms of reference.

[17] Some catholics broke away in the 1950s in protest at the close relationship between the DGB leadership and the SDP, establishing a separate organization, the CGB (*Christlicher Gewerkschaftsbund*); but this never became a significant body (Pasture, 1994: 60–1).

[18] In an exceptional arrangement, this fraction was able to affiliate to the International Federation of Christian Trade Unions (which in 1968 'deconfessionalized' to become the World Confederation of Labour – WCL), while the ÖGB as a whole affiliated to the International Confederation of Free Trade Unions (ICFTU).

[19] In France as in Italy, the cold war was soon to provide the occasion for a secession from the communist-dominated *Confédération générale du travail* (CGT) on the part of a section of socialists and republicans, who formed the CGT-FO (*Force ouvrière*).

[20] Formally completed in 1981.

[21] For a time, a merger between the ICFTU and WCL seemed possible. The CFDT, which had been one of the main advocates within the WCL of such a merger, disaffiliated in 1979 when the initiative proved abortive (Gumbrell-McCormick, 2000: 369–73), eventually joining the larger international a decade later.

[22] It is perhaps necessary to re-emphasize that the focus of this book is on western Europe: the role of trade unions under 'actually existing socialism' in the east is outside the boundaries of this analysis.

[23] Though this was not finally approved until 1991. Many believed that the CC.OO. had satisfied this political test significantly earlier; its admission was blocked partly because of opposition by the UGT, partly through fears that once its membership was approved it would no longer be possible to exclude the Portuguese CGTP or the French CGT. Indeed the CGTP was admitted two years later; as indicated below, the CGT had to wait longer.

[24] My use of the notion of social-democratic trade unionism overlaps, but only partially, with the 'Social-Democratic Model' of labour regulation discussed by Howell (1992: 22–3).

[25] It was argued in Chapter 2 that the notion of deregulation is tendentious and misleading: it denotes a change in the form and direction of regulation, not its abolition. Likewise, 'globalization' is a term often used to imply that changes in the international economy – which are indeed real and significant – are irresistible and necessitate a specific set of political responses. European trade unions have certainly proved vulnerable to such arguments. For a review of some of these debates see Hyman, 1999.

[26] At EU level, this supply-side emphasis can be seen in the 'four pillars' of the employment strategy adopted at Luxembourg in 1997: employability, entrepreneurship, adaptability and equal opportunities. With the (possible) exception of the last, none of these themes connects significantly to the traditional agenda of social-democratic trade unionism.

[27] Of course developments differed substantially across countries: 'New Labour' in Britain probably went furthest in rejecting the heritage of the past; the French socialists were among the most resistant to this trend.

[28] Marx gave a distinctive coloration to this interpretation by linking state power to conflicts within and between classes.

[29] These are ideal-type characterizations of positions in a very complex set of debates, shaped by the transition from mercantile to industrial capitalism. Very approximately one may relate the first approach to Ferguson, the second to Hobbes, Locke, Rousseau and later Hegel, the third to de Tocqueville.

[30] There is an interesting parallel here with the contrast drawn by Gramsci (1971: 238) between Tsarist Russia and the countries of western Europe. In the former, 'the state was everything, civil society was primordial and gelatinous', and this was both its strength and

its weakness. It was its strength in that this obstructed the development of alternative organizational structures which could challenge its legitimacy, but its weakness in that all discontents were likely to be directed against the state and this eventually resulted in its overthrow. In the west, by contrast, the dense network of institutions in civil society diffused conflicts and helped stabilize the state.

[31] There are evident affinities here with Durkheim's analysis of 'mechanical solidarity'.

[32] It is relevant that the German term *bürgerliche Gesellschaft* translates as both civil society and bourgeois society.

[33] Mouriaux (1985: 26–7) has noted that there are two opposing usages of the notion of 'the social' in French political debate: one treating social order as necessarily vested in the unequal distribution of private property; the other – particularly associated with the labour movement – aspiring to defend the interests of those with little or no property by imposing constraints on the exploitation of economic power.

[34] For Scott (1990: 9–10), social movements typically arise when the mainstream political system fails adequately to represent specific interests or to address specific issues.

[35] For one attempt to apply this mobilization theory to the study of trade unions see Kelly (1998: ch. 4).

[36] There are some parallels with the later discussion by Freeman and Medoff (1984: 5–11) of the 'two faces of unionism', in this case distinguishing between 'monopoly' and 'collective voice'.

[37] 'Every technological repercussion and economic transformation threatens stratification by status and pushes the class situation into the foreground' (Weber, 1968: 938).

5

British Trade Unionism

Between Market and Class

British trade unionism has a history dating back more than two centuries: the 'first industrial nation' gave birth to the first national trade union movement. While labour historians commonly identify distinct 'turning points' (if only to facilitate the organization of their narratives), and there have indeed been periods of significant transformation, by comparison with most other countries what is striking in the British[1] case is historical continuity – the persistence of many long-established traditions, in some respects specific to individual unions. 'British trade unions, more than those of most countries perhaps, are historical deposits and repositories of history. And anyone with close experience of trade unionism will be aware of the extent to which every union possesses a personality of its own' (Turner, 1962: 14).

Britain is recognized as the cradle of the 'industrial revolution' (in some ways a misleading term, since the rise of 'modern industry' was slow and uneven, and many aspects of pre-capitalist norms of work proved highly resilient). As was noted in Chapter 2, it was also the country in which the philosophy of *laissez-faire* – the insistence that social relations should be governed by the forces of supply and demand – took early hold. By the time that Marx was writing, the employment relationship in Britain was the closest approximation in any country to the 'free' market exchange of the commodity labour power which he analysed (though as was also argued earlier, it was impossible for actually existing employment relationships to match the models of fanatics of market liberalism). As the dominant mode of employment relations moved from one governed by status and tradition to that of a contract based on the balance of supply and demand, collective organization emerged more or less spontaneously, primarily among workers with distinctive skills and a relatively advantaged labour market position. For some writers indeed there was an organizational continuity between the pre-capitalist guild system and the 'trade societies' of the late eighteenth and early nineteenth centuries (though the Webbs among others strenuously disputed this). Certainly the main concerns of most of the early unions were limited and defensive: to protect customary standards of employment, including the monopoly of a particular function by those with the traditional job qualifications, against efforts by the new entrepreneurs to cheapen labour and simplify production.

The rapid expansion of large-scale industry in the middle decades of the nineteenth century, notably in coal mines, iron and steel mills and cotton factories, involving workers few of whom possessed traditional craft competences and many of whom had no background in urban manufacturing employment, brought a new dimension to British trade unionism. Here, collective organization was typically a reaction, often militant, against the tyranny of employer domination and oppression. But where unions became established, their orientations frequently changed: it was in such industries that collective bargaining conducted by professional union leaders and delegates became consolidated in the latter part of the century (Burgess, 1975; Webb and Webb, 1897). A similar process occurred, at the end of the century, with the 'new unionism' which extended organization to a wide range of trades and industries with a largely lower-skilled workforce. The 'new unions' were widely regarded (and defined by many of their own leaders) as radical and militant, but where they established bargaining relationships with employers a more pragmatic orientation soon prevailed (Hobsbawm, 1949: 135).

Workers' organizations in the nineteenth century absorbed many of the ideological influences of what may be termed Britain's passive bourgeois revolution. In contrast to the revolutionary crises which occurred in many other European countries, in Britain the rising entrepreneurial class achieved economic autonomy and political rights peacefully and incrementally; and did not need to mobilize the working class as fellow contestants of the established order (a mobilization which in many European countries then resulted in working-class assertiveness outwith bourgeois control). Central to the transition from feudalism to capitalism was the *negative* principle of detachment of the (relatively weak and undeveloped) state from economic life: the doctrine of *laissez-faire*. A further important feature of the British context is that ideologies have more often been implicit than explicit; against a background of anti-intellectualism, the English 'are incurious as to theory, take fundamentals for granted, and are more interested in the state of the roads than in their place on the map' (Tawney, 1921: 9).

Despite early state repression and often brutal resistance by large employers, by the second half of the nineteenth century British trade unionism had established deep roots and achieved both passive toleration within the law and grudging recognition by key employers. The typical form of association was localized and occupationally specific, and the typical objectives, as indicated above, were as much backward- as forward-looking: the defence of the right to the job, traditional methods of work organization, and established levels of wages. The most cherished principle became 'free collective bargaining': the right of unions and employers to resolve their differences on whatever basis they found mutually acceptable. What became known as the 'tradition of voluntarism' (Flanders, 1974), discussed in more detail below, implied a suspicion of the law and the courts, a reluctance to see individual employment rights legally regulated and a far greater resistance to statutory regulation of collective industrial relations. One symptom was the presumption that collective agreements should be open-ended, temporary, provisional, unenforceable except through a balance of industrial strength. Politics and industrial relations were regarded as largely separate spheres: the reason why, at the end of the nineteenth century, when unions felt the need for parliamentary representation to defend them from judicial attack, they established the Labour Party as an autonomous body.

Yet somewhat paradoxically, Britain is commonly regarded as a country with exceptionally powerful class identities and class divisions. From pre-capitalist popular struggles against feudal autocracy, the British labour movement inherited notions of plebeian independence which helped create an adversarial tradition in industrial relations (Fox, 1985). The British working class has been described as 'a class apart' (Meacham, 1977): displaying Touraine's principles of identity and opposition but without a totalizing vision of an alternative. 'Them and us' represented a natural, not a socially remediable, division. By the twentieth century, however, this class consciousness could inspire socialist perspectives among many union leaders and activists; and in the phase of organizational consolidation at the time of the 1914–18 war, many unions adopted an explicit commitment in their rules to the socialist transformation of economy and society. As Coates and Topham have commented (1980: 21), 'there are certain broad objectives which recur from one rulebook to the next, and from one generation to the next. These concern the issues of power, control and social accountability.'

Yet such ultimate goals rarely interfered with the more mundane day-to-day practice of trade unionism, which reflected the legal definition of a union that has persisted, with minor variations, since the 1870s: 'an organization whose principal purposes include the regulation of relations between workers and employers'. Nevertheless, there has been a constant tension between cautious bargaining and class assertiveness. The distinctive organizational and ideological configuration of the British labour movement has often been described as 'Labourism' (Saville, 1973). Unions in Britain (even if rhetorically committed to socialist aims) have in practice accepted and adapted to the existing social and economic system; but they have been prepared to fight determinedly in defence of their members' immediate economic interests within it. Traditionally they have recognized the need to rely on their own collective strength – 'industrial muscle' – rather than depending on external support; they have been more concerned with *de facto* than *de jure* rights. While unions' objectives in collective bargaining have for the most part been unambitious, threats to job security or to established norms of 'a fair day's wage for a fair day's work' have at times provoked uncompromising resistance. Occupying the terrain between class and market (see Figure 5.1), British trade unions have traditionally displayed a militant, but sectional and defensive, economism. But circumstances, and trade union identities, have changed despite the force of tradition.

The Formation of a Distinctive Trade Union Model

It is impossible to understand British industrial relations without some knowledge of the historical background. Like so many British institutions, those regulating employment are the product of a long historical evolution, in which governments,

FIGURE 5.1 *Britain – between market and class*

employers and trade unions fashioned modes of procedure which often perplex the overseas observer. The evolutionary inheritance involved a set of mutually supportive principles, practices and values. These may be described as the tradition of voluntarism, the tradition of unscientific management and the tradition of free collective bargaining.

The tradition of voluntarism meant that the state was reluctant to intervene directly in labour relations. This was reflected in part in the low level of legal regulation. Until the 1970s, an introductory account of British industrial relations might have briefly mentioned three parliamentary statutes – laws passed in 1871, 1875 and 1906 – before moving quickly to discuss the realities of employer-union and management-worker relationships. In most countries, collective organization and collective bargaining were legalized by creating a positive right to unionize, to bargain and to strike; and the courts acquired an important role in interpreting the nature and limits of these rights. In Britain, by contrast, ancient prohibitions were removed in a very different manner: by creating a set of legal 'immunities' covering a defined area of industrial relations, within which the courts were denied jurisdiction.

Hence in Britain there developed a major disjuncture between *de jure* and *de facto* employment rights. In the eyes of the law, while workers became free to organize collectively, the employer was equally free to dismiss those who joined a union; while unions were entitled to bargain collectively, employers were equally at liberty to refuse to negotiate or to recognize a union, whatever its level of membership; and while a union could lawfully call a strike 'in contemplation or furtherance of a trade dispute', individual strikers were still in breach of their contracts of employment and might therefore be summarily dismissed (or even sued for damages).

In the real world of industrial relations the situation was often very different. For most of the twentieth century, the majority of all but the smallest employers (at least in manufacturing and the public sector) accepted the right of their employees to organize and were prepared to recognize their unions. The ability of strikers to 'suspend' their contracts, though completely alien to British law, tended to operate in practice. However, *de facto* rights were subject to important qualifications. First, they tended to apply where employees enjoyed a relatively secure labour market position or were sustained by traditions of solidarity principally associated with a male manual working-class culture; other sectors of the labour force had little protection. Hence voluntarism probably encouraged and reinforced labour market segmentation. Second, as seen in Chapter 2 and as the Webbs (1897) noted a century ago, rights sustained only by collective strength tended to ebb and flow according to the general state of the labour market.

Other aspects of the voluntarist tradition may be identified. The separation between industrial relations and the law meant that the very notion of a collective contract, so important in many other countries, does not exist in Britain: collective agreements are 'binding in honour only', of legal relevance only to the extent that their terms may be incorporated (implicitly or explicitly) into employees' individual contracts. Likewise, trade unions have possessed a somewhat shadowy legal status: they are not formally agents of their members.

This is not to say that the law and the state traditionally had no impact on industrial relations. But while legislation on individual employment conditions has always been part of the British system, the rights have in general been far inferior to those in most continental European countries. Traditionally, most individual employment law covered either segments of the labour market not adequately regulated by collective bargaining, or issues (such as health and safety) with a clear-cut public interest. More systematic legal regulation which could be found in many other nations – a universal minimum wage, maximum working hours, protection against dismissal – was thought undesirable by most of those who shaped British industrial relations.

The treatment of public employees also reflected the tradition of voluntarism. A century ago the government accepted that the conditions of its own workforce should not be inferior to those established by collective bargaining for workers in the private sector. In the twentieth century there developed institutionalized arrangements ensuring 'fair comparisons' between pay and working conditions in the two sectors. Although (with very minor exceptions) the right of public employees to strike has never been subject to special restrictions, such arrangements helped sustain relative industrial peace. In general, then, the government as employer tended to follow rather passively what was established as 'good practice' in the private sector; only relatively recently did it assume a more active and initiating role.

Why did British employers – strongly represented in parliament, and influential in both main nineteenth-century political parties – accept so limited a role of the state in industrial relations? Because, in the main, they were confident of their own ability to handle labour relations; because their early ascendancy in world markets meant that they could afford to reach compromise settlements with trade unions; and because, above all else, the rise of British capitalism involved a struggle to exclude the state from detailed intervention in economic affairs. The philosophy of *laissez-faire*, so important in the rise and subsequent decline of British industry, left a powerful mark on industrial relations.

Employers were anxious to manage their own enterprises without state interference. How did they arrange this in practice? Here, the notion of unscientific management is important. While it is common to speak of an industrial revolution at the beginning of the nineteenth century, in fact the rise of British industry was not primarily based on large-scale factory production. The slogan 'workshop of the world' reflected a reality of large numbers of small-scale producers. The metal-working trades which figured so prominently in the success of Victorian capitalism manufactured an immense variety of commodities, often tailored to the specific requirements of individual customers. Vertical integration was low; complex products were often the outcome of a lengthy chain of supplier-contractor relationships. Technological innovation was intermittent and uneven: new machinery was often expensive, unreliable and inflexible. To cope with fluctuating and diversified product markets, employers in much of British industry relied heavily on the expertise and versatility of a labour force whose skills pre-dated capitalist manufacturing. Some firms might possess a formal hierarchy of managers, supervisors and chargehands; and some of the large cotton factories deployed the kind of military discipline which so struck Marx and Engels. But far more commonly, employers depended on the largely autonomous self-regulation of work teams, sustained either by systems of payment by results or by workers' acceptance of the ethic of 'a fair day's work'.

This system of unscientific management was attractive to small employers in uncertain markets, but was normally perpetuated also within those firms which grew larger and achieved greater market dominance. The costs of supervisory and technical staff – and of fixed capital – could be kept to a minimum, their functions performed by a skilled manual workforce which could be hired and fired with little notice. Training – while often dignified by the title of apprenticeship – was largely a matter of new recruits learning traditional techniques from established workers. To experiment with alternative systems of work organization and labour control was an unnecessary risk for companies which were already achieving acceptable levels of profit.

It is important to emphasize also the link between management preference and practice, and the structure of British companies and the capital market. The British system of share ownership has always been driven by concerns of short-term profitability; firms which failed to satisfy short-term stock market expectations suffered falling share prices and the risk of hostile take-over. Banks and other financial institutions never developed the long-term commitment to the firms in which they invested which was evident in many other countries. Companies were therefore discouraged from investing either in technical innovation or in enhanced workforce skills, if this was at the expense of immediate returns to shareholders.

Unscientific management encouraged the emergence of a system of labour relations in which firms delegated the formal conduct of collective bargaining to employers' associations, in the comforting belief that this excluded trade unions from direct involvement in the workplace. In practice, however, unionized workers in core sectors of the economy developed their own collective representatives – shop stewards – who became skilled in negotiating with first-line managers. In the middle decades of the twentieth century, in manufacturing at least, informal collective bargaining within the workplace became more important in determining pay and conditions of employment than were the official agreements reached at industry level. And because the real focus of collective bargaining shifted from the regulatory institutions at national level to the fragmented and informal pressure tactics of the shop floor, two key consequences were a significant degree of 'wage drift' and a large number of small, short strikes.

The third participant in shaping British industrial relations was the trade union movement. Why were unions traditionally so willing to accept the voluntarist principle, when their counterparts in many other countries were anxious to involve the state in regulating employment and in underwriting their own representative status? The answer can be found, in part, in three distinctive features of British trade unions: their complex and fragmented structure; their ambiguous attitude to political action; and the potent moral value they attached to the concept of 'free collective bargaining'. These derived in turn from the slow evolution of the British trade union movement, from the small local societies which existed before the industrial revolution to the very different pattern of more recent times. Over the years, unions developed a pragmatic relationship of mutual tolerance with employers. Experience showed them that collective bargaining could yield acceptable results; on the other hand they knew that politicians, and the judges who applied the laws which parliament enacted, came from a different class and often lacked sympathy or understanding towards workers' needs. For British unions, unlike those elsewhere in Europe, the state appeared largely irrelevant once their basic right to function had been legally established. Even after they had helped create the Labour Party, at the turn of the century, they normally treated political action as very subsidiary to their main preoccupation with collective bargaining; and were very jealous of any attempt by governments – including Labour governments – to intervene uninvited in their terrain.

The Craft Tradition

One narrative of British trade union history would identify a succession of waves of collective action, at times overlapping, and each resulting in a process of organizational sedimentation. The middle decades of the nineteenth century saw the consolidation of national unions of craft workers, notably in engineering, construction and printing, through the amalgamation of pre-existing local societies. This was followed by the first stable large-scale unionism among workers without formal craft status in the 'new' industries of industrial capitalism: coal, cotton, steel, railways. Around the turn of the century the foundations were laid for the giant 'general unions' of the twentieth century, recruiting across a vast range of industries and occupations. The twentieth century itself saw the change in trade unionism from an almost exclusively manual workers' movement to one encompassing a substantial number of white-collar occupations, and (a process in part interconnected) the development of the public sector as a major union stronghold. The same trends were linked to a growing feminization of a once overwhelmingly male movement.

The sedimented character of unionization helps explain the exceptional structural complexity of British trade unionism. Each wave of organization followed a distinctive structural logic, giving rise to a patchwork of cross-cutting membership constituencies. In consequence, all main unions in contemporary Britain have long been composite 'general' unions. At the same time, the evolutionary character of union development – the continuity of some organizations for two centuries – has had important ideological consequences. Each generation derived an understanding of the principles and purposes of trade unionism – of what it *meant* to be a member or activist – from pre-existing models. This is not in any way to deny the importance of change, creativity and conflict in British trade union development: phases of expansion and advance frequently involved explicit challenges to the prevailing models. Yet radical innovators often retained more of their ideological inheritance than they appreciated, and the outcome was typically a combination of diverse and at times contradictory orientations and assumptions.

There are two conflicting views of the British labour movement in the first decades of the nineteenth century. One emphasizes the crisis of a period when traditional rights of workers were trampled under the new imperative of profit above all else, when established skills were displaced or downgraded, when the capitalist 'rationalization' of agriculture drove much of the rural population into urban slums, and when a new political elite embraced the task of disciplining the 'dangerous classes' who toiled and suffered under the emerging industrial regime. Working-class reaction included the millennial Owenite 'general unionism' of the 1820s, the revolt against the New Poor Law of 1834, and the Chartist campaigns of the late 1830s and the 1840s. For the Webbs, this 'revolutionary period' inevitably failed and provoked among the surviving craft unions a 'reaction against the policy of reckless aggression which marked the Owenite inflation' (1894: 180). By the 1860s, they argued, these unions eschewed grandiose social goals, often prohibited branches from political discussion, deprecated strikes, encouraged processes of conciliation and arbitration of disputes, and pursued social respectability. This reading of trade union development was widely accepted, even though many writers have interpreted – and attacked – the trend as the outcome of the rise, perhaps deliberately encouraged by the ruling elite, of a 'labour aristocracy' of skilled workers with a secure economic position and a respectable social status (Foster, 1974).[2]

A contrary view (Musson, 1972) insists on the relative detachment in these early decades of the nineteenth century between popular radicalism and stable trade unionism. On this assessment, craft unions were largely unaffected by the social and political turbulence of the times, and were likewise little restricted by the oppressive legislation (including the notorious Combination Acts of 1800) which was primarily directed against more overtly militant working-class movements, viewed by the authorities as potentially revolutionary. For Musson, there was substantial continuity in craft unionism from the eighteenth century to the consolidation of national organization in the 1860s; what occurred in later years was 'not the creation of a "New Model", but the strengthening of the old' (1972: 50).

What requires emphasis is that the rise of industrial capitalism, and the responses of labour, involved complex, contradictory and uneven developments. Certainly many categories of skilled labour, embedded in pre-capitalist structures of job demarcation and work allocation, experienced no 'industrial revolution'; everyday work relations altered little. But this was not true of those whose status was undermined by technological innovation (the handloom weavers were the most obvious example), by the emergence of cheap standardized production for mass markets (as extensively in clothing and footwear), or by the challenge of new entrepreneurs with little or no respect for traditional practices (as, notably, in construction). In such contexts, skilled craft workers often embraced the radicalism of the more vulnerable emergent proletariat. This was the objective basis for Engels' assessment of the revolutionary potential of the British labour movements of the 1840s, and more recently for Thompson's somewhat parallel evaluation of collective action in the previous decades.

It is important to appreciate that in the first half of the nineteenth century, capitalist industrialization was widely perceived, and denounced, as a bizarre and indeed indecent social experiment. Resistance to this overweening threat to established social order – which could unite conservatives such as Cobbett with proto-socialist radicals – could appear not only morally appropriate but also practically reasonable. 'What above all differentiated the Chartist period from the post-1870 period was the general belief that the economic and political order brought into being by the Industrial Revolution was a temporary aberration, soon to be brought to an end'. The reasonableness of millennial aspirations was dissipated, not only by the defeat of the insurgency of the 1820s, 1830s and 1840s but also by the mere passage of time: 'capitalism had become an immovable horizon' (Stedman Jones, 1983: 237).

By mid-century, it was clear that capitalist production was not an ephemeral experiment but established reality. The 'Great Exhibition' of 1851 was a message that the dynamism of the new productive system would allow British entrepreneurs (with a little help from British military forces) to conquer the world. The capture of world markets in turn contributed to an expanding domestic economy which resulted in winners as well as (perhaps more than) losers within the working class. In the political sphere, the challenge to feudal rule – the regime of 'old corruption' which persisted well into the nineteenth century – resulted in a distinctively British form of class compromise. While in much of Europe the 'industrious classes' – workers, independent artisans and emergent capitalists – united against the political privileges of the landed classes, threatened and on occasion achieved revolution, in Britain the 'reform' of 1832 saw a pragmatic political accommodation between the old ruling class and the newly economically powerful. In this very partial extension of democracy, labour remained largely excluded. When this political betrayal could be plausibly viewed as cause of the material suffering of the victims of the new market economy and the new 'utilitarian' policies of the state, Chartism was able to pose a serious insurrectionary threat. Once British capitalism had survived its traumatic years of transition, the challenge largely evaporated: this, as much as the strategic competence of the government or the incompetence of its opponents, explains why the revolutionary uprisings of 1848 in much of Europe found so feeble an echo in Britain.

The year of the 'Great Exhibition' also saw the formation of the first 'new model union', the Amalgamated Society of Engineers (ASE). What was new about this amalgamation, a decisive event in the Webbs' account of the period, has long been a subject of dispute. The ASE drew most of its rulebook, and the bulk of its members, from a single component society. As Fraser has argued (1974: 221), 'the real significance of the ASE ... was as a *symbol*'. Its size, though trivial in modern terms, was remarkable at the time, and it enjoyed sustained growth; it survived an employers' lock-out shortly after its formation – an attack which would almost certainly have destroyed its predecessors – and went on to win at least the grudging acceptance of most of the larger employers; it consolidated substantial funds; it developed an administration which, by the standards of the time, was highly professional; and it pursued, and to a large measure achieved, a status as a respectable social institution. To differing degrees, these characteristics were widely imitated by craft societies in other industries, and later by non-craft unions as well, in the following decades. At their core was a conception of trade unionism in terms primarily of employment regulation, as far as possible through peaceful methods, and as far as possible also to the exclusion of involvement in political radicalism.

Craft unionism attempted to turn the rules of a market economy to workers' advantage – or at least, to the advantage of that minority of workers with a capacity to play the market. It rested on three fundamental principles: that craft training (typically involving a seven-year apprenticeship) gave craft workers a monopoly right to the relevant category of work; that wages should reflect this investment in training; and that the dignity of the craft entitled a high degree of autonomous control over the performance of the job. The craft worker was a professional rather than a hired hand. As the Webbs presented the view of the craft unionist (1897: 565), 'it seemed as outrageous, and as contrary to natural justice, for an unlicensed interloper to take his trade as for a thief to steal his wares'.[3] The craft society thus possessed a mission to defend the valuable market niche of those whose qualifications set them apart from labour in general – if necessary, by reinforcing the barriers against incursions by other members of the labour force.

Fundamental to the practice of the craft societies was what the Webbs termed the method of 'mutual insurance', which might otherwise be described as collective self-protection. The union prescribed unilaterally[4] the norms covering hours of work, minimum wages, job definitions and the ratio of apprentices to qualified workers (crucial to the control of the supply of labour). Should an employer attempt to evade these standards, union members would be constrained from accepting employment; if the defiance was sufficiently blatant, existing employees might be withdrawn, often singly rather than collectively, to find work elsewhere (the 'strike in detail'). If there were insufficient jobs available at any time on acceptable conditions, those unemployed would be entitled to support from union funds. Hence the craft societies could insist (as many did in evidence to the 1867 Royal Commission on Trade Unions) that they disapproved of strikes, and in some cases that they did not provide strike benefit. In sectors based on a multiplicity of small employers, it was unemployment benefit which offered the material support for the strike in detail. Moreover, the application of craft standards was defined by each union branch in the light of local conditions; the national craft 'amalgamations' were in large measure federations of local unions possessing a high degree of autonomy. National leaders could insist on their moderation of goals and methods while local branches remained far more uncompromising; as Clegg put it (1962: 9), 'their leaders could deprecate large-scale strikes while their members quietly put the screws on local employers'.

As indicated above, the consolidation of craft unionism from the mid-century involved in part a retreat from politics. In reaction against the divisive impact of the political controversies of the previous decades, several 'new model unions' banned political discussion from their branch meetings. In terms of political rhetoric, class antagonism was displaced in many other craft societies by an emphasis on the reciprocity of capital and labour.[5] Those union leaders who did engage in politics typically associated with the (newly consolidated) Liberal Party.

There was indeed one point in the 1860s when many craft unions were closely involved with large-scale political agitation, joining with the radical wing of the Liberals in the campaign for an extension of the franchise to the working class. For a moment, a repeat of the insurrectionary episodes of Chartism seemed a possibility (Harrison, 1965: ch. 3); but unrest was defused by the 1867 Reform Act which adopted the principle of 'household suffrage'.[6] The effect was to enfranchise the craft elite, and indeed the majority of better-off urban male workers. The right to vote ceased to be a significant issue in British politics until the women's suffrage movement nearly half a century later.[7]

A year after the Reform Act, the Trades Union Congress (TUC) was created. One of the objectives of the initial meeting was to bring together union leaders from London and the provinces in advance of the expected report of the Royal Commission on Trade Unions and to assist in pressure for legal changes to protect trade union activities and finances. Unlike previous meetings of this kind held during the 1860s, the explicit aim was to initiate a series of annual conferences. At first conceived as a semi-academic gathering to discuss 'carefully prepared papers', the Congress soon developed into an annual 'parliament of labour' (Martin, 1980; Musson, 1955; Pelling, 1963; Roberts, 1958). The need for such a body was confirmed by the long process of securing an acceptable framework of industrial relations legislation, eventuating in the Trade Union Act of 1871 and the Conspiracy and Protection of Property, and Employers and Workmen Acts of 1875. These laid the basis for the 'voluntarist' British system founded on the principle of negative immunities rather than positive rights. The unions were highly satisfied with this method of legalizing their status, and with the effectiveness of the TUC as a pressure group on behalf of their common interests. However, it should be emphasized that the TUC existed as an organization with limited capacity and competence, a forum through which affiliated unions found it useful to pursue certain of their objectives but an institution to which they were reluctant to assign significant resources or powers of initiative.

A quarter of a century after the first Royal Commission on Trade Unions, a Royal Commission on Labour was established in 1891. The contrast between the two situations indicates the degree to which a trade union movement embracing much of the logic of craft collectivism had achieved an accepted public status. When the first Commission was established, the unions were very much under attack. Their activities were widely viewed as responsible for the current period of economic recession; their reputation had been damaged by a much publicized series of acts of violence against non-unionists in the Sheffield cutlery industry; and the courts had ruled that unions were unable to sue an official who defaulted with their funds because their rules were 'in restraint of trade' and they were therefore illegal organizations. Union requests to nominate a member of the Commission were refused; they were merely permitted to send an observer to its hearings. By the time of the 1891 Commission, the unions were accepted as part of the solution rather than part of the problem, which was perceived as bad working conditions and poverty wages, and the economic inefficiency and explosive industrial conflict which these precipitated. Six of the Commissioners on this occasion were trade unionists (though the TUC, ambitiously, had asked to nominate half). The main report concluded in 1894 that 'peaceable relations are, upon the whole, the result of strong and firmly established trade unionism'. The task of government was to encourage and facilitate the development of effective collective organization on both sides of industry, assisting in their joint regulation of employment conditions by voluntary means. This was to remain the essence of British public policy for the next three-quarters of a century.

Economics and Politics: The Rise of Labourism

From the above account it is evident that while the ideology of craft unionism insisted on a separation between day-to-day job regulation and political involvement, the craft societies were nevertheless in part political actors. It could scarcely have been otherwise when unions were confronted by oppressive laws and a hostile judiciary, and when workers as citizens were disenfranchised while major employers were strongly placed to shape the legislative process. For some craft leaders, the labour movement was an appropriate vehicle to secure the working class (or at least its economically advantaged and 'respectable' segments) an accepted place within Victorian politics and society. This was, for example, the perspective of Robert Applegarth, the forceful secretary of the Carpenters and Joiners, though this brought him into conflict with the more narrow-minded representatives of the rank and file in the branches; and this conception was to shape the Webbs' own reading of nineteenth-century trade union evolution.

The recognition that some forms of political action were necessary components of the process of interest representation was reinforced by the extension of solid collective organization from the crafts to a wider constituency. The second half of the nineteenth century saw a major growth of trade unionism outside the craft trades, in particular in the coal and cotton industries. In the first half of the century there had indeed been frequent upsurges of collective organization in these focal industries of the industrial revolution, but for the most part these had proved ephemeral, either collapsing in defeat or withering away after having successfully resolved the immediate grievances which brought them into existence. In both industries, it was in the 1860s that the foundations were laid for stable trade union organization. In both cases, the contrast with craft collectivism must be qualified. The core constituency of mining trade unionism was constituted by the face workers or hewers, paid on the basis of the quantity of coal extracted, and enjoying far higher earnings than the majority of ancillary workers who received a fixed time-rate of pay. In cotton-spinning, there was an analogous situation: the spinners were far better paid than their assistants, and indeed often performed a contractor role and themselves employed the latter. Partial similarities existed in iron and steel, where a subcontracting system was common, and on the railways, where engine-drivers were the elite grade. In all these industries the strategic occupations required genuine skill; but this was acquired not through formal apprenticeship but through experience gained over time, often on the basis of an institutionalized system of promotion from one grade to the next on the basis of seniority. It was thus not an option for the emergent unions to shape the labour market to their advantage by controlling entry to the trade, as was often the practice of the craft societies.

Instead the unions in these industries pioneered two key forms of action which distinguished them from their craft predecessors. First, they can be seen as the initiators of collective bargaining. Unable to practise the craft societies' unilateral regulation of wages through the strike in detail, it was necessary to persuade (or compel) the employers to agree acceptable terms. This was the more necessary, but also more feasible, in industries where the product was standardized and where piecework payment was the norm: for here, standard conditions were in principle possible covering a whole locality or region. Hence 'it was the great piece-working trades that were responsible for the nineteenth-century development of collective bargaining' (Turner, 1962: 204).[8] Most notable perhaps were the elaborate piecework 'lists' negotiated in the Lancashire cotton industry specifying rates for every type of work: so complex as to be 'beyond the comprehension ... even of the investigating mathematician without a very minute knowledge of the technical detail' (Webb and Webb, 1894: 293). Their negotiation required a special class of representatives; aspiring officials of the weavers' unions were soon required to pass a technical examination.[9]

The nature of the production systems and employment patterns also encouraged unions in such industries to engage more extensively in political action than was the case with the craft societies. First, they had a particular need to regularize the legal status of collective organization and collective action. The craft unions, as has been seen, might highlight their role as friendly societies and disavow any intent to apply collective pressure on employers. Outside the craft environment the option of the 'strike in detail' was not available, and few workers could afford the level of subscriptions needed to sustain a wide range of friendly benefits; trade unions were bodies for collective bargaining and at times collective struggle or they were nothing. Miners' unions, for example, had often been the target of legal oppression, and played a major role in pressure for reform.

Second, employers in many of the new mass industries sought to maximize their return on capital investments by operating particularly excessive hours of work. From the 1830s the demand for legal regulation of working hours had been pressed by cotton workers, and resulted in the Ten Hours Act of 1847. The same demand was subsequently to become a major issue for unions in mining and on the railways. In such cases, 'their leaders recognised from experience that legislation provided the best form of control' (Clegg et al., 1964: 239).

More general questions of working conditions and health and safety were also linked to campaigns over working time in many of the new industries. In cotton, 'political action for limited ends [was] a method inherited from the Short-Time Committees of the 1830s' (Turner, 1962: 127). Eventually an umbrella body, the United Textile Factory Workers' Association, was established in the 1880s to coordinate such action in every branch of the industry. Factory legislation of a kind had been initiated at the outset of the nineteenth century, but was largely ineffectual. Subsequent Acts were stronger in principle, but lacked means of enforcement. A professional inspectorate was introduced on a very limited basis in 1833. For much of the rest of the century there was intermittent, and at times successful, pressure to increase the number and powers of the factory inspectors and to strengthen the content of factory legislation. While initially driven by the cotton workers and miners, unions in other industries followed suit.

An important question specific to coal-mining was the calculation of the output on which face-workers' earnings would be based. This was undertaken at the surface while the workers concerned might still be at the coal face; the owners might not be trusted either to weigh each hewer's coal accurately or to act fairly in rejecting small coals or stones included in the tubs. The unions therefore campaigned for legislation to require employers to permit the colliers to choose one of their number to check the weighing process, and this was achieved in an Act of 1860. But it proved possible for ruthless mine-owners to evade the original legal requirements, and the unions had to press repeatedly for improvements (Arnot, 1949: 50).[10]

Despite the preference of the craft societies for regulation on the basis of their own industrial strength – particularly over the 'core' questions of pay and hours – they increasingly saw the value of legislation on minor matters. 'It is probable that no one who is not familiar with Trade Union records has any adequate conception of the number and variety of trade regulations which the unions have sought to enforce by Act of Parliament,' wrote the Webbs (1897: 252). One reason why the TUC continued in existence after its original objective, the regularization of unions' legal status, had been achieved was to coordinate this pressure group activity. The annual Congress functioned in large measure as a forum within which individual unions could seek the support of the broader movement for their particular demands; and deputations to government ministers would then urge support for the approved measures. In 1872 the TUC elected what was to become in effect its executive body, the Parliamentary Committee: a title which was retained for half a century.[11]

Union participation in political action also involved attempts to elect leading officials to the House of Commons. Such efforts were influenced by factors of example and opportunity. Parliament contained a substantial number of colliery and mill-owners, directors of railway companies and other major employers from the new industries. There seemed an obvious need to seek some degree of counterbalance by electing working-class MPs. This was most feasible an objective in constituencies where there was a strong concentration of union members from a single industry: as was notably the case in coal and cotton (Clegg et al., 1964: 271–6). The 1884 Reform Act, which extended the franchise to a large proportion of workers in rural areas (where most coal mines were situated) increased the potential for such electoral politics; particularly since it was followed by a redistribution of seats which favoured concentrated mining districts (Gregory, 1968: 9).

Typically such efforts accepted the framework of the existing party system. Almost invariably union officials sought nomination as Liberals: an attempt easier to achieve in union strongholds because, at the time, many constituencies elected two separate members. Those successful were commonly described as 'Lib-Lab' MPs, and in most cases were by no means on the radical wing of their party. The union leaders, commented Engels somewhat despairingly, had become 'the tail of the great Liberal Party' (*Labour Standard*, 23 July 1881). The first of their kind were elected in 1874, Thomas Burt and Alexander Macdonald, both miners,[12] joined in 1880 by the TUC secretary, Henry Broadhurst. In the following dozen years there was a steady if unspectacular increase in numbers; in 1892 fifteen trade unionists (on a broad definition) were elected as MPs, the majority in mining constituencies (Humphrey, 1912: 193). But in the 1890s there was no further advance; on the contrary, numbers declined.

The limited achievements of 'Lib-Labism' had a number of causes. One was that 'in most areas ... the middle-class managers of local Liberal associations refused to accept trade unionists as candidates' (Clegg et al., 1964: 277). Another was that towards the end of the century the Liberal Party under the ageing Gladstone (84 when he stood down in 1894) had lost much of its earlier radicalism, was racked by internal division and showed little sympathy towards working-class demands. The idea of a separate political party to represent trade unionists' interests thus gained increasing support (Pelling, 1954: 49).

Several other developments encouraged this. One was the emergence of explicitly socialist organizations in the 1880s. H.M. Hyndman's Democratic Federation adopted a socialist programme in 1883, strongly influenced by continental Marxism, and changed its name to Social Democratic Federation (SDF) in the following year. Internal differences led soon afterwards to a breakaway, headed by William Morris, to create the Socialist League. Also in 1884, the Fabian Society was formed, again with an explicit commitment to socialism. The decade was one in which the rapid expansionary phase of British capitalism appeared to have come to an end, and when social investigators were revealing the depths of poverty and deprivation existing side-by-side with affluence and luxury. This provided fertile ground for arguments that wealth and income should be more equitably distributed, that competitive private capitalism should be replaced by public ownership and state regulation, and that an independent working-class party was the necessary vehicle to achieve these aims. In the same decade, a series of reforms of local government provided the basis for pressure politics at municipal and county level, where winning election for trade union candidates was far more feasible (and far less expensive) a prospect than at parliamentary level. The experience of local political mobilization was an important background to the creation of the Independent Labour Party (ILP) in 1892.

A development which was to some extent related was the upsurge of what became known as 'new unionism' in the late 1880s and early 1890s. Historians, like contemporaries, have debated the real significance of this wave of activity and organization, and recent accounts have often downplayed its importance (Clegg et al., 1964: ch. 2; Lovell, 1977: ch. 2). Yet in many respects this period was indeed a marked turning-point (Hyman, 1985: 251). Union membership, and strike activity, increased rapidly,[13] extending to many groups of workers not previously involved in collective mobilization. Generally the latter lacked recognized skills (though often possessing specialist aptitudes acquired through experience) and in many cases tended to move between jobs in different sectors and occupations; and most of the 'new unions' matched this pattern of labour market mobility by seeking to recruit extensively: they were the first of the 'general unions'. Socialists were prominent among the leaders and activists who spearheaded this expansion (even though their significance has often been exaggerated), and at times justified the expansionist character of their unions by an appeal to the logic of general class interest. And lacking confidence in their economic strength, they tended to put particular emphasis on political action (not least because many of the new recruits were municipal employees), sometimes linking this to socialist principles. In particular, the 'new unionists' pressed the demand for a universal eight-hour working day imposed by legislation, thereby coming into direct confrontation with the established union leaderships who saw this as a challenge to the principle of 'free collective bargaining'.

Another feature of the 1890s was important: a growing employer counter-attack and a series of hostile judicial decisions. The assertiveness of the new unions, indeed the very fact that the effort to organize workers without previous trade union experience and win recognition from hostile employers was a challenge to the *status quo* and required tactics which at times were none too gentle, provoked upper-class hostility (Saville, 1960). As the decade went on, this linked to growing concerns at the decline in British economic competitiveness, for which trade union restrictions served as an easy scapegoat. The employers' offensive was directed first against the 'new unions', most of which lost members almost as rapidly as they had previously recruited them, and several of which collapsed altogether. But established unions also became targets, particularly as the American 'open shop' (that is, non-union) model was seen as an example to many employers; and this process culminated dramatically in the protracted engineering lock-out of 1897–98. Likewise, hostile judgments in the courts initially targeted forms of collective action – in particular, picketing – which had been prominent in the 'new union' upsurge, but landmark decisions at the end of the decade involved craft unions. In consequence, 'the unions were provoked into considering ways and means of strengthening their defences' (Clegg et al., 1964: 178).

Independent parliamentary representation was a logical response to all these developments. Moreover, the unions had an obvious model for this: the 'Irish Party' of pro-independence nationalists elected in 1885 which had maintained tight collective discipline and for a time held the balance of power in Parliament. However, the 'big battalions' were largely hostile to such an idea: the miners, satisfied with their existing relationship with the Liberals, had no desire to participate in (and perhaps be expected to support financially) a political initiative by the broader movement; most cotton unions, their members drawn from both main camps in politically divided Lancashire, were anxious to maintain a politically non-partisan stance. The solution was a typical trade union compromise: a resolution was narrowly adopted at the 1899 TUC to convene a conference of those organizations willing to participate, in order to 'devise ways and means for securing the return of an increased number of labour members to the next Parliament'. This conference met in 1900, with delegates from unions encompassing less than half the total TUC membership, together with some from socialist organizations, and agreed to establish a Labour Representation Committee (LRC). This would attempt to achieve the election of 'a distinct Labour group in Parliament' which (on the Irish model) would 'embrace a readiness to co-operate with any party which for the time being may be engaged in promoting legislation in the direct interests of labour' or which opposed anti-labour legislation.

This decision, which owed much to the manoeuvres of Keir Hardie and Ramsay MacDonald of the ILP (the latter becoming first LRC secretary), carefully avoided linking the new body to socialism or defining it as a distinct new party, and showed some ambiguity on the extent to which it would be genuinely independent. This was tactically prudent but strategically questionable. The LRC had little time to organize for the snap general election of 1900, eventually endorsing fifteen candidates of whom only two were elected: Hardie and the railway workers' leader Richard Bell, who reached a local agreement with the Liberals. By contrast there were eight Lib-Labs elected, including five miners. The LRC might have been consigned to oblivion but for a further judicial attack on the status of the unions, the Taff Vale case, which ruled that a trade union could be held financially liable for the action of its members engaged in a strike. This created outrage among trade unionists, and affiliations to the LRC increased rapidly. Meanwhile the Liberal leadership – in opposition since 1895, and losing seats in 1900 – decided that cooperation with the new body would be an advantage, reaching a secret agreement in 1903 that an increased number of labour candidates would be allowed a clear run in the next election, while the LRC would try to discourage its own nominees from standing against Liberals in other constituencies (Bealey and Pelling, 1958: ch. 6). Against all expectations, the 1906 election resulted in a Liberal landslide; and to some extent on the Liberals' coattails, 29 LRC candidates were elected.[14] The new group soon adopted the title 'Labour Party'. A further 25 'labour' candidates were successful, including 14 miners elected as Lib-Labs.

In the next few years the 'Lib-Lab' group virtually disappeared, primarily as the miners voted, county by county, to affiliate to the new Party; the Miners' Federation as a whole did so in 1908 (Gregory, 1968). This was partly because there had been a generation shift among activists and officials of the miners' unions, with a stronger socialist influence; partly because the old elite of face-workers was increasingly outnumbered by lower-paid grades of labour with longer working hours; partly because, as a result, the various districts accepted the policy of the statutory eight-hour day and saw the unification of the union voice in Parliament as the best means to realize their legislative aims; but also because the politics of the new Labour Party differed so little from the Lib-Lab tradition. 'Labour rested its appeal before 1914 on its narrowly defined defence of the "trade union interest", both at local level (through support for clauses demanding that the local council should use trade union labour) and at national level (in demands for legal protection for trade unionism)' (Savage and Miles, 1994: 78). The goal of restoring trade union immunities by reversing the Taff Vale judgment was indeed rapidly achieved, despite reluctance on the part of the new government, in the 1906 Trades Disputes Act; but other advances were far harder to obtain. As for broader questions of social reform, the most radical pressure came from within the ranks of the Liberals themselves rather than from Labour. Certainly many socialists were rapidly disillusioned: 'by 1907 the essential irrelevance of the Labour Party in Parliament fuelled a growing dissatisfaction with the whole basis of Labour's political organisation' (Price, 1986: 152).

In electoral terms the Party failed to advance. It suffered a major blow from the courts in 1909, when it was ruled that trade unions were not entitled to spend money on political activities. This severely handicapped it in the two general elections of 1910, when it won 40 and 42 seats respectively: fewer than its previous total, after the accession of many Lib-Labs and several by-election victories. None of those successful in the first election was opposed by an official Liberal candidate, and only two in the second (Pelling, 1961: 24). As in 1906, the Labour leadership reciprocated by attempting to deter contests against sitting Liberals. As in the previous Parliament, the one distinctive political concern of those elected was to reverse the judicial decision which had limited the unions' freedom of action (as well as depriving the Party of resources).[15] They pursued no other common objectives; 'the Labour Party went into the First World War as it had been formed: as a Parliamentary expression of trade union aspirations which involved no coherent programme and no officially accepted socialist commitment' (Coates, 1975: 12). Paradoxically, a third of a century of pressure for independent working-class political action – in which trade unionists who were also socialists had played a prominent role – ultimately reinforced the traditional mind-set which segmented politics and industrial relations. 'The existence of an autonomous Labour Party in Parliament tended to further reinforce the sense of there being a political sphere distinct from the industrial world which was the province of trade unionism. And the development of two centres, the Party and the TUC – the one growing out of the other – seemed to imply the acceptance of two orders and two sets of functions' (Minkin, 1991: 9).

The Rise and Fall of Constitutional Insurgency

The main challenge to this segmentation originated from below. After the upsurge around 1890, union membership had for several years failed to keep pace with growing employment but then gradually recovered; by 1910 there were over 2.5 million union members, roughly one worker in six. Many of the 'new unions' had suffered badly but there were major advances elsewhere, notably in coal-mining. The new decade then saw an unprecedented phase of rapid expansion, with membership passing 4 million in 1913 and 8 million in 1920 – almost half the labour force. As so often in the past, union growth was associated with a resurgence of disputes. The number of officially recorded strikes, which had aver-aged 500 a year in the previous decade, rose to three times that number in 1913 and – after a lull caused by the wartime 'industrial truce' – reached a new peak in 1920. And many of these disputes were of a size and duration which had been exceptional in the past.

These developments are reflected in quantitative indicators; but there was also a qualitative shift in the nature of class relations, though its character was elusive and has been the subject of heated controversy among historians ever since. On one reading, the pre-war 'labour unrest' reflected an escalation of working-class discontent and the impact of new, anti-capitalist sentiments which but for the out-break of war might have exploded into a social and political breakdown; the years 1914–18 saw a growing gulf between a labour movement leadership, both indus-trial and political, committed to supporting the war effort and a rank and file which bore the brunt of harsh working conditions, shortages and deprivations at home, and the loss of relatives and friends in the trenches; while the massive post-war industrial confrontations saw Britain on the brink of revolution. This account has been firmly rejected by the great majority of scholars in recent decades; but though the refutations are cogent, they are often too comprehensively dis-missive. The complex dynamics of this turbulent decade reveal much about the contradictory synthesis of economism and class militancy underlying British trade unionism.

The pre-war unrest was often linked, by commentators at the time and by some subsequent historians, to the doctrine of 'syndicalism'. This took its name from the French *syndicalisme révolutionnaire* (revolutionary trade unionism), a move-ment whose leading theoreticians rejected any compromise with employers, advocated revolutionary violence and sabotage, and called for a general strike as the means to socialism. Their British followers – of whom the most notable was Tom Mann, famous as a leader of the 1889 London Dock Strike, and prominent across the world in industrial and political struggles for most of the intervening period – were more restrained. They advocated not violence but 'direct action', not sabotage but 'ca'canny' or going slow, an established element in workshop custom and practice. What they shared with their continental counterparts was disenchantment with parliamentary politics, an emphasis on industrial solidarity, and faith in the ultimate power of the general strike. Such sentiments proved attractive to some younger trade union activists and to socialists disillusioned with the mediocre achievements of the Labour Party; and some of these activists were prominent in the pre-war industrial struggles. Yet certainly the militant upsurge cannot be explained primarily in terms of the influence of such an ideology.

In fact the unrest had three distinct components. One comprised workers in transport and a variety of factory industries where trade unionism was weak or non-existent. To some extent this was a repeat of the upsurge of 1888–92, though this time the movement was more extensive and the achievements more durable, establishing the main general unions as the giants of British trade unionism. As two decades before, the fight to establish collective organization and win recognition from employers was often bitter; but once these goals were achieved, conflict usually subsided. A second element was a revolt from below in the industries which, half a century earlier, had pioneered the process of collective bargaining: coal and cotton.[16] In some of these disputes, intensified pressure of work was a major grievance; more generally, discontent resulted from modest wage agreements with a duration of several years negotiated just before the cost of living began to rise rapidly. National officials at times seemed totally unresponsive to their members' intense but often ill-articulated discontents (Phelps Brown, 1965: 229–34), firing a challenge to officialdom in the name of the rank and file which chimed with the arguments of the syndicalists. A third factor occurred in many of the craft trades, which (in the context described above as 'unscientific management') had customarily enjoyed considerable unilateral control over the labour process and conditions of employment more generally. While the American managerial craze for 'scientific management' was only partially and hesitantly imitated in Britain, there were sufficient attempts to impose new disciplines and new forms of rationalization of tasks to outrage craft trade unionists. Worse, their own national leaders – anxious, in a wide range of industries, to establish with employers a systematic framework of dispute resolution and to prevent independent action at branch or district level which might jeopardize this – often seemed to support this trend. Here too, appeal to the rights of 'direct action' by the rank and file was a frequent response;[17] though an additional factor was the problem of the structure of the unions themselves. For many activists, the failure effectively to confront the employers' challenge was rooted in the divisive and weakening effects of a multiplicity of competing organizations; the solution was to establish in each industry a single trade union (either by a process of amalgamation, or by launching a new industrial union which through its dynamism would win the adherence of most workers) which could stand up to the employers.

Such ideas gained a new lease of life under war conditions. Virtually every union executive responded to the declaration of war by agreeing to an industrial truce for the duration of the hostilities (initially expected to last only a few months). In this they were certainly not out of touch with their constituents: the popular pro-war enthusiasm is undeniable. When employers and the government called for the suspension of rules which might interfere with war production, the unions acquiesced (in the case of some craft societies, not without misgivings). The use of the strike weapon was suspended in return for a slow and cumbersome arbitration procedure. With greater reluctance, union leaders subsequently accepted the introduction of conscription.

Though most workers had endorsed the requirements of waging war in principle, there was less acceptance of the practical consequences, particularly as hostilities dragged on and 'war-weariness' set in. Production methods were often radically transformed; new forms of work discipline were introduced; new grades of labour, often without a trade union tradition, entered the workplace, eventually to displace existing workers called up to fight; vital protective practices were attacked; rents and other prices surged upwards; there were shortages of everyday necessities. Such grievances could often be redressed, if at all, only by pressure at grassroots level: the 'direct action' which syndicalists had advocated. And to channel such action there developed (as in all belligerent countries) a proliferation of workplace representatives: in the British case, shop stewards, who before the war had existed to a limited degree and with restricted functions in many of the craft societies.

There were two faces to shop steward activity. The one which captured the headlines was the emergence of a self-proclaimed shop stewards' *movement* with revolutionary socialist affinities. Left-wing stewards formed the core of the workers' committees established in many of the main munitions centres, which in turn combined during 1916–17 in the Shop Stewards' and Workers' Committee Movement. Many of its leaders developed an analysis which centred on the idea of workers' control of production. This was at odds with traditional conceptions of socialism, which rested on the nationalization of industry and the redistribution of wealth and income, but without significant change in authority relations at work. Having experienced the wartime spread of state regulation and control, there were growing fears that socialism on this model would simply mean exchanging one set of bosses for another. Socialism from below, built up on structures of management developed by workers themselves, seemed the preferable alternative; and this conception was developed into a theory largely consistent with the Russian idea of Soviet power. Many shop steward leaders enthusiastically supported the Bolshevik revolution of 1917, and subsequently helped establish the Communist Party of Great Britain (CPGB). (In consequence, under the stern prescriptions of Leninism, they disavowed much of the doctrine of workers' control which they had embraced during the war.) For a time, the movement's leaders succeeded in linking their political aspirations to the widespread support of shop-floor workers discontented with the impact of war conditions. But the strongest supporters of the movement were skilled engineers, motivated above all else by the defence of their distinctive status and prerogatives (including special exemption from conscription), if need be at the expense of all other workers; when this contradiction became no longer manageable, the movement fell apart (Hinton, 1973: ch. 10).

The other face of shop steward action was more mundane but more typical. 'Most of the stewards and other workshop representatives were concerned with the countless difficulties which arose in the readjustment of conditions which had to be made in order to adapt the industries of Great Britain to the needs of the war' (Cole, 1923: 3). Such spokespersons emerged more or less spontaneously to voice these grievances, either because they already enjoyed the trust of their fellow workers, or because there was nobody else willing to take on the task. Many employers found it useful to have such an interlocutor immediately available, so as to resolve minor disputes before they became major conflicts, or indeed as a means to negotiate change in advance. Yet conflicts often did arise over the recognition of shop stewards, and in particular of the right of senior stewards or convenors to have access to the whole of an establishment; and over the basis on which stewards could leave their own job to perform their representative function, and whether they should still be paid by the company in such circumstances. Some of these issues were formally regulated (in engineering) by national agreements of 1917 and 1919; though this was to some extent too late, since many of the most active stewards lost their jobs with the return to peace-time production.

After the end of the war, as has been seen, union membership rose to record heights; and so did the number of recorded strikes. What is notable is that militancy now took an official turn. As was seen earlier, consolidation of the fragmented British trade union structure had been widely seen as a means of building effective working-class strength, with the capacity to match the powerful combinations on the employers' side. Some activists viewed such centralization as a basis for more effective influence on government as well. The main pre-war success for advocates of amalgamation was the formation in 1913 of the National Union of Railwaymen (NUR); but after legal restrictions were relaxed in 1917, a series of major mergers followed, notably the Amalgamated Engineering Union (AEU) in 1921, the Transport and General Workers' Union (TGWU) in 1922, and the National Union of General and Municipal Workers (NUGMW) in 1924. The divisive effects of multi-unionism were also moderated by a number of federal arrangements: notably the National Transport Workers' Federation (NTWF), created in 1911 by the numerous unions of road and waterfront workers. In 1913 the NUR and NTWF joined with the Miners' Federation (MFGB) to form a Triple Alliance, which in combining workers in a range of strategic industries was widely seen as the most powerful weapon that British trade unionism had ever forged – even a potential instrument for the much vaunted general strike (Bagwell, 1971). Its capacity was barely tested before the outbreak of war, during which a new concept gained currency: the creation of a 'general staff of labour' through the rationalization of the TUC. This too was realized soon after the war, with the creation of a properly staffed departmental structure and the replacement of the Parliamentary Committee by a General Council.

Centralization, however, had many meanings, and the ambiguities were to become apparent in the turbulent post-war years. Coordination of action, particularly for the unions comprising the Triple Alliance, possessed a simple economic rationale. The mines, docks and railways were economically interdependent: a major dispute in any of the three soon resulted in lay-offs in the others. This depleted the funds of unions which paid unemployment benefit, while appeals for sympathy action could result in a spontaneous pattern of responses which union leaders were unable to control. To develop a common programme of demands and a common timetable for collective action was a means 'to end the wastefulness of unco-ordinated action' (Bagwell, 1971: 98–9). But in these industries, there was also a particularly fluid boundary between economic and political action. Since before long a large-scale stoppage would paralyse much of the economy, any government was bound to intervene in an effort to resolve the dispute. Governments were also closely implicated because of their own role in regulating prices and other aspects of business activity; in labour-intensive industries such as these, there was a close link between prices, profits and wages, and the government could therefore provide the material basis for conflict resolution. The aim of a union in industrial action might be explicitly to put pressure on government – a 'political' motive – but with the delimited objective of resolving an 'economic' grievance on acceptable terms. Governments frequently played their part in this sensitive interaction between politics and economics; but what if they refused?

The mining industry was to provide the test case. Like other strategic industries, the collieries had been under close state control during the war: the government had set production policy, specified prices and largely determined the process of collective bargaining, while guaranteeing the owners a generously defined level of 'normal' profits. The Miners' Federation – with some 800,000 members by far the largest union in the country – submitted to the government in January 1919 an ambitious programme of demands on wages and hours, together with their long-standing objective of nationalization. When the response was unsatisfactory a strike ballot resulted in a six to one majority in favour of action, at which point the government adopted a remarkable procedure to defuse the conflict. The MFGB was persuaded to postpone the strike and participate in a special commission to determine both the immediate issue of wages and hours and the longer-term question of nationalization; the chair, Sir John Sankey, was a judge acceptable to the Miners, who were able to choose half the other members. After a few months a majority reported in favour of nationalization; but the militant post-war mood had already ebbed, the Lloyd George government reneged on its agreement, and a year later the mines were returned to private control.

There followed a series of traumatic defeats for labour. In the months immediately following the end of the war, much of Europe was in social and political turmoil; there were widespread fears (and hopes) that the revolution in Russia would be imitated across the continent. In Britain the situation was far more stable: but here, too, there was a brief moment of uncertainty. Workers expected compensation for their restraint and sacrifice during the war; the armed forces had been promised 'homes fit for heroes' but instead experienced a slow and chaotic process of demobilization, provoking a number of mutinies; even the police went on strike. Many cabinet ministers feared, if not revolution, at least an uncontrollable explosion of militant discontent. But such fears soon subsided, as became evident to the government through its extensive and effective intelligence apparatus, which helps explain its readiness to disregard the Sankey report. During 1919 and 1920 the government indeed made substantial efforts to secure compromise in a variety of industrial disputes, to avoid as far as possible the possibility of common action across a number of strategic industries. But the brief post-war boom (partly reflecting the extent to which the economic structure of many European competitors was initially disrupted) soon collapsed, and with it the buoyant labour market conditions which had strengthened labour. Soon employers in export-oriented industries were seeking drastic wage reductions, while the government pursued deflationary budgetary policies which accentuated the economic crisis.

The miners were the first main casualties. The industry was 'decontrolled' at the end of March 1921 and on the same day the owners, having failed to persuade the MFGB to abandon national bargaining and agree to heavy cuts in pay, locked out the workforce. At first the other unions in the Triple Alliance agreed to take solidarity action; but amid confusion withdrew this support on 'Black Friday', 15 April. The miners fought on alone for three months before accepting defeat. In the following year the engineering workers, led by the new AEU, were in the firing line: the employers insisted on substantial pay cuts in March 1921, then demanded that the unions recognize their right to change employment conditions in the workplace before negotiating, imposing a national lock-out which lasted three months before the unions capitulated. The employers were quick to hammer home their victory, cutting wages once more – for some workers, to below 1914 levels. The onset of mass unemployment (which until the late 1930s remained almost continuously above ten per cent), the losses suffered by those who continued in employment and the costs of these and many other bitter defensive struggles were reflected in trade union membership, which between 1920 and 1923 fell by more than a third.

In 1926 the philosophy of the general strike was put to the test, in circumstances very different from the conceptions of those who had proposed it as an offensive weapon.[18] In the previous year, when the government had re-adopted the gold standard at the pre-war parity, coal exports were badly hit and the owners again demanded pay cuts and also an extension of the working day; this at a time when the economy generally showed signs of a mild recovery and unions in some industries were able to negotiate modest improvements for their members. Fearful of another 'Black Friday', the TUC agreed to block the movement of coal if the miners were locked out. The government responded by offering a nine-month subsidy to the industry while a new Commission was to draft proposals for the future of the industry. The unions hailed this as a victorious outcome – 'Red Friday' – and then did little while the Samuel Commission deliberated and the government prepared for a possible breakdown. The Commission reported in March 1926, recommending rationalization of the industry as the long-run solution to its economic difficulties; in the short term it rejected the proposal to increase working hours but accepted that there should be some reduction in wages. Talks between the two sides brought no settlement, and at the end of April the TUC decided that if the miners were locked out a strike would be called in their support, involving workers in transport, printing and much of heavy industry. Efforts to involve the government in negotiating a compromise broke down.

Union members responded to the strike call on 4 May with considerable enthusiasm. At national level a network of TUC committees coordinated action, while at local level a network of the existing trades councils ran the strike in their localities. However, the government had developed a more systematic organization than that improvised by the unions, using troops and specially recruited strike-breakers to maintain a rudimentary transport system. It also conducted an impressive propaganda offensive, in particular making effective use of the new broadcasting system. It argued that the strike was a 'challenge to the constitution' and that no further discussion of the mining situation could take place until the TUC surrendered unconditionally. As Miliband puts it (1961: 133–4), 'with unerring precision, the Government and its supporters concentrated on the one issue which was, above all others, certain to unnerve the Labour leaders: the issue of revolution and unconstitutionality. Concentration on that issue had another immense advantage – it made it unnecessary to discuss the miners' case at all.' Faced with this intransigence, the union leaders who had called the strike had no idea how to proceed. They had entered into a coordinated form of national solidarity action, expecting that the government would as in the past be stimulated to encourage an acceptable settlement; but their bluff was called, and they were denounced as revolutionaries.[19] With the failure of desperate efforts to find a face-saving outcome, after nine days the strike was called off unconditionally (ironically on the same day that a second wave of workers had been called out). Many strikers were victimized, while a number of activists were prosecuted and imprisoned. The miners remained locked out for another six months until starved back to work on the owners' terms.

This heroic disaster was a brutal demonstration of the limits of what can be called constitutional insurgency. Far more union leaders and activists were prepared to use fiery rhetoric and militant action than were willing seriously to contemplate a confrontation with the political and social order. A telling example is given by Aneurin Bevan (1952: 20–1) who recounts an occasion when the MFGB president, Robert Smillie, had spoken of a meeting in 1919 between the Triple Alliance representatives and the prime minister, Lloyd George. The latter, according to Smillie, 'said to us: "Gentlemen, you have fashioned, in the Triple Alliance of the unions represented by you, a most powerful instrument. I feel bound to tell you that in our opinion we are at your mercy. The Army is disaffected and cannot be relied upon. ... We have just emerged from a great war and the people are eager for the reward of their sacrifices, and we are in no position to satisfy them. In these circumstances, if you carry out your threat and strike, then you will defeat us. But ... if a force arises in the State which is stronger than the State itself, then it must be ready to take on the functions of the State."' Lloyd George was, of course, bluffing;[20] if necessary, the government could have responded as forcefully in 1919 as in 1926. But he knew that the union leaders were negotiators, not revolutionaries. Bevan continues: '"from that moment on," said Robert Smillie, "we were beaten and we knew we were." After this the General strike of 1926 was really an anti-climax. The essential argument had been deployed in 1919.'

One of the consequences of the defeat of 1926 was to expunge from the official perspectives of British trade unionism the belief that concerted industrial action was a legitimate or effective means to force a government to alter a policy to which it was constitutionally committed. As a corollary, it became a priority to establish at the macroeconomic level procedures for peaceful accommodation of interests which had long been the function of collective bargaining at workplace and local (and sometimes sectoral) levels. In some respects, this was working with the grain. As noted in the previous chapter, the wartime Whitley reports had initiated procedures of industry-level negotiation, primarily in parts of the economy without strong traditions of collective bargaining – particularly in the public sector, where 'Whitleyism' became the conventional label for a system of centralized, bureaucratic and conflict-free industrial relations. Much more generally, the inter-war decades saw a consolidation of national collective bargaining; the pre-war patterns of district negotiation, often more volatile and more subject to rank-and-file influence, virtually disappeared. After the traumatic conflicts of the 1920s, which in large measure reflected the painful adjustment of traditional export industries to severe price fluctuations and the loss of their former dominance in international trade, peaceful settlement became the norm; for twenty years after 1932 there was not one single official national strike. The abortive Mond-Turner talks of 1928–29 can be seen as a premature exercise in what, in later decades, would elsewhere be described as 'social partnership'. For some of the new generation of TUC leaders, a broader partnership between unions and state was the logical objective of a labour movement which could no longer aspire to overturn existing structures of political and economic power but might legitimately aim to influence the outcome of the prevailing decision-making institutions.

From such a perspective, the notion of a 'general staff of labour' assumed a significance very different from that envisaged by its original protagonists. The process of trade union amalgamation itself demonstrated how meaning could be transformed: the concentration of forces was the objective of left-wing radicals, but its accomplishment resulted in a formalization of trade union structures which strengthened centralized discipline. The pre-war resilience of rank-and-file autonomy was submerged in a process of consolidation, the supporters of which had often been the most strenuous advocates of rank-and-file initiative. Increasingly it was the national leaderships who were authorized to act.

Here, the notion of Labourism has some relevance. According to Saville (1988: 14–15), 'Labourism was a theory and practice which recognised the possibilities of social change within existing society, and which had no vision beyond existing society. ... On the one hand, there was an "economist" class consciousness continuously renewed from within the industrial sector; on the other, a pervasive sense of and practice of collaboration in political affairs.' This dichotomy was reinforced by the rise of the Labour Party from the representative of a 'sectional interest' (even though the majority of the population!) to the status of a party of government. Labour had 'come of age', first by supporting the war (despite its previous anti-militarist commitments), then through token representation in Asquith's coalition government of May 1915, subsequently by more substantial membership of the Lloyd George coalition in December 1916. Then, when (despite the preferences of many of its national leaders) the Party decided to leave the coalition after the armistice, Labour emerged from the 1918 election as the main parliamentary opposition. This was in a sense a double accident. The Liberals, in seeming political ascendancy in 1914, had fragmented: between those who opposed the war (and in many cases gravitated to the Labour Party); Asquith loyalists, unable to forgive Lloyd George for his coup in 1916; those who for whatever reason failed to gain the 'coupon' of government endorsement in the

1918 election; and Lloyd George followers who were to become a minority in a Conservative-dominated post-war coalition. Among the opposition parties, Labour was actually second to the Irish nationalists; but these refused to take their seats in a British parliament.

In other respects, 1918 saw the emergence of Labour as a potential party of government. Detailed discussion had resulted in a new constitution, adopted in February of that year. This made Labour for the first time a national party with individual members (membership was previously indirect, through affiliated trade unions, socialist societies or autonomous local labour bodies). The constitution also included the famous Clause 4, section 4, committing the Party 'to secure for the workers by hand or by brain the full fruits of their industry and the most equitable distribution thereof that may be possible, upon the basis of the common ownership of the means of production ...'. The unions retained a dominant (indeed, probably enhanced) numerical preponderance in the Party's decision-making structures. An attempt was also made to establish joint administrative machinery for the Party and the TUC. However, in practice the long-standing disjuncture between 'politics' and 'industrial relations' was reinforced through these organizational reforms. Trade unionists elected to the national executive committee of the Party came from minor unions, or were second-tier officers of the larger ones; all important union leaders sat on the new TUC General Council (membership of both bodies being precluded). In general, affiliated unions were willing to leave Party policy to the parliamentarians.

This was evident in 1924 when Labour under MacDonald first assumed government office (even though as a minority). The unions were marginalized, with TUC secretary Fred Bramley complaining that he 'never had more than five minutes' conversation with the Prime Minister throughout' (Pelling, 1961: 172). Ernest Bevin of the TGWU was likewise unimpressed when threatened with military intervention during a dockers' strike. Similar problems occurred during the second Labour government of 1929–31, which collapsed when the majority of the cabinet – their resolve stiffened by the belated intervention of the TUC leadership – refused to accept MacDonald's proposed cuts in unemployment benefit.[21] In the rest of the 1930s Bevin, together with Walter Citrine of the TUC, tried to assert a stronger guidance over key political objectives. If they were effective, however, it was largely because the parliamentary Party – reduced to a rump in the 1931 election and deprived of almost all its previous leadership – had neither the will nor the competence to shape its own policies. By the end of the decade this had changed, and the union leaderships were content to operate the traditional division of functions.

It would be foolish to imply that more radical perspectives on trade union action were eclipsed: the CPGB, and the Minority Movement which it launched in 1924, embodied a conception of the relationship between economic and political struggle which sustained many of the anti-capitalist principles developed in previous generations. But the CPGB was one of the tiniest in Europe in relation to the size of the country: it claimed 4,000 members on its formation in 1920, but this figure soon slipped; just over 10,000 for a brief moment after the end of the General Strike, but falling below 3,000 by the end of the decade. Only in the latter 1930s, with the campaigns in defence of the Spanish Republic and for a popular front, did membership again exceed 10,000.

To some extent activism and commitment compensated for small numbers: the CP exerted an influence out of proportion to its size. Yet influence was won at a cost: to an important degree, communists sought to shape union policy by proxy. There was a persistent tension between, on the one hand, the effort to inspire radical, and potentially revolutionary struggle from below, and on the other the attempt to gain election to official positions, win conference debates, and attract the support of potentially sympathetic leaders. In the circumstances of the 1920s in particular, when the CP consolidated its own traditions, the latter was the more attractive approach. And this was the line of least resistance, for most communist militants were trade union loyalists first and revolutionaries second[22] – and indeed were frequently denounced from Moscow for their 'trade union legalism'. The charge was correct: in what other country would the general secretary of the central union confederation have written a guidebook to constitutional procedure (Citrine, 1939), or would such a book have become a trade union best-seller, as popular on the left as on the right?

In a number of respects, the 'revolutionary pragmatism' of the CPGB was remarkably effective (Fishman, 1995). With the economic revival (largely boosted by rearmament) in the 1930s, communists proved dedicated recruitment agents for their unions, played a major part in the reconstruction of shop steward organization, and were rewarded by increasing success in official elections. This carried over into the 1939–45 war and the post-war era. But like the socialists of the 1880s and 1890s, typically their leadership was accepted despite rather than because of their politics; and also like socialist radicals of an earlier era, their revolutionary pretensions became dissociated from the day-to-day immersion in the realities of interest representation and compromise.

The New Order: Between High Politics and Low Industrial Relations

It was noted in the previous chapter that one account of British trade union development identifies a progressive development of collaborative relationships, at least at national level, from the 1914–18 war onwards. Such a narrative, however, presents a minor sub-plot as the main story; or to make the point rather differently, it overstates the 'corporate bias' within a field of tension in which the adversarial tradition died hard.

Certainly the unions acquired a new public status during these years. As was seen earlier, Applegarth had set a precedent in being appointed a member of a Royal Commission; since 1874 there had been trade unionist MPs; Broadhurst became the first of these to be appointed a (very junior) government minister in 1886. By the end of the nineteenth century a number of trade unionists had been elected as local councillors or appointed as magistrates. The 1914–18 war, however, brought a quantum shift. In the 1915 coalition government Arthur Henderson, the Labour leader, became a member of the cabinet and two other trade unionist MPs were given junior offices. When the Lloyd George government was formed the following year, Labour obtained three cabinet appointments and several junior posts. 'Trade unions became part of the recognised scene' (Allen, 1957: 25). This advance brought union leaders into the ambit of the 'honours' system. Membership of the cabinet carried with it the status of Privy Councillor; in accepting this, Henderson expressed the hope that 'it is the only honour that any Labour man will ever accept' (Allen, 1957: 31). However, various union leaders were to accept other decorations, and retired union leaders were subsequently knighted. A new precedent was, however, set in 1935 when Walter Citrine, the TUC secretary (together with the steelworkers' leader, shortly to retire) accepted a knighthood.[23]

This, remarked Citrine later (1964: 315), could be regarded 'as a recognition of services which I believed had been valuable to the community'. It was an expression of the extent to which, by the 1930s, 'the TUC was accorded a standing in government circles which was quite unprecedented in the case of non-Labour governments' (Martin, 1980: 241). The trade union movement was well on the way to the status announced by Labour prime minister Harold Wilson in 1968: 'the TUC has arrived. It is an estate of the realm, as real, as potent, as essentially part of the fabric of our national life, as any of the historic estates' (quoted in Taylor, 1978: 37).

Yet this is to neglect Bagehot's famous distinction (1963: 61) between the 'dignified' and the 'efficient' parts of the political process. The transformation in the status of the labour movement involved, to a large degree, the ceremonial status of its dignitaries and the integration of its representatives in an elaborate web of consultative mechanisms. Neither could be simply equated with decision-making power. Here, indeed, barriers of class were more resilient. And the authentic class assertiveness of Labourism likewise remained powerful. 'Organized labour will henceforth be satisfied with nothing less than full partnership with the State [another rendering of partnership!]' wrote a leading union official in 1940 (Price, 1940: 167). Bevin, anything but radical yet fiercely class-conscious, expressed this soon after his appointment as minister of labour in Churchill's wartime coalition, denouncing the fact that 'unions ... are tolerated as long as they keep their place and limit their activities' (1940: v). A real impact on policy was a different matter.

Nevertheless, 1940 is widely regarded as a watershed: the point at which the recognition of labour moved from the 'dignified' to the 'efficient'. By contrast to the experience of 1915–18, Labour was now offered a far more substantial stake in government, with party leader Clement Attlee becoming deputy prime minister. The appointment of Bevin himself, never previously a parliamentarian, also implied a new concern to incorporate the unions in the decision-making process.

Even more than in 1914–18, the 'home front' was of decisive military importance. To reverse the disastrous defeats of 1940 demanded massive supplies of aircraft and other armaments; and 'rearmament on such a scale required nothing less than reorganising the whole economy of the country, and doing this not only as fast as possible but under the handicap of black-outs and air raids and of the steady withdrawal of younger men from industry to serve in the Armed Forces'. The implications ranged 'from state control of industry and industrial relations to inflation, fair shares when supplies were short and equality of sacrifice' (Bullock, 1967: 3). Trade unions had a vital mediating role to perform, in defusing discontent and sustaining civilian morale. As in the previous war, the job of union official was a 'reserved occupation', exempt from conscription: a symbol of their perceived importance for the war effort. As in that war also, union membership increased substantially (though by no means as rapidly): from 6 million at the beginning of the war to 8 million at its end.

Most recent accounts stress the ambiguity of the trade unions' wartime position. Their commitment to industrial peace and to maximizing production was evident. The CPGB (reluctantly on the part of many of its leaders) accepted the Comintern's anti-war line in 1939 but toned down any opposition to the war effort (Fishman, 1995: 256–7). Once the line changed, following the German attack on Russia in June 1941, it became perhaps the most fervently patriotic and productivist of all political forces and gained membership rapidly.[24] In contrast to 1914–18, there were no significant organized groups opposed to collaboration in the interests of national survival and the defeat of fascism.[25] Yet paradoxically there were far more industrial disputes: on average, roughly double the annual number of stoppages recorded in the first war, and for the first time ever passing the 2,000 mark in 1944.

Most stoppages were in coal-mining, where the extreme conditions of production were an exceptional provocation to unrest, and where the complexities of the payment system were a recipe for unstable industrial relations. But in some respects, mining epitomized the duality of trade union consciousness in 1939–45: the sense of a war on two fronts. Officials and activists who had lived through the inter-war years carried a heavy load of grudges: being outmanoeuvred by Lloyd George in 1919–20; defeat in the General Strike in 1926; the vindictive Trade Disputes Act the following year; the betrayal of the movement by MacDonald in 1931; the scandal of mass unemployment and the degrading treatment of the unemployed by the public authorities. Now there was a widespread feeling that workers striving to boost war production were at the same time boosting the private profits of the factory owners, and a resentment at being subject to the dictates of the 'little Hitlers' who exercised management on the shop floor (Croucher, 1982). In circumstances when labour was once again scarce and employers dependent on workers' cooperation, the occasion existed to shift the balance of power. 'Management simply had to listen and the foremen lost their right to hire and fire and dispense personal favouritism' (Jones, 1982: 44). One expression of this new assertiveness was (as in the previous war) the rapid spread of shop steward organization, this time linked from the outset to the official trade union machinery. Another was the campaign for Joint Production Committees (JPCs) at workplace level. These were favoured by Bevin 'as a way to further the corporatist compact that remained his central reformist goal' (Weiler, 1993: 125). For many trade union activists, on the other hand, they were a potential vehicle for limiting managerial autonomy and exposing managerial incompetence. Not surprisingly, many companies resisted the whole idea, making the campaign to establish JPCs a means for trade union activists at one and the same time to proclaim their commitment to the war effort while denouncing their employers.

After the end of war production, as a quarter century earlier, there was a disruption of employment and an opportunity for employers to push back the frontier of control on the shop floor. But on this occasion there was no slump, and union membership remained stable. Moreover the political circumstances were the opposite of those after 1918, when war prime minister Lloyd George had won a decisive electoral victory to head a conservative (and increasingly right-wing) administration. In 1945, against all expectation, the Labour Party under Attlee won a massive victory over Churchill and formed the first majority Labour government.

Two accounts of the experience of this government (re-elected with a narrow majority in 1950 and defeated the following year) are familiar. One stresses the achievements: rehabilitating a disrupted economy; presiding over relatively full employment; nationalizing coal, gas and electricity, railways and other sectors; creating the National Health Service and extending other areas of public welfare provision. The other focuses on the limitations: 'a view widely held among active rank-and-file supporters of the Labour Movement, and one which I shared, was that the Labour government, though it had introduced many good social changes during its period of office, had "run out of steam", had committed itself to a rearmament programme which Britain could not afford without sacrifices in living standards, reduced investment in industry and cuts in living standards' (Mortimer, 1993: 243–4). These perspectives are not incompatible. The reforms were substantial (particularly in contrast to the patterns set between the wars), and were enthusiastically received within the labour movement; though it should be added that they attracted support across a far wider political spectrum. The welfare measures followed the war-time Beveridge Report, and have been described as 'the last and most glorious flowering of late Victorian liberal philanthropy' (Stedman Jones, 1983: 246). Most of the industries nationalized – with crippling levels of compensation – were virtually bankrupt and had long been seen as requiring systematic restructuring; even some conservatives thought public ownership the only solution. The key debates concern whether the government could have been more radical at the outset; whether the early reforms could have been the springboard for further advance; and more generally, whether Labour could have been less subservient to the political and economic priorities of the US government (and of its own, very conservative, civil servants).

Whatever the answers – which are beyond the focus of the discussion here – what is undeniable is that the trade unions were not prominent among the advocates of more adventurous policies. Their top officials constituted a 'praetorian guard' committed to warding off any challenges from the left: 'a tight alliance between major Ministerial figures and major trade union leaders ... from 1949, organised and co-ordinated every major vote at the [Party] Conference' (Minkin, 1978: 24). Most unions had four main expectations from the government: first, a smooth and equitable process of demobilization and a transition to a peace-time economy without the unemployment which followed the previous war; second, those extensions of the social and economic role of the state which Labour's manifesto promised; third, the abolition of the hated 1927 Act; finally, that their status in the 'corridors of power', already greatly enhanced during the war, should be maintained and extended. All these expectations were met, and most union representatives were grateful, not least because all these factors contributed to the steady if undramatic growth in their own membership and finances.[26]

The most sensitive issue was the defence of 'free collective bargaining'. As minister of labour in the war cabinet, Bevin had stressed the principle of 'voluntaryism' (Bullock, 1967: 44–6). While strikes were prohibited and compulsory arbitration machinery established, the content of wage bargaining was not directly controlled; the government relied on the self-restraint of union negotiators. This principle was continued under the Labour government (in which Bevin himself became foreign secretary). Circumstances changed, however, in 1947 with the fuel crisis and consequential economic crisis, the development of the Marshall Plan and the onset of the cold war. Until then, the very limited opposition to the sanctity of 'free collective bargaining' had come mainly from the left: those who called for 'socialist planning' and saw the planned development of wages (including a minimum wage) as the logical corollary. But a strange reversal ensued. Early in 1948 the cabinet (in the absence of Bevin, who up to that date had remained vehemently opposed to interference in wage bargaining) adopted a policy statement calling for limitations on pay increases; if its norms were not voluntarily observed it would enforce restraint. The TUC, by a substantial majority, endorsed (relatively flexible) guidelines on pay negotiations; now, it was the communist-oriented left that denounced interference in 'free collective bargaining'.

Voluntary restraint proved remarkably effective, but its impact was uneven and inequitable. Workers in the public sector felt its impact most rigorously; workers whose existing agreements provided for automatic cost-of-living adjustments, or who had the benefit of piecework or other supplementary payments, were far less affected. The resultant grievances weakened support for the policy, and by the 1950 Congress it was narrowly rejected – though the General Council still urged restraint. For some observers, this experience contributed to a gulf between union members and officials. 'The unions are at present the bulwark of industrial peace and lawfulness. With the employers' federation and associations ... they have developed a whole code of industrial behaviour,' reported Zweig (1952: 180–2). 'This often breeds suspicion on the part of the workers. In Lancashire you can hear an uncensored expression about the bosses and the union secretaries: "They piss in the same pot."' Certainly this disenchantment – reinforced perhaps by the degree to which former union officials and activists had become part of the new nationalized management – can be seen as linked to the growing independence of action on the part of shop-floor union representatives.

The 1951 change of government brought remarkably little alteration to trade union perspectives. The fear had been that a Conservative government would herald recession, mass unemployment and union-bashing. But the British economy continued to grow, notwithstanding the intermittent minor recessions of the 'stop–go' cycle, allowing prime minister Harold Macmillan to proclaim 'you've never had it so good'. Nor was the unions' status challenged by legislation; and their relationships with ministers and participation in official committees remained as strong, or even stronger, in the 1950s as in the 1940s. '*Ad hoc* consultation at all levels of government remained frequent and, for the most part, free of difficulty' (Martin, 1980: 301). When in the early 1960s the Macmillan government decided to introduce an incomes policy, it was anxious if possible to avoid alienating the unions; and as part of its effort to win their assent, in 1962 it established the National Economic Development Council (NEDC) with six members directly nominated by the TUC. This was acclaimed by TUC general secretary George Woodcock, reporting to the 1963 Congress: 'we left Trafalgar Square a long time ago. ... We have to deal ... with affairs of the moment in committee rooms, with people who have power.'

The Labour government of 1964 maintained the dynamic. A centrepiece of its economic strategy was an incomes policy: or rather, as it was officially proclaimed, a 'productivity, prices and incomes policy'. It could be presented as an expression of the philosophy of socialist planning and as a vehicle for growth. Hence, notably, Frank Cousins, general secretary of the TGWU and an opponent of wage controls under the previous government, was brought into the cabinet in the new post of minister of technology and could defend the policy as entailing not wage restraint but the 'planned growth of incomes'. A National Board for Prices and Incomes was established to make both general and specific recommendations to government. Initially voluntary, the policy was given statutory backing in 1966, despite TUC objections. Relationships soon deteriorated sharply, as the pay norms became increasingly rigorous, and bore particularly severely on public-sector workers; the TUC also strongly criticized the government's restrictive budgetary policy; and mutual recriminations culminated in the controversy, discussed below, over industrial relations legislation.

The 1960s may be seen as a decade of complex transitions. Workers had by now discarded the 'depression mentality' and were coming to take job security and rising incomes for granted. Yet the British economy, with its 'stop-go' cycles, its poor investment record and its continuing tradition of 'unscientific management', was being outperformed by a growing number of competitor nations. Incomes policy, linked after 1964 explicitly to the encouragement of 'productivity bargaining' through which pay increases were traded off against the reorganization of working practices, became central to government efforts to escape the dilemma. But was incomes policy an instrument to be applied with or against the unions? Until the latter 1960s, the priority of governments of both parties was to gain unions' cooperation – or at least, as after 1966, their 'reluctant acquiescence'. Yet it was unclear what union cooperation entailed. Those who analysed industrial relations in other countries in terms of 'corporatism' defined this as a form of 'political exchange' whereby unions cooperated in wage restraint in return for (possibly) substantive concessions over broader social and economic policy and also for government reinforcement of their own representative status. Such reinforcement in turn enhanced their own capacity to guarantee their side of the bargain. In the British case, this was doubly problematic.

First, as has been seen, the TUC itself possessed only limited authority over its diverse membership. Certainly it was not totally powerless, and in the 1960s it was given enhanced capacities; 'it did more than merely urge affiliates to comply with its official wage policy: it scrutinized and passed judgement on many hundreds of their specific pay claims' (Martin, 1980: 320). Nevertheless its capacity to pursue any major policy initiative usually depended on a consensus among its major affiliates, and implementation could not typically be imposed coercively.

Second, the structure of individual unions limited the scope for their 'incorporation' in government policy-making. A key feature of post-war development was a growing 'bifurcation' within trade union decision-making between the conduct of collective bargaining on the one hand and the 'political' commitments which fed into TUC and Labour Party conference resolutions on the other (Undy et al., 1981: 42). The formal hierarchical structures still determined the latter; but in key sectors of the economy, the former was increasingly devolved to grassroots level. Shop-floor organization and bargaining, which had steadily increased in importance before and during the war, were forced onto the defensive in many workplaces for the next ten years or so (Price, 1986: 201). But from the 1950s there was a sustained revival, first in a limited number of manufacturing industries with strong trade union traditions, then much more extensively. By 1970 it was estimated that there were some 300,000 shop stewards representing workers in manual occupations, and over 50,000 staff representatives as well. In many industries it was collective bargaining at plant level – often fragmented across different departments and occupational groups – which determined the larger share of earnings increases, and also regulated production methods, the organization of working time, hiring and firing and a host of other issues. This process was perhaps most elaborately developed in the motor industry, where researchers in the 1960s (Turner et al., 1967: 222) wrote of 'what might be termed "parallel unionism". For the car workers, in effect, the unions proper have become mainly a society for obtaining occasional general wage-increases and for demonstrating class and occupational solidarity by means of membership. ... The shop stewards' organization has become the real union.'

These conditions informed the report of the Donovan Commission, set up by the Wilson government in 1965. Its creation followed several years in which the status of trade unions had attracted considerable controversy. From the late 1950s some Conservatives had argued that unions should be far more strictly regulated by statute, and as if in response the courts had begun to make a much hostile interpretation of the law, narrowing and eroding many of the immunities laid down in 1906. More generally there was concern at the trend in strikes: numbers were beginning to rise rapidly (despite a sharp decline in mining, which had previously dominated the statistics), reaching almost 4,000 in 1970. Shop-floor 'anarchy', constant pressure on wages, and 'restrictive practices' which obstructed innovation were all presented as scapegoats for the mediocre performance of the British economy.

The TUC helped ensure that the Commission was not merely an exercise in union-bashing. On its insistence the terms of reference covered employers' associations as well as unions, and it nominated two of the commissioners including its own secretary, George Woodcock. After intensive investigation, the Donovan report concluded that the problem of British industrial relations involved systematic institutional deficiencies. There was a 'formal system', constituted by the national organizations of workers and employers and generating national collective agreements which were increasingly detached from the realities of workplace industrial relations. The latter, in the words of Flanders (1970: 169), were 'largely informal, largely fragmented and largely autonomous'. The main problem with trade unions was not that they were too strong but that they were too weak. Most shop stewards were 'more of a lubricant than an irritant'. Without institutional reform no changes in the law could work much effect, and the main instrument of reform must be management; it should recognize that most issues could not be effectively addressed above the level of the company itself, and therefore that domestic industrial relations should be much more systematically coordinated.

The government accepted much of the analysis and prescription but was anxious to show some signs of greater toughness; so in its draft legislation it included proposals for compulsory strike ballots and for powers to delay major strikes. Though relatively modest (particularly with hindsight) these 'penal clauses' provoked massive opposition from the unions and within the parliamentary Party itself; the government was forced to back down, its face only partially saved by a 'solemn and binding' undertaking by the TUC to police strikes itself. Soon afterwards, Labour went down to defeat in the 1970 election.

The Heath government adopted a much more offensive strategy, but without wholly abandoning the objective of union cooperation in its policies. Its Industrial Relations Act of 1971 introduced for the first time detailed external regulation of unions' internal affairs; limited the traditional immunities to unions which followed the new, tougher registration procedures; imposed major restrictions on the legality of strike action; and virtually outlawed compulsory union membership (the 'closed shop'). Yet it introduced for the first time a remedy for unfair dismissal, and also a statutory procedure for union recognition. The Act was strongly opposed by the unions, though initially there was no clear strategy of resistance. Pressure from below led however to an instruction that affiliated unions should not register under the new procedures or cooperate with the institutions established by the Act, and a small number of unions which failed to comply were eventually excluded from the TUC.

What followed seemed to demonstrate the limits of a coercive approach to industrial relations (Weekes et al., 1975), and the truth of the slogan that 'the workers united will never be defeated'.[27] Resistance to the Act coincided with efforts by the government to impose restraint on public-sector pay; while abandoning Labour's attempt to impose a general incomes policy, it announced that settlement levels for public employees would be reduced in a step-by-step process (described as the 'n − 1' formula). This came to grief in 1972 with disputes in coal-mining and on the railways. In the first case, the National Union of Mineworkers (NUM) had initiated an overtime ban at the end of the previous year; this was followed by the first national strike in the industry since 1926. Eventually the government, desperate to end the economic disruption which ensued, appointed a court of inquiry which resulted in major gains for the union. In the rail dispute, involving a work-to-rule and overtime ban, the government used its new legal powers to impose a 'cooling-off' period and then a compulsory ballot. The latter resulted in large majorities in support of the rail unions' action (even non-unionists voted in favour), assisting them in obtaining a more substantial increase than might otherwise have been forthcoming. This was followed by a bitter struggle by the dockers, involving resistance to the loss of their traditional work with the development of containerization. The gaoling of five dockers who had helped coordinate the picketing of container terminals provoked massive protests and the threat of a general strike; the crisis was defused only after a series of bizarre judicial manoeuvres resulted in the dockers' release.

To restore order in industrial relations the government felt obliged to seek a return to consensus: it 'offered the TUC a place in the formulation of economic policy, based on NEDC, which went further than anything offered by any previous Government, in exchange for active support of an incomes policy' (Kessler and Bayliss, 1995: 21). Negotiations came close to agreement but the TUC finally drew back; the government imposed statutory wage limits at the end of 1972; and the TUC, though protesting, made little effort to challenge the legislation: 'all unions, however militant, preferred to find loopholes in the policy rather than direct confrontation with the state' (Crouch, 1977: 223). After a year, however, the NUM again challenged pay restraint, on this occasion making systematic use of 'flying pickets'. Once more there was serious economic disruption and Heath called a general election, with the central question: 'who governs?'. The outcome was a parliamentary stalemate, with Labour marginally the largest party; and it formed a minority government.

The events of these four years created a widespread sentiment – both among trade unionists and the wider public – of trade union power. The Industrial Relations Act had proved largely unworkable in the face of concerted union non-cooperation (though also, as was little emphasized at the time, because large employers on the whole were reluctant to use their new legal rights to drag unions before the courts).[28] Efforts to achieve wage restraint, by consent and by compulsion, had appeared equally unsuccessful. And when the government attempted to restore its mandate by going to the country it was defeated (albeit narrowly).

Initially, the Labour government elected in 1974 made no attempt to repeat the experiment; the miners' demands, as well as several other impending flash-points in the public sector, were resolved on (by previous standards) very generous terms. At least programmatically, Labour had adopted a range of radical policy commitments and had developed a closer relationship with the TUC leadership. A priority was to repeal the Industrial Relations Act, achieved through the 1974 Trade Union and Labour Relations Act and (after a second election in which Labour had achieved a parliamentary majority) the 1975 Employment Protection Act – both of which provided workers with new individual and collective employment rights. But soon a drastic inflationary and foreign exchange crisis (driven in part, ironically, by the cost-of-living wage indexication included in the Heath government's compulsory incomes policy) led to a new and more draconian phase of pay controls, in which wage restraint was supposedly to be rewarded by progressive social and fiscal policies. The notion of a 'social contract' used to legitimate this initiative marked a significant shift in the rhetoric – and the underlying assumptions and perspectives – of British unions: a recognition that militant economism had its limits. The agreement between government and unions, brokered to an important degree by the TGWU secretary Jack Jones, provided for an initial flat-rate norm for pay increases which was relatively favourable for the low-paid but far more restrictive for more advantaged employees. The TUC also supported a second phase of restraint in 1976, this time on a percentage basis. The following year the unions did not endorse, but acquiesced in, a tighter percentage limit; but in 1978 the government imposed an extremely low norm which provoked a wave of conflict – popularly termed the 'winter of discontent' – and was quickly followed in May 1979 by the electoral victory of an aggressively anti-union Conservative party newly led by Margaret Thatcher.

In retrospect the dominant interpretation of the 1970s – on much of the left as well as the right – was that overbearing trade union power, deployed increasingly arbitrarily, had led inexorably to the nemesis of Labour. This assessment is questionable on a number of grounds. How far the industrial conflicts of 1978–79 can be blamed for Thatcher's victory is problematic: 'Labour had given the electors so many reasons to vote against it that it was impossible to discern the critical factor' (Cronin, 1984: 206). Conceptions of trade union power in general rested on dubious empirical foundations. Opinion surveys showed that Jack Jones was widely regarded as the most powerful man in Britain; but for a union leader to endorse wage restraint is not self-evidently evidence of overbearing power: 'publicity is never the most reliable index of influence' (Coates, 1980: 203). In effect the unions were pursuing, with considerable self-restraint, their traditional role of defending the living standards of their members in circumstances of escalating economic adversity – circumstances made worse by the terms of IMF support in 1976, which resulted in severe budgetary stringency for the remainder of Labour's period of office.

In essence, 'trade union power' consisted in the continuing capacity to block the deterioration in workers' real incomes, social benefits and employment security which governments and their economic advisors increasingly insisted was unavoidable. This was a negative or oppositional power. This well encapsulated the tradition of Labourism, and was poignantly demonstrated in another controversy of 1974–79: the debate over 'industrial democracy'. In line with its policy commitments, the government established a committee of enquiry under Lord Bullock to advise on how (not whether) employees might obtain representation on company boards. In 1977 it reported with recommendations for a procedure whereby recognized trade unions might initiate the election or appointment of worker directors. This was fiercely resisted by employers' organizations but received only lukewarm trade union support. On the left, worker directors were seen as a threat to militancy and class struggle; much more generally, they were viewed as potentially compromising trade union independence. This scepticism had echoes of the arguments of Clegg a quarter of a century earlier (1951: 24, 131): 'the trade union is industry's opposition, [but] can never hope to become the government. ... Trade unions owe their existence to the need felt by the workers for an organization to oppose managers and employers on their behalf. The trade union cannot then become the organ of industrial management; there would then be no one to oppose the management, and no hope of democracy. Nor can the union enter into an unholy alliance for the joint management of industry, for its opposition functions would then become subordinate, and finally stifled.'[29]

British unions, as 'industry's opposition', continued to conceive their role in primarily economic rather than political terms. Most union leaders accepted the 'distinction, fully understood though logically inexact, between "industrial" and "political" issues. Roughly speaking, any issue that the unions consider to lie within their own preserves and to be best dealt with either by themselves or by the TUC General Council is "industrial"; the rest are "political"' (Flanders, 1970: 34). Yet this was a conception increasingly at odds with the changing roles of governments, employers and trade unions. The 'inexact' distinction was not, ultimately, for the unions themselves to draw. 'It was the state who defined "political" and when it exercised this definition against the unions a whole structure of rights and protections was in danger' (Fox, 1985: 435–6). Against their will (in most cases), union representatives had become enmeshed in politics: 'the unions did not seek a new political role by themselves. This was thrust upon them by the incomes policy of the state, but since the state's demand that, in effect, the unions operate as its agents could not be accepted, the unions' response had to be one of increasing political militancy' (Crouch, 1977: 226). British trade unions demonstrated in the 1970s that they could wield substantial veto power, but they lacked the organizational capacity and for the most part the will to seek to translate this into a more positive strategy for economic transformation. The challenge posed by Lloyd George in 1919 had returned to haunt the movement: 'if a force arises in the State which is stronger than the State itself, then it must be ready to take on the functions of the State. ... Have you considered, and if you have, are you ready?'

A Transformation of British Trade Unionism?

The opportunity, if such there was, passed rapidly; the 1979 election was to bring the climax of a 'Copernican revolution' (Fox, 1985: 373). The Conservative Party under Thatcher embraced the philosophy of the newly ascendant economic right and sought a break with the consensual bias of all post-war governments in order to instal a regime of economic liberalism. This required the imposition of strict monetary disciplines, the end of direct state intervention in the functioning of markets and the removal of institutional constraints on their 'free' operation. Among these, trade unions were the most important. 'Solving the union problem is the key to Britain's recovery' was the title of a pamphlet published by Keith Joseph, one of Thatcher's most senior colleagues, immediately before the election.

Few believed at the time that the Conservatives, once in office, would pursue such a project; or, if they were to start on the projected course, that they would persist. Heath's failure was an object lesson. Clegg (1979: 378), writing shortly before the election, took it for granted that a Thatcher government, like Heath's, would be forced to turn from market liberalism to an incomes policy: 'the relevant question therefore is not whether Britain will soon see the last of incomes policy, but whether the future will bring another series of short-lived policies or one lasting one.' Even 'a social contract between the unions and a Conservative government' could not be excluded (1979: 381–2). Another academic observer, writing immediately after the election, argued that previous decades had seen a growing development of corporatism in Britain which was unlikely to be reversed. 'The Tories ... cannot afford to be seen as anti-union. ... It would be surprising indeed if the Thatcher government does not attempt at some point to forge a policy consensus among the major interest groups; if it does, and especially if it attempts to negotiate an incomes policy, the price will be the sort of incorporation of the union movement here described. The tide of union influence may ebb and flow, but ... will not easily be eroded' (Thomson, 1979: 48, 54). If the dominant mood within the unions was that they could stand up to Thatcher as they had to Heath, trade unionists were in good company. But the assumptions were wrong: the tradition of militant economism, the distinctive British synthesis of class and market, was to be tested to destruction.

First, the legal framework was altered dramatically; but not, as in 1971, through a single Act which could provide a concentrated focus for resistance. From 1980 there were eight major acts of parliament as well as other lesser pieces of industrial relations legislation. The main effect was to weaken still further the limited legal protections available to individual workers, while overturning the tradition of trade union 'immunities'. The scope for legal strike action was drastically narrowed, while the internal procedures of trade unions were subjected to detailed and onerous regulation. From one of the least legalistic industrial relations systems in the world, Britain became one of the most legally prescriptive; and in a form bearing asymmetrically on workers' organizations as against employers.

Second, the labour market was transformed. For the first two post-war decades, the average rate of unemployment had been less than 2 per cent. There was a gradual deterioration in the 1960s and 1970s; while in the 1980s the level rose to one of the highest in Europe. At the same time, the structure of workers in employment altered substantially. The long-term decline in manufacturing accelerated; manual workers were outnumbered by white-collar staff; public employment was substantially reduced by the government's privatization of most of the nationalized sector and compulsory contracting-out of many elements of public services. The traditional norm of full-time permanent employment gave way to a far more 'flexible' workforce, with a rapid growth in part-time working (almost a quarter of all employment), in temporary contracts and in self-employment.

Third, partly in consequence there was a sharp fall in trade union membership, which had peaked at over 13 million in 1979 but fell year by year to under 8 million in the late 1990s (TUC membership fell to under 7 million). While more than half of all employees were union members at the earlier date, the proportion dropped to less than a third. In part this reflected the high unemployment; in part, the restructuring of employment. Union membership was traditionally high among manual workers, in large manufacturing plants (and in similar work contexts such as docks, coal-mines and railways) and in the public sector: precisely the areas where employment fell sharply. Conversely, new jobs were created mainly in small firms, in private services, often for a largely part-time and female workforce: precisely where unions were traditionally weakest.

Fourth, also important were the policies and practices of employers. Arguably, one reason for the failure of the 1971 Act had been that most main employers saw little need for a revolution in industrial relations. A decade later, in far more difficult economic circumstances, attitudes had changed. British employers (and indeed also academics) had absorbed much of the American vocabulary of human resource management (HRM). As in most of Europe, there was intense discussion of the need to harness employee commitment to company objectives, to improve channels of communication, to invest in skills, to integrate the management of the workforce within more general corporate strategy. Whether this implied a rejection of traditional industrial relations was a much debated question; but what was undeniable was the degree to which individual companies explicitly assumed the role of major industrial relations actors. Most employers' associations disintegrated; or at least ceased any attempt to regulate employment conditions. In what remained of the public sector, the government strenuously encouraged a devolution of managerial authority and the breakdown of national bargaining. Increasing decentralization of pay determination and of other aspects of employment regulation had important implications for the overall coverage of collective bargaining in a context of declining trade union membership. By the end of the 1990s, the official Labour Force Survey showed that only 44 per cent of employees were in workplaces where unions were recognized, and only 36 per cent had their pay and conditions determined by collective bargaining.

The fifth change which deserves emphasis is in overt industrial conflict. The number of strikes fell to the lowest levels since records began over a century earlier, and the numbers of workers involved and days lost also declined substantially. At the same time, there was a marked shift in the distribution of major disputes, from the private to the public sector. The causes and significance of this change were disputed. One relevant factor was the state of the labour market: the number of strikes tends to vary inversely with unemployment. Another was the change in employment structure: jobs disappeared substantially in traditional strike-prone industries. The legislative changes which narrowed the traditional immunities and introduced an obligation for unions to hold strike ballots were seen by some commentators as a key explanation. Whatever the reasons, the role of British unions as bearers of militant economism was eclipsed.

This eclipse was confirmed by four symbolic defeats. In 1979 what was then the main British-owned motor vehicle company (British Leyland) dismissed the shop steward convenor at its largest plant. Management effectively exploited workers' fears for the survival of the company and their jobs, as well as playing on political differences (the convenor was a member of the Communist Party), and a protest strike attracted very limited support. The distinctive British system of shop steward organization, traditionally regarded as a basis of collective strength, proved to have feet of clay. Second, in 1980 a new hard-line management in British Steel faced out a three-month national strike in order to dismantle the traditional industry-wide system of pay negotiation, humbling a once powerful union. Third, even starker was the defeat of the miners in 1984–85 in their year-long strike against pit closures. Divided by regional jealousies and differentiations of economic interest, confronted by the full resources of state power, and – some argued – under a strategically inept leadership which failed to appreciate the limits of economic militancy in hard times, the miners' struggle was seen by many trade unionists as a demonstration that traditional forms of resistance were doomed to failure. The fourth example was the success of news magnate Murdoch in breaking the influence of the printing unions within his empire, by moving production to a new works, withdrawing union recognition, and dismissing employees for striking in protest. Murdoch successfully exploited the armoury of new legal rights given to employers, and after suffering heavy legal penalties in the courts the unions abandoned their resistance. The notion that unions, given sufficient determination and solidarity, could successfully defy the law seemed to have been discredited. Trade unionism was 'confirmed as the bearer of a secondary, derivative, negative, limited power, severely circum-scribed by economic change and state initiatives' (McIlroy, 1995: 398).

Loss of membership and economic effectiveness led also to a dramatic weak-ening of trade unions' influence within the Labour Party. In the folk memory of the Party leaders of the 1980s and 1990s, the unions were largely to blame for the defeat of 1979 and the long hegemony of Thatcherism; renewed electability required a radical redefinition of the traditional linkage. In the main, union leaders accepted the need for 'a new subordinate role' (McIlroy, 1995: 301), abandoning the traditional assumption that at least on questions of industrial relations legislation their influence on party policy would be decisive. In 1993, after a fourth succes-sive electoral defeat, the new Party leader John Smith pushed successfully – despite resistance from several major unions – for substantial curbs on trade union voting power within the Party. His successor, Tony Blair, carried the process much further, as well as forcing through the elimination of the 1918 commitment in the Party constitution to the social-democratic goal of common ownership of the means of production. While most trade union leaders were far from happy at these changes, their response was nevertheless one of 'grudging acquiescence' (McIlroy, 1995: 389).

Nor, much more generally, was there significant union opposition as it became clear that the substantive industrial relations policies of 'New Labour' would involve no major break with those pursued since 1979 by the Conservatives (McIlroy, 1998). Fearful of Conservative charges that a Labour government would be 'soft' on trade unions, leading figures in the party often attempted to sound as anti-union as their opponents in the expectation that this would be to their electoral advantage. In somewhat more nuanced but still ambiguous fashion, Blair insisted that the unions would receive 'fairness not favours' from a Labour government. Thus the election of May 1997 brought no radical transformation for British unions.

First, the economic environment of industrial relations remained largely unal-tered. Labour maintained the monetary regime adopted by the Conservatives, including its tight public expenditure limits, and indeed increased the autonomy of the Bank of England in setting interest rates. Against the background of the appreciation of the pound in relation to currencies of competitor economies, this reinforced the recessionary pressures already generated by global economic trends, adversely affecting production; although high domestic demand brought some recovery in employment. Like the Conservatives, Labour strongly emphasized the need for labour market 'flexibility'. This commitment – together with an evident desire to maintain the goodwill of big business and the employers' organizations – made it resistant to most proposals for new employment rights and to most aspects of the social agenda developed by the European Commission.

In the sphere of industrial relations more narrowly defined there was considerable continuity with the previous government, but with some shifts in policy. Labour ended the UK 'opt-out' from the social protocol agreed at Maastricht. In consequence the working time Directive was incorporated into British law, a significant change since average working time in Britain is the highest in the whole EU. However, the government exploited to the full the scope for exemptions contained in the Directive, and even allowed individual workers 'voluntarily' to opt out of its requirements. The European Works Council Directive was also transposed into British law, though here too in a minimalist manner.

In addition, the government implemented the Party's commitment to introduce a national minimum wage, appointing a Low Pay Commission to oversee the process. The rate recommended by the Commission, £3.60 an hour, took effect in April 1999; its level was well below trade union demands but was nevertheless likely to entail pay increases for two million workers.[30] Modest increases were approved the following year.

The government was committed to introduce a law on trade union recognition. The proposals outlined in the White Paper *Fairness at Work* in May 1998 were more restrictive than had been hoped by the trade unions but were nevertheless strongly opposed by the main employers' organizations. The Employment Relations Act which was passed in July 1999 made substantial concessions to the employers; not only did recognition require majority support in an employee ballot, but 40 per cent of all employees covered had to vote in favour (a rule which would disqualify most members of the British parliament). According to the 1998 WERS survey (Cully et al., 1999), in only 1 per cent of all British workplaces did unions lack recognition despite having majority membership.

Other continuities may be noted. The separate Employment Department was not re-established (leaving Britain as one of the very few European countries without a separate ministry of labour). The 1980–93 legislation regulating and restricting unions was not altered significantly, and limitations on strike action remain virtually unchanged. Even the statutory requirement for the Advisory Conciliation and Arbitration Service (ACAS) to promote collective bargaining – uncontentious when adopted in 1975, but abolished in 1983 – was not restored on the grounds that ACAS should not be 'seen to be biased by statute'.

Reconstructing Trade Union Strategy: Leaner but Fitter?

The faith of British unions in the virtue and effectiveness of 'free collective bargaining' has, not surprisingly, altered radically. Even before the onslaught of the Thatcher years there was growing recognition of the limitations of a 'voluntarist' model of industrial relations. For example, there was increasingly vocal argument by feminists that the dynamics of collective bargaining did little to counteract, and perhaps even reinforced, gender inequalities in the labour market. It was a reflection of such criticism, though also of the requirements which followed UK accession to the European Community, that legislation on equal pay and sex discrimination was passed in the 1970s. Another important factor was the abortive Industrial Relations Act passed by the Conservatives in 1971; while largely anti-union in intent this introduced for the first time legislation (albeit largely ineffectual) on union recognition and unfair dismissal. Even if few unions had asked for such positive rights, the new consensus was that these should be strengthened rather than abandoned, and the laws adopted under the Labour government elected in 1974 produced a far more comprehensive legal framework for British industrial relations than ever before.

Under Thatcher it became obvious – not least because of the clear declarations of the Labour leadership – that there would be no return to 'collective *laissez-faire*'. It was also evident – much as the Webbs had argued almost a century earlier – that the changes in the labour market had in any event shifted the balance of advantage within 'free collective bargaining'. Given high unemployment, job insecurity, the decline of the old union strongholds and the shift in economic structure towards contexts where traditional collective militancy was extremely hard to mobilize, statutory rights were perceived in a new light. A symbolic shift came in 1986 when for the first time the TUC accepted the principle of a national minimum wage. Two years later the TUC reversed its long-standing opposition to British membership of the EC, perhaps on the logic that anything so bitterly opposed by Thatcher must have much to recommend it. Thereafter, adoption of core elements of the 'European social model' became a clear objective of most British unions.

More specifically, unions responded to hard times in six distinct ways. The first was initiated in particular by organizations attempting to recruit higher-skilled or professional and managerial employees, but was embraced more generally and was endorsed by the TUC at the end of the 1980s. This approach assumed that traditional appeals to collective interests and solidarity were no longer relevant to workers who were confident in their individual capacity to work the labour market. What was therefore necessary was to offer a range of individual incentives: cheap holidays and motor insurance, cut-price financial services, pensions advice and other benefits not directly linked to the employment relationship (Bassett and Cave, 1993). While often presented as the modern face of British trade unionism, this strategy in fact harked back to the earliest forms of craft unionism, in which individual 'friendly benefits' were the material foundation of the 'method of mutual insurance'. Research was to show (Waddington and Whitston, 1997) that this approach was largely misconceived: new recruits to trade unionism, even among those favourably placed in the labour market, were primarily concerned with the traditional union functions of collective improvements in wages and conditions and protection against arbitrary action by the employer.

Another significant ideological shift, as noted above, was in attitudes to the law. As unions' bargaining power was reduced, so there was increasing enthusiasm for employment rights underwritten by law rather than enforced by collective strength. Though the key landmark was the acceptance of the principle of a statutory minimum wage, more radical still was the proposal in 1994 to move from the long cherished principle of a 'single channel' of employee representation. Hitherto, virtually all British unions had resisted any notion that workplace representative structures should be created separate from trade union organization and within which non-unionists might hold elected positions. This constituted a major obstacle to union support for continental models of 'industrial democracy'. The taboo was now breached; in its report (1994, 1995) on representation at work the TUC accepted that non-unionists – a minority of the workforce in the 1970s, but by then almost two thirds of all employees – should receive a statutory right to workplace representative structures.[31] The shift was of immense symbolic importance, and remained controversial.

A third response also implied a pessimistic view of the capacity for collective mobilization of members in a world where employment of male manual production workers in large workplaces was no longer the norm. If it was no longer possible to wield 'industrial muscle' in the traditional manner, employer goodwill seemed a necessary condition for achieving and sustaining effective organization. This encouraged a resort to a concept hitherto totally alien in British industrial relations: 'social partnership'. Following the election of John Monks as general secretary in 1993, the pursuit of partnership became a central theme of the TUC, underlying a succession of policy documents. From 1996 onwards, resolutions acclaiming social partnership were adopted by each annual Congress, usually with very little debate; while *Partners for Progress* was the optimistic title of the TUC's proposals (1997) for industrial relations under a new government. The General Council established a partnership Task Group at the end of 1998 to oversee the new policy orientation.

At company level, a large number of 'partnership agreements' were negotiated during the 1990s, for the most part involving an exchange of job guarantees and possibly union-based consultation machinery in exchange for more flexible working arrangements. More generally, however, the notion of 'partnership at work' was widely embraced (not least by the Labour government of 1997) without any acceptance of the principle of union involvement which is integral to continental norms of 'social partnership'. This is considered in more detail below.

A fourth initiative, again associated with the 'relaunch' of the TUC under Monks, was to raise the public profile of trade unionism through active campaigning. This involved in part a process of mobilizing for stronger rights for employees – not least by backing European-level regulation – but also involvement in a variety of other campaigns. For example, the TUC became active in high-profile anti-racist initiatives.

Fifth, there was considerable emphasis on the need to develop (or rediscover) an 'organizing culture'. For much of the post-war era, unions could benefit from broad social support for collective organization, reinforced increasingly by employer willingness to reinforce or even impose a norm of union membership (the 'closed shop'). To a large degree, unions lost the habit and indeed the capacity of active recruiting. In the 1980s, as the closed shop was systematically outlawed and employers increasingly sought to marginalize or exclude trade unionism, it became obvious that active recruitment was again essential. In the late 1980s the TUC attempted to encourage coordinated recruitment by member unions, but to little effect. Traditional inter-union rivalries inhibited cooperation, and most existing union officials were too overwhelmed by the demands of servicing existing members to devote much time to recruitment (Kelly and Heery, 1994: 103–5, 190–1). This led the TUC in the 1990s to emulate the efforts of its US counterpart, establishing in 1997 an 'organising academy' to develop specialists able to work with local union activists and officers to build up membership and organization. As yet it is too early to evaluate its success.

Finally, unions came to realize that in the past they often took their membership too much for granted. Many of the legislative initiatives of the Conservatives reflected a view that union leaders were out of touch with their members, industrially more militant and politically more left-wing. Hence the laws of the 1980s required the direct election and re-election of top officials and executive bodies; ballots before strikes or other industrial action; a vote every ten years to maintain a political fund; and individual confirmation every three years to permit deduction of union subscriptions by the employer from a worker's pay (the 'check-off'). The underlying premise of these initiatives was misconceived. Few incumbent union leaders have been defeated in elections, and those that were more often lost to challengers from the left than from the right; strike ballots have been overwhelmingly positive, ironically serving to strengthen the hand of union negotiators; all political fund ballots have been won, and the process has encouraged some unions without political funds to establish them; the campaigns over the check-off (one of the few aspects of the Conservative legislation to be repealed in the Employment Relations Act) allowed some unions to increase their membership. Nevertheless, the whole experience of responding to the legislative offensive obliged unions to improve (or in many cases, to develop for the first time) their communications to meet the circumstances of the modern age: both to discover their members' feelings and aspirations, and to argue for the policies which the leadership believed important.

Conclusion: In Search of an Identity

Trends in British trade union ideology remain uneven, uncertain and contested. But experience since 1979 has clearly shaken the stability of a model of trade unionism founded on the market-class axis. The opposite pole of the eternal triangle – encapsulated in the notion of social partnership – has exerted increasing attraction: the geometry has shifted.

Nevertheless, there has been a major contradiction within the ideological reorientation of the TUC and most main unions. The aim was 'to recreate an encompassing trade unionism which can speak on behalf of a broadly conceived labour interest' (Heery, 1998a: 356). On the one hand, appeals to social partnership became almost a reflex response to every industrial relations issue. On the other, reversing union decline was also seen as requiring a 'new unionism' centred around active campaigning and mobilization, particularly among the expanding sectors of marginalized workers. The launch of the TUC 'Organising Academy' in 1997 coincided with the opening of a 'Bad Bosses' Hotline' for aggrieved workers to report exploitative wages, oppressive conditions and harassment at work. Yet as Heery has emphasized, there is a fundamental incompatibility 'between an aggressive campaigning unionism and attempts to develop social partnership in relations with the government and with employers' organizations' (1998b: 348). This was indeed noted by the General Council in its 1999 report to Congress: 'inevitable tensions can exist between the active promotion of partnership and the "anger, hope, action" model of organisation. ... Partnership may not be the right model when confronted by a bad employer.'

A more fundamental paradox underlies the British unions' conversion to the idea of social partnership. As indicated in the previous chapter, ultimately this concept has achieved a purchase in (some) other European countries on the basis of collective employee strength, typically buttressed by a powerful array of legal representational rights. It is where the disruptive mobilization of workers' power is an available tactic that unions' interlocutors have been constrained to embrace partnership as a preferable option. But for unions which lack substantial collective strength or significant legal rights to call for partnership is to submit aspiration to a sterner test. Even before the 1997 election, the Labour Party suggested a very different conception of partnership, in its 1996 statement on industrial strategy: 'in modern world class companies the relationship between employers and employees must be based upon partnership and trust and the recognition of a shared stake in the success of the enterprise'. There was no explicit role, in this formulation, for collective representation of employee interests: management itself could function independently as the trustee of partnership. Since the 1997 election this has been the perspective of the Labour government: the objective is 'partnership' between employers and employees, with no necessary role for trade unions, rather than 'social partnership', in which a recognized status for union representation is inherent. Many employers proved happy to assent to this diluted understanding of partnership – which indeed reinforces the legitimacy of management as protector of the common interests of workers and employers.

'Employers are now beginning to appreciate that as partners trades unions can add value to their business and business performance,' declared the mover of the social partnership resolution at the 1998 Congress.[32] Trade unions as agencies for the enhancement of shareholder value? Of course employees have no obvious interest in the business failure of their employers. This still leaves the question, however, of the price which unions may properly pay to contribute to business success, and the rewards – both substantive and procedural – to be demanded in return. On these points, the new rhetoric of British trade unionism is in general evasive. Whether other trade union movements, operating at least in some respects from a basis of stronger entrenched rights, have proved more successful is the concern of the following chapters.

Notes

[1] Constitutionally there is a distinction between Great Britain (England, Scotland and Wales) and the United Kingdom, which also includes the six counties of Northern Ireland

(and before 1921, the whole of Ireland). It is, however, common practice to use the two terms interchangeably. While most of the main British unions have members in Northern Ireland, many workers there are in unions based in the Irish Republic or in exclusively Northern Ireland organizations. In some respects the troubled relationship between the two communities has coloured the nature of trade unionism there; I am unable to address this in the present work.

[2] The notion of a 'labour aristocracy' was part of everyday discourse in Victorian England, was employed by Marx and Engels, and was later used by Lenin to explain the 'bribery' of the working class and its leaders in imperialist countries. While adopted by some modern historians it has been contested by others; for some contributions to the debate see Fraser, 1974; Gray, 1981; Hobsbawm, 1964: ch. 15 and 1984: chs. 12–13; Moorhouse, 1978; Pelling, 1968: ch. 3; Reid, 1978; Stedman Jones, 1983: ch. 1.

[3] They quote the 1845 rules of the Journeymen Steam Engine Makers, incorporated into those of the ASE in 1851: 'the youth who has the good fortune and inclinations for preparing himself as a useful member of society by the study of physic, and who studies that profession with success so as to obtain his diploma ..., naturally expects in some measure that he is entitled to privileges to which the pretending quack can lay no claim ... and has the power of instituting a course of law against him. ... But the mechanic, even though he may expend nearly an equal fortune, and sacrifice an equal portion of his life ... has no law to protect his privileges.' The role of the union was to protect the rights of its qualified members in the same manner that the law protected those of the certified professional.

[4] Or rather, in normal circumstances, sought to protect traditional regulatory standards.

[5] According to T.J. Dunning, secretary of the Bookbinders' Society, 'the true state of employer and employed is that of amity' (Jefferys, 1948: 48).

[6] The Act, which virtually doubled the British electorate, was a far more substantial instalment of democratization than generally anticipated at the time; it reflected in part a complex set of manoeuvres between and within the two main political parties, but also a recognition within the ruling class that respectable artisans were no longer a threat and could provide important support to the constitutional order.

[7] One should note that at this period trade unionism was still subject to severe repression in many European countries, while the working class was excluded from the vote. The incremental legalization of unions and enfranchisement of workers was a distinctive British phenomenon, which almost certainly served to dampen the violence of class antagonisms.

[8] One may note that in the craft-based shipbuilding industry, where piecework was the norm, collective bargaining undertaken by full-time union officials became established earlier than in most other craft industries.

[9] The Webbs (1894: 294) describe such officials, with approbation, as 'a combination, in the Trade Union World, of the accountant and the lawyer'. Turner, however, adds a necessary caution (1962: 132–5): technical expertise was ineffectual without solid collective organization, and much of the work of the early full-time officials was directed at membership recruitment and the consolidation of local union structures. It should be noted that while the spinners were exclusively male, the weavers (whose union by the end of the century was the largest in the industry) were overwhelmingly female; their officials, however, were predominantly male. The same was true of the other main female-dominated occupation, the cardroom workers involved in preparatory stages of the spinning process.

[10] The issue was not fully resolved until 1911. Once established, the office of 'checkweigher' often served another function: a miner victimized for union activity might be selected by his fellows to fill the position, becoming in effect a full-time pit-level union representative.

[11] The second Congress in 1869 elected a similar committee, but it did not appear to function (Roberts, 1958: 58). Only in 1875 did Congress decide to appoint a paid (though only part-time) secretary, Henry Broadhurst of the Stonemasons. The Webbs (1894: 471–2) were scathing in their criticisms of the rudimentary and amateurish organization of the TUC: 'the whole organization is so absurdly inadequate to the task, that the committee can hardly be blamed for giving up any attempt to keep pace with the work.

The members ... preoccupied with the affairs of their societies, and unversed in general politics, ... either confine their attention to the interests of their own trades, or look upon the fortnightly trip to London as a pleasant recreation from hard official duties. In the intervals between the meetings the Secretary struggles with the business as best he can, with such clerical help as he can afford to pay for out of his own meagre allowance.'

[12] Burt was to retain his seat until 1918, when he was over 80 years of age.

[13] In a few years union membership roughly doubled, reaching a million and a half (out of a labour force of some 12 million).

[14] The status of one other successful candidate was ambiguous.

[15] Despite the subservience of the Labour Party to the Liberal government, the latter was in no hurry to remedy the legal situation, doing so only in the Trade Union Act of 1913.

[16] For mining see Francis and Smith (1980) and for cotton see White (1978).

[17] Price (1980: ch. 7) gives a detailed account of this tension in the building industry, though he mistakenly takes this as typical of the 'labour unrest' more generally.

[18] The threat had already been employed once, in the summer of 1920, when it appeared that the government might send troops to support Poland in its war against the Soviet Union. The TUC and Labour Party both agreed to use 'the whole industrial power of the organized workers' to prevent an unpopular military adventure seemingly intended to restore capitalism in Russia. As Clegg comments (1985: 294), the circumstances were totally exceptional: 'to enter upon a war by an act of aggression against a country which, whatever the merits of its regime, was offering no direct threat to Britain, was ... repugnant' to the labour movement irrespective of political ideology.

[19] Once the government and its supporters had made the radical connotations of the idea of a general strike a propaganda issue, the TUC began to insist that what was taking place was not a general strike (not all workers being called out) but a 'national strike'. But as Allen wryly comments (1957: xiii), 'it was as general in its scope as any strike could afford to be in this country'.

[20] Assuming that this incident, reported at third hand, did indeed take place (presumably at the time of the appointment of the Sankey Commission). There is no particular reason to doubt the accuracy of the account.

[21] MacDonald continued as prime minister in a coalition 'national' government in which he and a few of the previous Labour ministers were far outnumbered by Conservatives.

[22] 'We Communists ... work as loyal but *militant* trade unionists,' declared Party secretary Harry Pollitt in a pamphlet in 1937 (quoted in Fishman, 1995: 203).

[23] Ernest Bevin, who received a similar offer, refused (though only after requesting time for consideration) (Citrine, 1964: 313–15). A number of union leaders, then and after, have refused to accept 'honours' – and, in particular, from Conservative governments.

[24] It reached a peak of over 50,000 members in 1943 (still trivial by continental standards) before going into gradual but persistent decline.

[25] There were indeed Trotskyist groupings which maintained the position abandoned by the CPGB in 1941; but their membership was minute.

[26] I have discussed this period in detail in Hyman, 1993.

[27] This rallying cry, very popular on picket lines in the 1970s, would be put to empirical test in the 1980s. Or was it? If workers were defeated, they must have been disunited. ... Indeed.

[28] Those cases which did occur were either, in the early period, government-inspired, or else initiated by small firms. In one notorious case, in 1974, the AUEW refused to pay a fine imposed by the courts and, as the possibility of a widespread strike loomed, this was paid instead by an anonymous benefactor (generally assumed to be a large employer anxious to avoid a stoppage).

[29] Clegg's conception of industrial democracy was strongly influenced by Schumpeter's theory of political democracy in terms of the existence and legitimacy of opposition. Ironically, he subsequently became a fervent advocate of incomes policy, was a member of the National Board for Prices and Incomes in the 1960s and later chaired the

Comparability Commission established by the 1974–79 Labour government to advise on public-sector pay determination.

[30] A lower rate of £3.00 applied to workers aged 18–20 (the Commission proposed £3.20); younger workers and trainees were excluded altogether.

[31] Presenting the report to the 1995 TUC, Bill Morris insisted that 'we do need new laws guaranteeing rights of representation. The era of the voluntary system of industrial relations in Britain has been buried by the employers.'

[32] Bill Connor of the shopworkers' union USDAW, subsequently appointed chair of the TUC Social Partnership Task Group.

6

German Trade Unionism

Between Society and Market

In both Germany and Italy, modern trade unionism is in many respects a product of the second half of the twentieth century. Under Hitler and Mussolini, free trade unionism was brutally suppressed; in each country a new movement was created by design and from above after the defeat of the dictators. This does not mean that nothing of the former traditions survived to inform post-war identities and actions; but in contrast to the British case, it makes sense for the following two chapters to focus on the post-war era. Accordingly, each will be substantially shorter than the last.

The theme of the present chapter is the shifting geometry of German trade unionism.[1] In the immediate phase of post-war reconstruction there was an uneasy tension between a vision of trade unions as vehicles of class mobilization which could build a society and economy of a new type on the ruins of the old; and a conception of unions as a force for social integration with the capacity and the duty to avoid the destructive cleavages of the Weimar period. Initially there was a strong communist presence within the newly re-emerging labour movement, as well as a substantial marxist-oriented left among the social democrats; with the collapse of the Third Reich, a non-capitalist route to reconstruction seemed conceivable – perhaps even inevitable. But such a course faced powerful – and ultimately overwhelming – resistance both within the German labour movement itself and from outside.

Following the political defeats suffered by the labour movement in the early post-war years, and in a climate of cold war anti-communism (the communist party (KPD) was outlawed in 1956), it was the integrative view which came to predominate. As the German 'economic miracle' unfolded, so this approach appeared to yield material benefits. The idea of a 'social market economy', originally a conservative slogan, became for several decades a stable point of reference for trade union identity. But as the economic and political environment became less favourable, so the balance between social regulation and market forces encountered new tensions and issues of class identity resurfaced.

The Reconstruction of Trade Unionism and the Eclipse of Radicalism

The economic history of the first post-war decades centres around the rapid transformation from massive devastation to unexpected success. Following Germany's unconditional surrender, the country was divided into occupation zones governed by the four victorious powers (Britain, France, the USA and the USSR). Roughly a third of the country's former territory disappeared from the map of Germany,[2] and economic relations across the zonal boundaries were difficult; hence former production chains were disrupted. Some five million Germans had died in the hostilities or had perished in the concentration camps. Bombing had destroyed much of the industrial infrastructure; some of what remained was seized by the victors as reparations. Dislocation was increased by a massive influx of refugees and of those expelled from the countries of central and eastern Europe; roughly one person in five was homeless. There were desperate shortages of food, fuel and other necessities (Krips, 1958: 101–3).

Initially, each of the four occupying powers developed its own political and economic regime within its specific zone. With the emergence and intensification of the cold war in 1947–48, the four-way division was succeeded by a two-way polarization: the three western zones were integrated within the new Federal Republic (*Bundesrepublik Deutschland*, BRD) in 1949, followed by the constitution of the German Democratic Republic (*Deutsche Demokratische Republik*, DDR) in the east. The inclusion of (west) Germany in the European recovery programme (Marshall aid) contributed significantly to economic revival. So did the rearmament boom at the time of the Korean war.

German trade unionism was reconstructed through the interaction of pressure from below and from above. In many workplaces, unofficial works councils created some kind of order out of chaos, helping oversee the renewal of production and addressing workers' lack of the necessities of life. For many on the left, such councils could form the embryo of a new social order: a vision which perturbed the occupying powers, who attempted to formalize and domesticate them. At the same time, former officials and activists who were released from the prisons and camps, who returned from exile, or who had simply kept their heads down during the Nazi years, rebuilt the labour movement within each zone and devised blueprints for an integrated German trade unionism.

It was generally agreed that the new structure should transcend the former ideological divisions which had seriously weakened the labour movement in the Weimar era. The principle of trade union unity (the idea of the *Einheitsgewerkschaft* – a single union in each workplace) was taken further by some who advocated the formation of 'one big union' organized into industrial sections. This was a model implemented in east Germany (and also in many respects in Austria) but was viewed with suspicion by the occupying powers; in the British case, the TUC was persuaded to add its own opposition (MacShane, 1992: 218–19). The outcome was the formation in 1949, soon after the BRD itself, of a structure of sixteen industrial unions largely autonomous in the formulation of their own policy but united in a central confederation, the *Deutscher Gewerkschaftsbund*

(DGB).[3] The total membership was roughly five million, covering about a third of the labour force: a density level significantly higher than that of all the main unions immediately before the Nazi era.

Though the new unions were largely run by social democrats, the corollary of the principle of unity was that they should avoid too close a formal identification with the revived social-democratic party (SPD) so as to prevent a breach with the christian-democratic minority among their members and activists. But conversely, they could not ignore the strong left-socialist or communist sympathies of many rank-and-file militants; and this was reflected in the relatively radical 'basic programme' (*Grundsatzprogramm*) – calling for the reorganization of the economy and society on the basis of social ownership – adopted by the founding conference in Munich. In many respects this was in tune with a widespread popular mood: even the christian democrats (CDU), at their 1947 Ahlen congress, approved an economic programme (soon abandoned in practice) with strong socialist overtones, rejecting the profit motive and demanding the socialization of the basic industries.[4]

Ambitions for a new social and economic order were encouraged by the shadow of the past. The industrial tycoons who had made their peace with Hitler – indeed had helped him to power – were discredited, and initially there was consensus among the occupying powers that the former concentration of economic ownership in private hands must never again be permitted. The trade unions were seen as the most reliable guarantors of a new, democratic Germany, not least by the Labour government in Britain. Hence the socialization of the 'commanding heights' of the economy seemed a realistic objective; and the struggle over ownership and control was to be the overriding issue for the new DGB.

During the years of allied occupation, the conglomerates which had dominated the strategic industries of iron and steel and coal (the so-called *Montan* industries) were broken up into separate companies under tight control by the occupying authorities. Particularly in the British zone – which included the main centre of these industries in the Ruhr area – the principle of codetermination or *Mitbestimmung* was implemented, with employee representation on the company supervisory boards[5] and the appointment of a trade unionist as 'labour director' in the management team (Spiro, 1958: 32–5).

The 'basic programme' adopted by the DGB in Munich in October 1949 called both for the public ownership of all key industries (mining, iron and steel, chemicals, energy, transport and finance) and for 'codetermination of the organized workers in all the personnel, economic and social questions of economic policy and management' (Schneider, 1989: 457). In May 1950 it elaborated its demands: a universal system involving parity representation for union nominees on supervisory boards. But the political climate was unfavourable: at the first parliamentary elections in September 1949 the SPD had won just under 30 per cent of the vote, less than the CDU, and Adenauer headed a conservative government committed to economic deregulation and privatization. This policy was consistent with the goal of 'normalizing' capitalist production relations which underlay the Marshall plan. The demand for board-level parity codetermination, strongly resisted by the employers, received a cool response from the new government.

The unions of steel and coal workers, fearing the loss of the rights which they had gained during the period of allied occupation, held strike ballots in late November 1950 and early 1951 respectively, in both cases winning over 90 per cent support for industrial action. A compromise was then reached in direct negotiations between DGB president[6] Hans Böckler and chancellor Adenauer: a special law would be passed confirming parity codetermination in these two industries.[7] This was implemented in May 1951 (Schuster, 1974: 37–8).

By then Böckler – already aged 74 when elected to head the new DGB – had died. Under new leadership, the unions pressed strongly to extend the *Montan* scheme to the whole economy. Again there were threats of militant action, and protest stoppages and demonstrations indeed took place – including a strike by newspaper printers. But within the DGB itself there was opposition to the use of industrial militancy for seemingly party-political ends; while the miners and metal workers, the vanguard of the movement, were in practice disinclined to risk the settlement already achieved in their own industries by pursuing a general strike. The government proceeded with legislation in July 1952 giving a token one-third employee representation on supervisory boards in firms with over 500 workers outside the *Montan* industries; there was no provision for a labour director. The same Works Constitution Act (*Betriebsverfassungsgesetz*) gave a legal foundation to works councils, but again on a basis opposed by the DGB. In particular, the government rejected its demands that trade unions should have a direct input to works council proceedings, and that the councils should have significant veto power over management decision-making. The new law largely reaffirmed the relatively modest framework introduced in 1920. The unions had been 'tamed' (Pirker, 1960: ch. 6).

Following the failure of its 'half-hearted resistance' to the government's plans (Otto, 1975: 124), the DGB sacrificed a scapegoat; at its congress in October 1952 its president, Christian Fette, failed to achieve re-election. The DGB went on to campaign against the government in the 1953 elections, causing protests from its christian-democrat wing; Adenauer was re-elected with an increased majority. There was then a marked shift away from political radicalism. An important symbol of this reorientation was the dismissal in 1955 of Viktor Agartz, the popular left-wing head of the DGB economic research institute (Mühlbradt and Lutz, 1969: 74–6; Niethammer, 1975: 357). The action programme adopted by the DGB in the same year concentrated on pragmatic immediate demands; structural changes to the economy and society were retained as at best a distant goal. In 1959 the SPD adopted the 'Godesberg programme' which abandoned its former commitment to the socialization of industry and accepted the capitalist market economy; in the same year the DGB initiated a revision of its own constitution, and agreed changes on similar lines four years later in its 'Düsseldorf programme' to replace that of 1949.

Ironically, the consequence of this depoliticization was to downgrade the DGB's own status: the main focus of trade union activity was now the collective bargaining undertaken by the individual industrial unions. The latter allowed the DGB no effective role in shaping their goals and tactics in this sphere; indeed in 1959 its president complained that he discovered their initiatives only from what he read in the newspapers (Mühlbradt and Lutz, 1969: 81). Hans Böckler, who had emerged from 'hibernation' at the end of the Nazi era (Borsdorf, 1982: 323) to play a key role in the reconstruction of the movement, was among the most prominent of all German trade unionists when elected first president of the DGB; his successor was head of the printing union, followed in turn by the leader of the metalworkers. Thereafter, no president of an important industrial union would regard election to head the DGB as a promotion.[8]

The Social Market and Concerted Action

The ruling christian democrats under Adenauer and economics minister Erhard proclaimed the goal of a 'social market economy' (*soziale Marktwirtschaft*). The meaning of this term was open to conflicting interpretations. The emphasis initially was on the word 'market' rather than 'social': the slogan reflected the new government's commitment to private ownership and to minimal state intervention in the organization of production. Hence the German unions explicitly rejected the concept. But for many christian democrats, a market economy was not enough: if markets were the basis for productive efficiency they could not ensure distributional equity; moreover, market dynamics might also result in undue concentration of economic power through the growth of monopolies and oligopolies. Hence government initiative was required to correct both tendencies (Gourevitch et al., 1984: 106–7; Wallich, 1955: 114–19).

Once the principle of a market economy was no longer contested within mainstream German politics, the concept of *soziale Marktwirtschaft* tended to become used in ways which stressed this 'social' dimension. For some, it became equivalent to the idea of organized capitalism: market forces should in general prevail, but within a framework of coordination and regulation directed primarily to enhancing economic efficiency. An alternative understanding stressed the need for a balance between market autonomy and state intervention, between employers' pursuit of profit and workers' right to dignity and well-being. An extensive welfare state was a corollary of this perspective. This second emphasis, common to both social democrats and the 'social' wing of the christian democrats, may be regarded as the emergent ideology of most German trade unions from the end of the 1950s. The point of reference became the axis between market and society. (see Figure 6.1).

A 'social market' orientation was institutionally supported by the distinctive German 'dual system' of industrial relations. Under a law of 1949, trade unions were assigned the exclusive right to represent workers' interests in negotiations with employers; and the principle of 'free collective bargaining' (*Tarifautonomie*) became, as in Britain, a cherished value which was later to inhibit any formal acceptance of incomes policy. But the German term had a significantly different meaning from its analogue in English. The latter implied an adversarial model of industrial relations: an assertion of the right of workers, through their unions, to pursue their economic interests as they saw fit. But *Tarifautonomie* denoted the *mutual* autonomy of unions and employers' organizations as 'bargaining partners' (*Tarifpartner*) (Kaiser, 1956: 182): as indicated in Chapter 4, this was consistent

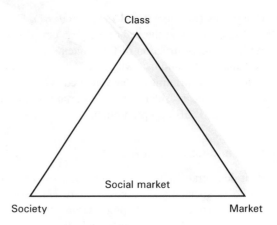

FIGURE 6.1   *Germany – between society and market*

with a model of social regulation informed by the catholic principle of subsidiarity. At times this form of industrial relations might involve conflict, but within the framework of clear (and partly legally prescribed) rules of the game.⁹ Dahrendorf, writing in the 1960s, declared the paradox that 'the German labour movement needed conflict but it sought order' (1965: 220). A more nuanced comment is that 'unions have been conflictual participants in German economic life since the war but their conflict perspectives, thus far, have remained confined within a broader consensual framework shared with other actors about basic social goals' (Gourevitch et al., 1984: 91).

The other institutional support of a 'social market' orientation was the works council system. Councils possessed closely defined legal powers to represent employees at plant and company level but were also prohibited from inter-fering in the sphere of collective bargaining or exerting collective pressure on the employer. The principle of 'collaboration in mutual trust' (*vertrauens-volle Zusammenarbeit*) within a juridically prescribed 'works constitution' (*Betriebsverfassung*) might not always be observed in reality; and certainly the formal idea of a dual system with separate spheres for unions and works councils misrepresented the reality of close interaction and interdependence between the two. Yet it is important to note the extent to which the practical operation of the works council system came to complement the 'responsible' wage bargaining of the unions by encouraging a collaborative search for positive-sum out-comes at company level (Thelen, 1991). As Streeck described it (1984a: 110), 'co-determination has proven an effective mechanism to bring about an accom-modation of class interests at the level of the individual enterprise – a "syndicalist" version of "social partnership" – resulting in a commitment of labour … to com-petitiveness, productivity, and profitability'.

As this comment indicates, another integrating feature of the post-war German system was what may be termed productivism. Streeck has also regularly argued that the degree of employment protection (socializing the market) provided by individual labour law and by the rights of works councils in respect of hiring and firing created a favourable environment for flexible workforce responses to production reorganization and innovation.[10] Windolf has concluded that within the German institutional structure, workplace trade unionists (through the works councils) were encouraged to seek 'productivity coalitions' whereby 'cooperation with management and commitment to the firm's central goals are exchanged for greater job security and participation in strategic decision making'. The concept, he adds, 'revives the ideology of community – *Gemeinschaft* – propagated by employers in many countries during the interwar period in reaction to radical Marxist ideology' (1989: 3). Evidently the idea of community relates closely to the trade union understanding of a social market. Consensual productivism was widely regarded as the basis for a successful, high-skilled, high-quality, high-performance economy from which unionized workers could derive their share of the advantages. For many German trade unionists this was an explicit ideological point of reference; even those who articulated more oppositional views – counterposing class to social market – nevertheless seemed implicitly to embrace productivism. In effect, unions were both guarantors and beneficiaries of the German 'economic miracle': 'The "Keynesian compromise" in which growth, full employment and price stability were underwritten by government economic policy established the preconditions for sectoral unions to pursue successfully their core bargaining functions' (Schauer, 1994: 120).

The 'economic miracle' of the 1950s was based initially on government efforts to restrain consumption and encourage investment, with priority assigned to production for export. Monetary stability was embraced as an essential foundation of economic policy (in part because of the memories of hyperinflation in the Weimar years); the *Bank deutscher Länder*, established by the allies in 1948, which in 1957 became the *Bundesbank*, was charged with ensuring this. This strategy proved successful: there was a rapid increase in productivity, a reduction in the initially high levels of unemployment, and hence the capacity for significant wage increases without price inflation. This was the background for the revival of collective bargaining.

Writing in the early years of the BRD, Kerr (1952) noted how rapidly the processes of collective bargaining had become institutionalized along familiar lines. Anxious to negotiate on a comprehensive basis, the unions themselves encouraged the re-establishment of employers' associations; in the main, moreover, they had neither the will nor the resources to engage in militant economic struggle. Experience would soon show that this assessment was only partially correct. The metalworkers' union *IG Metall* (which comprised some 30 per cent of total DGB membership) commonly exercised wage leadership, developing a shrewd ability to assess what the market could bear: how much metal employers could afford without compromising their competitiveness in export markets. Since the settlements reached set the pattern for the whole economy, union negotiators had also to take account of the macroeconomic consequences of their policies. According to Streeck (1994: 124), this encouraged a 'self-interested wage moderation'; but again, up to a point only. In the German unions' rapprochement with the social market, class radicalism was never fully sublimated. Its continuing latent potential is evident in the evolution of the bargaining policies of the metalworkers' union.[11]

In the internal controversies of the mid-1950s, a highly influential text by Agartz expounded the principle of an 'expansionary wage strategy' (*expansive Lohnpolitik*); he developed a Keynesian argument that high wages would contribute to demand-driven employment growth by increasing purchasing power: exactly the opposite of the economic philosophy of the government. The strategy was embraced by Otto Brenner, president of *IG Metall* from the end of 1952; and together they won support for this at the 1954 DGB congress and were assigned to draft a set of collective bargaining objectives for the movement as a whole (Bergmann et al., 1975: 132–4, 156–60; Gourevitch et al., 1984: 112–13; Grebing, 1970: 258–9; Schmidt, 1971: 49–50).

The 'maximalist' approach embodied in this plan was pursued by the metalworkers with considerable initial success. Under Brenner, the union imposed firm central coordination on the regionally-based collective bargaining process. In 1956 a national agreement was reached on the introduction of the 45-hour week (a 2¼ hour reduction) with a modest weekly wage increase; two years later there was a more substantial pay increase together with agreement on a 44-hour week from 1959. Both deals were won without the need to strike, but in parallel the union targeted the Schleswig-Holstein region with demands for paid sick leave, longer holidays and improved holiday pay; most of these goals were achieved after a four-month strike. Nevertheless, *IG Metall* suffered a setback when the strike was ruled illegal on the grounds that a strike ballot had been held before negotiations had formally broken down; the employers were awarded DM 100 million damages. By 1960, however, the union was able to gain agreement in principle on a phased move towards the 40-hour week by 1965, in addition to large wage rises. Though its vanguard role was temporarily restored, *IG Metall* faced increasing opposition from more right-wing union leaders (notably Georg Leber of the construction union *IG Bau*); and its militant stance in 1962 and 1963 (in itself a response to the tougher and more concerted tactics of the employers), though largely successful, brought it into conflict with the SPD. In a significant change of line, by 1964 Brenner showed greater willingness to compromise and even signed an arbitration agreement making strike action more difficult (Gourevitch et al., 1984: 123–6). This may well have reflected a pragmatic assessment of a shifting balance of forces: confrontational bargaining had simply become too risky now that employers had succeeded in coordinating their own forces more effectively (Mühlbradt and Lutz, 1969: 112).

The shift towards a social market orientation was confirmed as a generally dominant principle with the formation of the 'grand coalition' between CDU and SPD in 1966 and the introduction of 'concerted action' (*konzertierte Aktion*, KA) in the following year: 'At the latest with its participation in KA, the cooperative character of *IG Metall* bargaining is manifest' (Bergmann et al., 1975: 150). Concerted action was a response to the apparent faltering of the economic miracle, which up to the mid-1960s had brought unemployment below the 1 per cent level while allowing regular increases in real wages and social benefits. The entry of the SPD as junior partner in government also signalled a stronger Keynesian dimension to public policy[12] and a redefinition of the social market on more 'social' lines. The 1967 law for the 'promotion of stability and growth' required the government to involve unions and employers' organizations in the formulation of economic policy and to produce quantitative data which might inform collective bargaining. It is questionable how much impact KA had on the actual process of wage negotiation (Flanagan et al., 1983: 280–6); nevertheless, the combination of coalition government and formal concertation was an important symbol of the firm integration of the labour movement within the German social and political, as well as economic, order. Rightly or otherwise, KA was widely regarded as an important contribution to the economic recovery, enabling the SPD to achieve sufficient gains in the 1969 election to head a new coalition with the much smaller free democrats (FDP) which was to survive uneasily until 1982. A number of prominent union leaders became ministers in the new 'social-liberal' government.

The often bitter debates within German trade unionism during the 1960s had centred around two radically different conceptions of purpose and identity: as a mechanism of social order (*Ordnungsfaktor*) or as an oppositional force to employers – and perhaps to capitalism as such (*Gegenmacht*). For most observers the conflict was personified in the confrontation between Leber and Brenner (Markovits, 1986: 96–8; Schneider, 1989: 276–7). When, at the beginning of the decade, the building workers' leader insisted that the unions should identify fully with the post-war German state and act as defenders of a capitalist market economy, his vision was assertively at odds with the dominant ethos of the movement. By the end of the decade, his encompassing conception of social partnership seemed to have defined the practice (if not necessarily the theory) of German trade unionism as a whole. But the conversion of most unions into implicit or explicit protectors of the social market economy was to provoke in turn a reaction.

Challenges from Below

Across much of western Europe (and indeed beyond), the late 1960s and early 1970s saw radical challenges to the industrial relations order consolidated in the two previous decades. Germany did not escape this 'resurgence of class conflict' (Crouch and Pizzorno, 1978). The centralized disciplines which underlay the new 'German model' of industrial relations (both in the maintenance of workplace peace and in the procedures of collective bargaining with their occasional ritualized accompaniment of conflict) were put temporarily in question.

In 1969 'the wave of grass-roots strikes that had been sweeping over the continent reached Germany. ... It is true that the German wildcat was pretty small beer, internationally speaking'; but the unofficial militancy delivered a shock to the system (Flanagan et al., 1983: 242, 252). In the month of September there was an upsurge of spontaneous strikes, primarily in the metal industries, involving some 140,000 workers. Similar outbreaks occurred at intervals during the following years, notably in 1973. The immediate motive was to protest against falling real wages: the unions had negotiated modest pay increases during the recession at the beginning of KA, but now the economy was booming and prices were rising sharply. Also associated with economic expansion was an intensification of work pressure (Bergmann et al., 1975: 322–3; Müller-Jentsch and Sperling, 1978: 261–3; Schumann, 1971). A background factor which some observers considered important was a disaffection (as in many other European countries, linked to the rise of left-wing student activism) with the political consensus which the grand coalition seemed to embody. A particular target of criticism involved the emergency laws (*Notstandgesetze*) adopted as a constitutional amendment in 1968, following earlier initiatives during the 1960s. This empowered the government to suspend various civil liberties, including the right to strike; SPD support was part of the price of coalition membership. The majority of German unions were opposed, but offered only verbal reaction; others on the left attempted more militant resistance.[13]

In some cases the militancy reflected an explicit challenge to the consensual policies of the established workplace leadership. From the 1950s various unions, notably *IG Metall*, had established a structure of workplace union representatives known as *Vertrauensleute* (literally, 'trust people'), partly with the aim of controlling the activities of works councillors. Such ideas were stillborn: lacking legal powers or collective bargaining functions the *Vertrauensleute* (where they existed at all) usually had only a token role; and since they were often appointed directly by the local union apparatus they lacked the elective legitimacy of the works councillors themselves (Markovits, 1986: 187–8). But in the late 1960s there were attempts, particularly by left-wing activists influenced by the British shop steward model, to reconstruct the *Vertrauensleute* system as a directly elected representative structure: an effort which helped give impetus to, and was in turn reinforced by, the unofficial strike action. A further consequence was that in the 1972 works council elections, there were many 'confrontations between long-serving works councillors and candidates from among the *Vertrauensleute*. ... The social partnership policies of many works councils were increasingly criticised, and many *Vertrauensleute* committees decided to nominate new candidates ... in order to achieve a more militant interest representation' (Schmidt, 1973: 43). This was to be repeated in 1975 (Müller-Jentsch, 1975).

A central focus of dissent in many of the disputes was the fact that workplace 'productivity coalitions' often *excluded* many sections of the working class: women, migrant workers (known euphemistically as *Gastarbeiter* or 'guest workers'), the lower-skilled. Such groups commonly perceived the policies of works councils and trade unions as favouring the interests of the relatively skilled male workforce in better paid and stable employment, while marginalizing their own concerns over such issues as work intensification in routine jobs, insecurity, and arbitrary and oppressive discipline. Such grievances fuelled a number of the spontaneous disputes (Kirchlechner, 1978). Reaction to exclusion was reflected in oppositional candidatures in the works council elections, notably by Turkish workers. Some observers also perceived an age factor: the rise of a generation which had not experienced the hard times before the German 'economic miracle' and had higher ambitions than their parents. In these respects, the new militancy contested the consolidation of industrial relations processes moulded by the principles of the social market, but also transcended simple ideas of class.

Official trade union responses were ambivalent and contradictory (Bergmann et al., 1975: 330–4). According to Markovits (1986: 208), 'for IG Metall the strikes provided both a genuine learning experience and an opportunity to coopt the militancy of the workforce'. This was part of the story, but another aspect of union reaction was the attempt to discipline shopfloor activists, particularly those suspected of communist sympathies;[14] many were expelled. 'Criticism and opposition' could result in 'exclusion, the dissolution of elected committees, or the dismissal or removal of troublesome functionaries or secretaries' (Müller-Jentsch and Sperling, 1978: 296).

The positive response had three main elements. First, *IG Metall* in particular returned (at least temporarily) to a more assertive collective bargaining stance. 'The strikes of September 1969 ... began a five-year mobilization period during which the German labour movement won substantial wage increases'. To avoid being again outflanked by workplace militants, official negotiators had to demonstrate that they too were willing to be tough. This was particularly apparent in the next bargaining round in 1971, when 'work stoppages evolved through most branches of the German economy under the aegis of the unions' (Gourevitch et al., 1984: 135–6). The return to aggressive wage policy was brought to an end with the oil shock and the global economic crisis after 1974. However, this was followed by a significant shift in tactics described as *neue Beweglichkeit* (literally: new mobility or agility), again pioneered by *IG Metall*. This involved calling public demonstrations and brief 'warning strikes' *before* negotiations broke down, as a means of stimulating rank-and-file support for the union's objectives and strengthening the hand of the negotiators (Kowol, 1981). Such action was judged legitimate by the federal labour court in 1976 following a complaint by the employers (Jacobi et al., 1992: 254), and 'the general level of mobilization accompanying pay negotiations rose' (Lang, 1992: 24).

A second element in union responses was to supplement wage bargaining by an increased attention to the 'qualitative' demands which lay behind some of the unofficial stoppages. The quality of work itself, and the ability to exercise direct influence over the day-to-day relationship with management (*Mitbestimmung am Arbeitsplatz*), became issues of debate within trade unions. The optimistic productivist orientation to technological innovation of previous years[15] was increasingly questioned: new technology, while increasing output, might destroy jobs and degrade those that remained. Even before the September strikes, the unions in printing, metalworking and chemicals had negotiated 'rationalization protection agreements', later extended to the public sector (Brandt et al., 1982: 140). The more positive concept of *Humanisierung der Arbeit* (HdA: humanization of work) was adopted in the early 1970s, leading to a notable official strike in Baden-Württemberg (a small but important centre of the motor industry) in 1973. The outcome was a 46-page framework agreement known as *Lohnrahmentarifvertrag II* (LRTV II). This defined basic principles to regulate payment by results, shift-work and overtime, and also specified rules to determine track speeds, minimum hourly rest periods and minimum task times on assembly-line and repetition work (Schauer et al., 1984). While in general the collective agreements reached in an individual bargaining district are extended across Germany, in this case employers were bitterly opposed to the encroachment into managerial prerogatives and LRTV II remained an isolated achievement (Gourevitch et al., 1984: 137). But in 1974 the DGB embraced the demand for HdA, and the government also offered its support (Thelen, 1991: 186–92).

A third response, partly related, was the demand for a greater shopfloor role in collective bargaining. The slogan *betriebsnahe Tarifpolitik* (bargaining policy close to establishment level) in part reiterated the old aspiration for a German version of shop steward organization and for greater union authority over works councils; but it also reflected the logic that HdA and 'social control of rationalization' required a system of union regulation in the workplace (Brandt et al., 1982: 154). This logic indeed underlay LRTV II, which defined general principles the application of which was delegated to company-level agreement. Arguably, official union support for a radical decentralization of bargaining was mere rhetoric: the last thing the central leaderships wanted was the emergence of a structure of workplace representatives with the right to strike and the capacity to define their own collective bargaining priorities. While union policy gave new emphasis to the role of *Vertrauensleute*, in practice they were consolidated as representatives with few powers or functions, mere ancillaries of works councils.

The 'cooption' of the grassroots revolt was linked to important changes in the codetermination laws in the 1970s. In 1968, with the SPD a junior partner in government, the DGB returned to the battleground of the early 1950s and called for an extension of parity codetermination; the government appointed a committee of investigation which reported in 1970. By then the SPD was the main governing party; but its junior partner, the FDP, opposed any extension and insisted that the issue be deferred until after the next elections in 1973 (Gourevitch et al., 1984: 134). Progress was, however, made over workplace codetermination: the new *Betriebsverfassungsgesetz* of 1972 implemented many of the measures which the unions had failed to achieve twenty years earlier: enhanced powers for works councils, including influence over the working environment; and closer formal links between unions and councils. The number of works councillors entitled to release from their normal duties was increased, and a new institution – the central works council – was made mandatory in multi-plant companies (Streeck, 1992: 146–7). A new law on board-level codetermination was finally enacted in 1976. This gave the unions a victory in form but a defeat in substance: parity was notionally achieved in all firms with over two thousand employees; but on the insistence of the FDP, one employee representative was to be chosen by middle managers (*leitende Angestellte*); while the chair of the supervisory board, who possessed a casting vote, could be appointed by the shareholder nominees alone if there was otherwise no agreement. Even this, however, was too much for many employers: many large firms subdivided their operations in order to evade the high size threshold, while in 1977 a number of companies and employers' associations brought a complaint to the constitutional court (rejected in 1979). The DGB took this as an invitation to withdraw formally from concerted action, which in adverse economic circumstances was all but dead already.

In some respects the struggle over *Mitbestimmung* signalled a revival of class as a driving force of industrial relations. During the 1970s, conservative elements complained that Germany was becoming a *Gewerkschaftsstaat* (trade union state), supposedly discerning undue union influence on the SPD-led government. In response, some union leaders insisted that what existed was rather an *Unternehmerstaat* (employers' state): in the formulation of economic and social policy, government was increasingly a hostage of the owners of capital. At least the rhetoric of class antagonism was heightened further in 1978–79, when 'social partnership was emphatically and repeatedly put in question' (Jacobi et al., 1978: 8). There were bitter disputes over rationalization and working time in printing, steel and engineering, with evidence that – as the unions had long suspected – the employers' confederation BDA operated a 'taboo catalogue' which proscribed member associations from reaching agreements with unions on sensitive, and notably qualitative issues (Schneider, 1989: 363, 388). Partly in response to the unions' new mobilization tactics, employers also resorted increasingly to lock-outs, again provoking vehement denunciations from the labour movement (Jacobi et al., 1992: 254–5). On the initiative of the unions concerned, there followed a mass campaign of legal complaints by members suing their employers for loss of wages. Thus industrial relations struggles acquired a sharp class and political profile (Markovits, 1986: 143–4). Subsequently, class antagonisms were rekindled in a different form when the FDP, which had pressed for increasingly restrictive economic and budgetary policies, decided at the end of 1982 to withdraw from the government and form a new right-wing coalition with the CDU.

German Unions on the Defensive

Unions in most European countries faced a difficult political and economic environment in the 1980s, reflected in a widespread pattern of membership decline. German unions experienced some of these challenges, but to a less radical degree. De-industrialization, which in many countries brought a sharp contraction in traditional union strongholds, was much less marked in Germany; and the Kohl government showed less hostility to trade unions than did some conservative counterparts elsewhere. The entrenched rights of works councils proved a stabilizing factor in hard times, and union membership altered little during the decade: numbers affiliated to the DGB, which in the 1970s had risen from 6.7 to 7.8 million, fluctuated around this level throughout the 1980s; given the growth in the labour force, this entailed a slight decline in density.

In some respects, there was a dangerous tendency towards complacency. German unions remained predominantly organizations of male manual workers, despite the changing profile of the labour force as a whole. They were also failing to attract significant numbers of new entrants to employment. Their public image suffered during the 1980s, partly because of the propaganda offensive of their opponents, but also because of their own strategic inadequacies and organizational deficiencies. Particularly serious were the scandals surrounding the unions' wide-ranging business activities. In 1986 the unions' property agency

Neue Heimat – for several years the subject of rumours of corruption and maladministration – collapsed spectacularly; the government refused to bail the unions out, and they were forced to dispose of most of their commercial activities. The scandal 'cost the DGB and the unions much public esteem and almost caused a crisis of identity' (Schneider, 1989: 359). But despite debates over the need for a strategic reorientation, there were only modest signs of policy innovation.

Though the German economy fared better than those of most other European countries, it did not escape the effects of a far harsher international competitive environment. There was a sharp deterioration in the labour market: unemployment at the beginning of the 1970s had been only 1 per cent; but rose to over 4 per cent in the middle of the decade; after a slight improvement there was another rapid increase, to more than 9 per cent in 1983, and a high level persisted throughout the decade, though with some recovery towards the end. One key consequence for the unions was that company rationalization and technological change were now regarded even more explicitly as threats rather than opportunities. Another was that the labour market became increasingly polarized between the 'core' workforce dominating the ranks of union members, and a growing 'periphery' of lower-skilled and insecure. This confronted unions with 'the dilemma that what has served the interests of some of their members well, may increasingly clash with the interests of other members or, more likely, of an increasingly unorganised marginal labour force' (Streeck, 1988: 19).

The more difficult economic environment spurred the DGB to adopt a new action programme in 1979 and to revise its 'basic programme' once more in 1981, in a document which 'combine[d] socialist rhetoric with pragmatic accommodation to capitalism' (Jacobi et al., 1992: 235). The action programme identified unemployment as the key challenge facing the unions, and expressed a pessimistic view of the employment effects of technological and organizational change. Disappointment with the deflationary economic policies of the Schmidt government was also apparent: in place of the traditional union aspirations for partnership with the state in defending and extending the social market, the emphasis was now on the unions' own bargaining strength as the means to regulate the labour market. 'With unemployment continuing to grow and with the unions beginning to criticize German industry more stridently for its contributions to structural and cyclical unemployment via capital export, automation [and] rationalization ... "Keynes-plus" was the answer towards which the DGB and its constituents began to move' (Gourevitch et al., 1984: 171). While still advocating expansionary macroeconomic policies, their emphasis was increasingly on the need to persuade or compel employers to mitigate the adverse effects of rationalization for workers.

Despite a broad consensus on these themes, there were nevertheless marked differences between a more militant group of unions led by the metalworkers and a more cautious group led by the formerly left-wing chemical workers. Both wings placed emphasis on job-sharing as a solution to the employment crisis; but while the latter group identified early retirement as the main solution, the former gave priority to reducing the work week. In the late 1970s, after sharp internal argument, *IG Metall* adopted the objective of a 35-hour week without loss of pay and then persuaded the DGB to endorse this goal. Many unions however regarded the target as unattainable – particularly as the employers' 'taboo catalogue' precluded any agreement on less than 40 hours a week – and were unconvinced that this was an appropriate means of job-saving (Markovits, 1986: 149–50).

The new strategy of *IG Metall* was first put to the test in 1978 in the steel industry (where job losses had been severe); strike action failed to breach the employers' united front, but did achieve other gains – including increased holiday entitlement, also included in the taboo catalogue, and additional free shifts. In 1983 the 35-hour demand was revived in the engineering industry; the protracted strike which ensued the following year ended in a complicated compromise. Average working hours would be reduced to 38.5, but the standard week for individual workers could range between 37 and 40; the implementation of this formula in each company was to be negotiated between management and works council. Following this breakthrough, 38.5 hours soon became the general norm in German collective agreements. A partial victory for trade union militancy; but procedurally the agreement significantly shifted the division of labour between unions and works councils and allowed employers far greater scope in pursuing increased flexibility in work arrangements (Markovits, 1986: 438–9). This was to facilitate what Streeck (1984b: 297) had termed 'wildcat cooperation', the implementation of company-level productivity coalitions in ways which could undercut the unions' own official policies. In any event, the trend continued, with employers bargaining further hours' reductions against increased flexibility: in 1987 there was agreement on a staged reduction to 37 hours, and in 1990 for further cuts culminating in the 35-hour week in 1995. The achievements of the metalworkers were soon matched (at least in part) in much of the rest of the economy (Bosch, 1994: 134–8; Smith, 1998: 56; Thelen, 1991: 172–5).

The significance of the working-time campaign can be assessed in a variety of ways. The principle of the social market had been embraced in the long phase of economic success and progress towards full employment: social ideals and market principles had indeed appeared compatible, even complementary. Rising unemployment, and a more aggressive employer insistence on flexibility in work organization, challenged the society-market synthesis. In the political sphere, growing commitment to market liberalism and fiscal discipline in the final years of the social-liberal coalition prefigured the adverse climate of the Kohl era.

Yet the conservative government after 1982 was marked by the same internal contradictions as its predecessor. The FDP, junior partner in both governments, was strongly committed to 'free markets'; but the position of the CDU was far more ambivalent. Notably, the minority of christian-democrat trade unionists had a significant influence within their party and constituted an effective force for continued social regulation of the labour market. Norbert Blüm, minister of labour throughout the Kohl years, was himself a member of *IG Metall*. The government's policies have been described as 'half-hearted deregulation' (Jacobi et al., 1992: 240–1): mainly relaxing restrictions on temporary employment contracts and on night and weekend working. By far the most contentious initiative, as far as the unions were concerned, was article 116 of the Employment Promotion Act, adopted in 1986, which was directed against the new strike tactics of the metalworkers in particular.[16] Less inflammatory but still strongly resented was a change, pressed by the FDP, which in 1988 provided new rights for representation of minority interests on works councils and created special committees for junior and middle managers.

In a period of increasing tension within the principles of social partnership and the social market, more radical union policies were open to two different interpretations: either an insistence on the reconstitution of the social market; or a recognition that its two elements had become irreconcilable, and that unions should reject the market in favour of more traditional notions of socialization. *IG Metall* appears to have come closest to the latter position, but straddled the duality somewhat uncomfortably. The union's rhetoric became increasingly militant in the 1980s. The demand for HdA was given a more aggressive character in its 1984 action programme 'Der Mensch muss bleiben',[17] which stressed the antagonism between employer-driven rationalization and the needs and interests of workers, and called for stronger organization and intervention at workplace level. A militant, class-oriented trade unionism seemed confirmed in 1986 when Franz Steinkühler, who as head of the Stuttgart office had negotiated the LRTV II agreement, was elected president. He possessed some of the fluency and charisma of Brenner a quarter of a century before, though his taste in pin-stripe suits and more general affluent life-style distinguished him from an earlier generation of radicals. However, rhetoric and reality diverged. In many respects, *IG Metall* under the elegant militant Steinkühler exemplified Wright Mills' classic characterization of the union leader (1948: 9): 'he organizes discontent and then he sits on it, exploiting it in order to maintain a continuous organization; the labor leader is a manager of discontent.' Perhaps the last flowering of the innovative strategic radicalism of the 1980s – drawing also on the themes of humanization – was the policy document *Tarifreform 2000* (IG Metall, 1991). This ambitious programme, embracing principles of workplace equity and democracy within the collective bargaining agenda, was no sooner adopted than overtaken by the economic pressures of unification and deteriorating international competitiveness: 'pushed increasingly into the background and finally run into the sands' (Bahnmüller and Bispinck, 1999: 77).

United – and Divided

The Berlin wall fell in November 1989. Currency union between the two German states took place in July 1990, followed in October by full unification. This was not a merger of equals but a takeover: the smaller DDR ceased to exist and its territory became part of the *Bundesrepublik*. Laws and institutions were transferred overnight from west to east. But compared to the west, the eastern economic infrastructure was very backward and productivity extremely low; production chains were internalized within giant combines which were broken up in preparation for privatization; and former markets in eastern Europe were lost with the disarray of the whole region and the introduction of the *Deutschmark* in the DDR. The result was rapid de-industrialization and a surge in unemployment:

16 per cent in the east by 1992, a figure which would have been far higher but for subsidies for short-time working and early retirement, migration of many east Germans to the west, and the withdrawal by many others – particularly women – from the labour market. But for massive transfer payments from west to east, the political fallout would have been potentially disastrous (Hyman, 1996b: 605–6).[18]

German unions faced a series of challenges which for a number of years overshadowed all other concerns. First, how to extend their own organization to the east. Second, how to develop familiarity with a whole system of institutions (works councils, labour courts, employment offices) previously unknown in the east. Third, how to reconcile the long-established principle of standard wages and employment conditions across all of Germany with the reality of far lower productivity in the east. Fourth, after the immediate post-unification boom, how to respond to the deterioration in the German economy and labour market of which the cost of subsidizing unification was at least in part a cause. These challenges were reinforced, as the 1990s developed, by the intensification of international competitive pressures and growing doubts concerning the viability of the postwar 'German model'.

The highly centralized east German confederation FDGB was democratized after the fall of the wall and transformed into a system of industrial unions on the western model; individual DGB affiliates provided considerable advice and assistance during this restructuring period. For a time it seemed that the eastern and western unions might merge, but eventually it was agreed that the eastern unions would dissolve and encourage their members to join their western counterparts *en masse*. This was unexpectedly successful: a far higher level of union density was achieved than in the west, and DGB membership rose from just under 8 million in 1990 to almost 12 million. But as unemployment began to bite, many of the new members were lost; and because jobless workers were allowed to pay only a token subscription but required extensive advice and assistance, many unions suffered serious financial losses and were forced to make economies which affected members in the west also (Fichter, 1997: 86; Jacobi et al., 1998: 201–2).

The unions were required to fill a vacuum of representation at individual, workplace and sectoral levels. Individual workers needed help in challenging unfair treatment by employers, appealing against refusal of social benefits, pursuing training in new skills and job-seeking. At workplace level the key issue was to establish functioning works councils and also to ensure the election of *Vertrauensleute*. Most researchers have argued that this was an uphill struggle: the latter existed in far fewer workplaces than in the west, while the former tended to be more distant from the union and to be willing to ignore union policy if this was seen as necessary for company survival.[19] At sectoral level, there were similar institutional difficulties. The principle of the standard multi-employer collective agreement applying to the great majority of firms and (even if formally based on regional bargaining units) uniform across the whole country – the *Flächentarifvertrag* – rested upon strong employer collective solidarity and discipline. These foundations were difficult to establish in the east: firms proved less willing than in the west to affiliate to employers' associations and more liable to withdraw if they faced difficulties, or simply to ignore the terms of agreements negotiated on their behalf.

From the outset a burning substantive issue was the wide disparity in wage levels (and also working hours) between east and west. For varying reasons, the western-dominated unions, employers' organizations and government were at one in balking at the persistence of a low-wage region within the new Germany and saw a rapid narrowing of the differences as essential. In the negotiations around the time of unification, substantial pay increases were awarded; and in 1991, *IG Metall* secured agreement to equalize nominal wages in metal-working by 1994.[20] But this virtually guaranteed that many eastern firms would be uncompetitive. With unemployment mounting, the government changed its mind; and faced by a revolt from its own members in the east, the employers' organization *Gesamtmetall* had second thoughts and in 1993 unilaterally (and unlawfully) abrogated the agreement. *IG Metall* had little option but to call a strike, which – to the surprise of most observers and probably its own officials – attracted massive workforce support. After two weeks a compromise was arranged: the date of equalization was put back two years, and a so-called 'hardship clause' opened the possibility for firms facing serious financial difficulties to pay under the required rate (Jacobi et al., 1998: 220; Turner, 1998: 4–16).

The 1990s saw unprecedented uncertainty, controversy and pessimism concerning the German 'social market' model and its future. The debate was encapsulated in the slogan *Standort Deutschland*: Germany as a location for production. It was widely argued that the virtuous circle underlying economic success in previous decades – workplace productivity coalitions with a skilled and committed workforce able to negotiate continuous but incremental improvements in performance in order to compete successfully in high value-added markets (Streeck, 1997: 41) – had lost its efficacy. In the past there had been a trade-off between high performance and (relatively) high wage levels, and the additional labour costs resulting from a generous welfare state financed in large measure by payroll taxes. But Japanese producers had now shown that it was possible, and therefore necessary, to compete on both price and quality; the collapse of the iron curtain had opened a reservoir of skilled but low-paid labour on Germany's eastern borders; the single European market seemed linked to a weakening of major employers' commitment to a specific German identity. Finally, the new international competitive regime seemed to require rapid and systemic rationalization, to which the institutions of workplace codetermination could be regarded as an obstacle. The post-war industrial relations settlement faced serious challenge: there was 'a crisis of social partnership' (Turner, 1998: 117). How far the costs of unification were a major precipitating factor of this crisis is a matter of dispute (Silvia, 1999: 86; Streeck, 1997: 44; Turner, 1998: 117).

Unfavourable economic circumstances had a series of adverse consequences for trade unions. One was a delayed process of de-industrialization. Between 1975 and 1990, the proportion of the labour force employed in industry had fallen only from 45 to 40 per cent; in 1998 the figure was 34 per cent, still significantly above the European average but a sharp decline nevertheless (EC, 2000: 130). For a trade union movement more rooted than most in traditional industries, this was a serious challenge. De-industrialization was linked to levels of unemployment unknown for almost half a century: by 1994 the rate had risen to 10 per cent for Germany as a whole, climbing further to almost 13 per cent in 1997; while the level remained far higher in the east than in the west, even here the 10 per cent threshold was breached (BMA, 2000).[21] The relaxation of statutory regulation in the 1980s was also reflected in a growth of temporary employment, contributing – again, later than in many other countries – to the emergence of a two-tier labour market: 'a clear rift in terms of prosperity between the bulk of the permanently employed (the core workforce) and that of the "rest" of the marginalized working population' (Müller-Jentsch and Sperling, 1998: 78).

These labour market changes presented dilemmas of both organization and policy. Numerical decline was one evident indicator of the problem: from the peak of 11.8 million in 1991, DGB membership fell year-on-year to 8.3 million at the end of 1998. Were German unions condemned – and perhaps content – to represent a diminishing core workforce? Or if not, how could they appeal to a broader constituency? The working-time campaigns of the 1980s had been presented as a work-sharing and hence job-creating strategy. The outcome may have been some positive labour market effects, but according to most observers rather modest; the more obvious consequence was a rapid increase in hourly pay, allowing the union movement to 'have its cake and eat it too' (Silvia, 1999: 100). Unions also called for 'creative supply-side policies' (Hoffmann et al., 1990: 181) designed to reduce unemployment through skill enhancement and other active labour market measures. While clearly a progressive response to the unemployment crisis, such demands also served as an implicit rejection of claims that the standardized, and in comparative terms rather egalitarian, system of labour market regulation was itself an obstacle to job creation outside the old manufacturing sectors. Resistance to greater differentiation of employment conditions could be construed by critics as protecting the standards of the core out of largely rhetorical concern for the less skilled and marginalized (Streeck, 1991: 323–4). Some within the trade union movement also argued that the choice, for many of those in the secondary labour market, was between social regulation albeit at a lower level than for core workers, or no such regulation at all.

A different challenge was the continuing differentiation of industrial relations' regimes at company level. During the 1990s there was a persistent decline in the proportion of workplaces covered both by works councils and by collective agreements; by 1997, only 14 per cent of establishments had both. Though larger workplaces were more likely to be institutionally regulated, this still implied a serious weakening of the German institutional model (Hassel, 1999). In addition, the trend to decentralization facilitated by the sectoral agreements of the 1980s continued. The dilution of sectoral regulation in Germany as a whole was encouraged by developments in the east. The 'hardship clauses' which in 1993 permitted eastern firms in economic difficulties relief from the requirements of the sectoral agreement were soon echoed in the west by 'opening clauses (*Öffnungsklauseln*): 'a turning point in the history of German industrial relations' (Jacobi, 1995: 47). More flexible work arrangements, particularly in the organization of working time, were often pioneered in eastern plants of German firms which viewed 'the new *Länder* as a testing ground, where they could try out new strategies and concepts without any risk' (Bispinck, 1998: 13). Concessions obtained from 'more tolerant' eastern workforces could then become a precedent for managements in the west (Schmidt, 1998: 57).

A trend already significant in the 1980s was management enthusiasm for the devolution of operational responsibilities to working groups. Japanese ideas of team-working and quality circles were particularly influential in the motor industry and were widely embraced by German employers. Such forms of 'direct participation' were a significant challenge to existing institutional regulation, bypassing the representative structures of works councils and *Vertrauensleute*, and for this reason were at first resisted by unions such as *IG Metall*. But by the 1990s attitudes had changed, and union policy became the regulation of such initiatives as a potential step towards the objective of task-level codetermination (Flecker and Schulten, 1999: 94–5; Müller-Jentsch and Sperling, 1995: 17–25).

Economic adversity reinforced the pressures towards 'wildcat cooperation' identified by Streeck in the 1980s. Again, eastern Germany served as a pace-setter: in companies facing the threat of closure in the immediate aftermath of unification, management and workers' representatives felt obliged to cooperate in a tacit 'survival pact'. As western workers came to face similar dangers, 'cooperative company egoism' and 'concession bargaining' (Dörre, 1998: 126–7; Kotthoff, 1994) became more widespread. By the late 1990s, fragmentation and heterogeneity seemed increasingly characteristic of German industrial relations (Flecker and Schulten, 1999); the formal institutions of the traditional system remained in place, but their regulatory effect was significantly reduced. This diversity – both between and within sectors – could in itself be seen as an obstacle to a coordinated trade union response.

A different challenge came from government efforts to reduce the costs, to employers and to the public budget, of the welfare state. Though far less radical than in many European countries, these initiatives were nevertheless seen as raising fundamental questions of principle. The most explosive issue concerned sick pay. By law an employee unable to work for health reasons was entitled to full pay (including overtime, where this was regularly worked) for up to six weeks. Legislative changes approved despite bitter union opposition in 1996 reduced the amount of payment to 80 per cent of normal wages (without overtime) and the length of entitlement to four weeks. However, full payment of wages was also prescribed in most collective agreements. *Gesamtmetall* attempted unilaterally to abrogate this obligation, provoking forceful union reaction which proved successful. When employers sought to renegotiate the terms in the next bargaining rounds, the unions were also in general successful in maintaining the existing principle, though at the cost of other concessions to the employers. Coinciding with this challenge was the effort by the government (in the shadow of the convergence criteria for European monetary union) to enforce a wide-ranging set of expenditure cuts through an 'economy package' (*Sparpaket*). Efforts to push through significant changes in taxation and pension arrangements were, however, largely blocked by the government's lack of a majority in the upper house of parliament (the *Bundesrat*).

Though the main challenges to German unions were external, some wounds were self-inflicted. After the scandals of the 1980s, their public status suffered another severe shock in 1993 when Steinkühler – the most prominent and probably most charismatic of their leading figures – was found to have abused his position on company supervisory boards to engage in insider share-dealing and had to resign as president of *IG Metall*. A perceptive analysis in the DGB's theoretical journal (Arlt and Hemmer, 1993: 332–5) drew sombre conclusions. Starting from the familiar thesis of the 'dual character' of trade unions (Zoll, 1976), the authors stressed the difficulties for any union representative to manage the contradictory tension between the roles of 'conflictual opposition and cooperative partner'. To be effective, a union leader had to use militant rhetoric to encourage the collective commitment of the membership, but had also to be willing to compromise on the best available deal. This always invited accusations of insincerity and of 'selling out' the members; the only defence against such charges was 'exemplary personal integrity'. Not only had Steinkühler undermined union leaders' general credibility; the marginal members of the labour force in particular would be encouraged to regard the unions 'as rhetorical advocates but not practical champions of their interests' and would be embittered by the sight of officials, already enjoying a standard of living above the average, exploiting their position for their personal enrichment.

Given its elaborate organizational resources, its traditional concern to base practice on theoretical analysis, and the relatively high degree of internal consensus on its own identity and mission, the German trade union movement might have been expected to respond to the manifold challenges of the 1990s with a significant measure of strategic vision. But there was little evidence of this; rather, the reaction involved 'great uncertainty and lack of clarity' (Bispinck, 1998: 20). Part of the reason was an evident crisis of confidence; associated with this was broad agreement that German unions needed to redefine their role, but sharp disagreement on the direction of change. In particular, as noted earlier, there was an underlying conflict on whether to reaffirm the social market or to transcend it.

In the late 1980s the DGB had launched an ambitious debate on future strategy and structure, the so-called *Zukunftdebatte* (Hoffmann et al., 1990; Leif et al., 1993); but any hopes for a strategic reorientation soon ran into sands. Observers regarded the DGB as an 'impotent giant', unable to pursue significant initiatives because of the veto power of its member unions all concerned to prevent any reform which might shift the balance of power within the movement to their own disadvantage (Klein et al., 1993).[22] The end result was a new *Grundsatzprogramm*, the first since 1981, agreed at Dresden in 1996. Its central theme was a reaffirmation of support for the social market economy, but accompanied by demands for more effective social regulation and for stronger links between social and economic policy. On more specific objectives 'it frequently resorts to the language of compromise, which blurs its focus' (Silvia, 1999: 108).

Driven by financial difficulties, the unions sought primarily organizational solutions to their problems. Most notably, there was a trend towards mergers and amalgamations: in 1989 the tiny artists' union joined the print workers to form

IG Medien; in 1996 the miners, leather and chemical workers amalgamated to form *IG Bergbau, Chemie und Energie* (IGBCE); in 1996 the agricultural workers joined with the construction union. In the main, these mergers involved small and struggling unions seeking survival with a larger partner. This was also the case when the textile and wood workers joined *IG Metall* in 1998 and 1999. Most ambitious of all, agreement in principle was reached in 1998 for six unions in public and private services to form the giant *Vereinigte Dienstleistungsgewerkschaft* (ver.di); one subsequently withdrew, but in November 1999 the others agreed the basis for a merger to be completed in the spring of 2001.

One consequence is that the concept of industrial unionism, already eroded by the growth of conglomerate employers and the rise of new products and processes straddling traditional sectoral boundaries, has become an evident fiction; the pattern of amalgamation reflects political affinity and rivalry more than an industrial logic (Streeck and Visser, 1997). Another is to put the role and status of the DGB increasingly in question. By the year 2000, the sixteen (for a period, seventeen) affiliates had reduced to eleven. Should ver.di be created as planned the number would fall to eight (with the new super-union also embracing the DGB's smaller rival DAG – with the risk of potentially serious jurisdictional conflicts); the three main affiliates would embrace roughly four-fifths of total DGB membership. This would put in doubt the confederation's continuing purpose; and since part of the rationale of merger is for the combined unions to take over some of the activities hitherto undertaken by the DGB, pressure to reduce further the confederation's already depleted resources seems inevitable. Not surprisingly, since the mid-1990s economies have been the order of the day.

Collective bargaining policy in the 1990s was largely reactive and marked by an unpredictable oscillation between militancy and moderation. One tendency has been to resort to the language of class while still striving for the compromises of the social market. An index was that while strike threats remained common, actual stoppages were infrequent. The most serious dispute of the decade, in terms of workers involved and days lost, was in the public services in the spring of 1992. This was in fact precipitated by the government, concerned at the economic impact of unification, and hoping to enforce a low pay settlement which would set the terms for the private sector. The public service union ÖTV (*Öffentliche Dienste, Transport und Verkehr*) had little option but to organize a series of strikes (the first in the sector for eighteen years), and after two weeks the government was forced to back down.

After the failure of coercion, the government sought a return to concertation, proposing a 'solidarity pact' whereby wage restraint in the west would be linked to government aid to the east (Webber, 1997: 232–3). The intensive series of bilateral negotiations brought no formal agreement on incomes policy, but the settlements reached in the 1993 bargaining round were notably modest. This could be interpreted as a pragmatic adaptation to the collapse of the post-unification boom: 'in view of the difficult environment the German unions, including *IG Metall*, aimed only to match the rise in the cost of living; even this could they only partially achieve' (Bahnmüller and Bispinck, 1999: 77). In effect, hard times encouraged concession bargaining. This presented particular dilemmas for the metalworkers' union: after the fall of Steinkühler his successor, Klaus Zwickel, was under considerable pressure to demonstrate working-class credentials and a militant orientation. 'The societal interests of labour cannot be guaranteed by market logic and deregulation,' he declared (1993: 739). 'As in the past, the principle must be: living labour takes precedence over dead capital.' But dead capital could still bite: the costs of German unification, and escalating anxieties over German engineering's international competitiveness, created forceful pressures for restraint.

A dramatic instance was the crisis which hit Volkswagen at the end of 1993, soon after Zwickel's election. Under considerable duress, an agreement was reached allowing the company to reduce weekly wages in return for job guarantees and a shorter working week. Making a virtue of necessity, *IG Metall* presented this formula as an imaginative response to what was regarded as a temporary crisis for a major employer of the union's members. But the agreement contradicted the principle of the integrity of minimum standards applying to the industry as a whole, and the union's firm insistence that reductions in working time should not involve loss of weekly pay. While in theory 'without precedent', the Volkswagen settlement set the guidelines for the industry-level agreement reached in spring 1994 after a high-profile build-up towards strike action: a settlement which allowed companies greater flexibility within the context of overall wage restraint. 'An agreement for jobs,' declared Zwickel. In 1997 he went further, calling for a 32-hour week without full pay compensation as a job-creating measure; this was backed by some other unions, notably ÖTV, but was viewed askance by many others.

The principle of job-saving pay curbs was enthusiastically embraced by employers' organizations in the run-up to the 1995 bargaining round. Some other unions went further towards concession bargaining in 1994 than did the metalworkers; for example, *IG Chemie* accepted reduced pay rates for new employees. But after its diplomatic retreat the previous year, in 1995 *IG Metall* could not easily afford a second climb-down (not least because of forthcoming leadership elections); and the employers' intransigence virtually guaranteed a conflict. With the breakdown of negotiations, demonstration stoppages gave way to full-scale strikes. Yet hostilities were bounded ('it is easier to start a strike than to end one,' commented Zwickel). The bargaining region selected for action was Bavaria – according to the union, the home of some of the more hard-line employers – and the number of firms targeted was small. In any event, the conflict was resolved speedily by German standards and the settlement was sufficient to allow the union to claim a significant victory while leaving the employers in disarray (Turner, 1998: 118–19).

Soon, however, the mounting labour market difficulties led to a reaffirmation of social partnership. At the union's conference in December 1995, to general surprise, Zwickel proposed the creation of a *Bündnis für Arbeit* (alliance for jobs). He offered to agree to a pay settlement no greater than the rate of inflation, and reduced starting pay for long-term unemployed, if employers pledged to create new jobs and apprenticeships and if the government abandoned plans for cuts in social benefits (Bispinck, 1997). This was certainly a public relations coup, and after the DGB had endorsed the proposals the government and employers agreed to discussions. These proceeded with little concrete outcome in the early months of 1996; but when the government insisted on pursuing its programme of welfare cuts the unions abandoned the exercise.

In the more confrontational environment provoked by the fight over sick pay, in 1997 Zwickel called for 'an end to modesty' in pay bargaining. The metal-workers' settlement of that year, providing an increase of roughly 4 per cent over two years, could be seen as in part a trade-off for the maintenance of the previous payments for sickness absence and for progress in negotiations over partial early retirement, increasingly viewed as a means of work-sharing. For the 1999 round he announced a target of 6.5 per cent. However, any serious reconsideration of collective bargaining strategy was effectively put on hold in the run-up to the parliamentary elections of September 1998.

The Red-Green Coalition: Lifebelt or Straitjacket?

Dissatisfaction with the social and economic policies of the Kohl government placed increasing strain on the formal political neutrality of the German unions. In the months before the federal elections the DGB ran a massive campaign on the theme 'jobs and social justice', while its conference in June 1998 was 'little more than a five-day electoral rally for Gerhard Schröder,' the SPD candidate for chancellor (Silvia, 1999: 97). Whether or not this was a contributory factor in the outcome,[23] the social democrats made significant gains and after several weeks of negotiation with the Green party agreed a programme for a red-green coalition government. Walter Riester, deputy leader of *IG Metall*, became minister of labour.

The new government was committed to a range of positive actions very welcome to the unions. First, it would re-launch the *Bündnis für Arbeit*. Second, and linked to this, there would be an active labour market policy. Third, a number of legislative changes of the previous government – notably on sick pay – would be reversed. Fourth, there would be some new improvements in employee protection. Fifth, there would be a review of the existing law on co-determination and on industrial conflict. Two major questions remained unclear and were to prove contentious: whether, and how, there would be a shift from a restrictive monetarism to a more expansionary macroeconomic policy; and whether, and how, the effort to curb the cost of the welfare state would be pursued in different guise.

The government did indeed deliver on its immediate commitments. In December 1998 an initial summit meeting of the new *Bündnis* reached agreement on a set of objectives for tripartite discussions and established a series of working groups. Simultaneously the promised legislative changes were introduced and took effect the following month. Otherwise progress was slow. What became ponderously entitled the alliance for jobs, training and competitiveness soon became an established institution: but its very name indicated important differences between the participants. Jobs and apprenticeships were the priority for the unions; there was far less agreement on how to achieve these goals. Some argued that an expansionary macroeconomic policy combined with active labour market measures could deliver employment growth while also being consistent with generous pay increases; but this case was never systematically developed. The employers by contrast had a clear agenda: to improve competitiveness they wanted tax cuts for business and they wanted wage restraint. Most unions (despite reservations by the metalworkers) signed up to the first demand; and while rejecting any formal incomes policy as an infringement of free collective bargaining, they agreed that bargaining policies should support job creation and should be 'reliable' (Arlt and Nehls, 1999). What seemed to guarantee the continuity of the 'alliance' was that all parties to the discussions were anxious that, whether or not agreement on policy could be achieved, they at least should not be blamed for failure.

For its part, the government offered no substantial initiatives and appeared to hope that the other participants would find a solution. This might be regarded as symptomatic of a more general vacuum of policy, an outcome of serious internal divisions. Most notably the finance minister, Oskar Lafontaine, favoured neo-Keynesian expansionism and argued in particular for curbs on the ability of the *Bundesbank* to impose monetary restraint; but after losing the internal argument in the cabinet he resigned in early 1999, much to the chagrin of the unions. Schröder himself appeared to share many of the perspectives of the Blair government in Britain,[24] including tight budgetary discipline and a 'modernization' of the welfare state.

In a withering contribution to the debate on employment, Streeck (and Heinze, 1999) denounced what he regarded as a lack of vision on the union side. The main recipe to combat unemployment was to encourage job-splitting and early retirement. Yet this assumed a fixed demand for labour which could only be redistributed: unions were pursuing an 'alliance for pensions' rather than for jobs. Streeck's plea was for an expansion of employment in the service sector, which is far less developed in Germany than in otherwise comparable countries. But, he argued, given the low productivity of much service work compared to manufacturing, this would be possible only with a differential tax regime, a more flexible institutionalization of the employment relationship than that developed in Fordist manufacturing, and wage determination which took account of productivity differences. This proposal was a frontal challenge to the established principles of German trade unionism; and the general union response was to denounce the idea of creating a 'low-wage sector'. But there was little indication of a plausible alternative.

Reviewing the first twelve months of the Schröder government, Zwickel (1999) declared that there was 'no cause for rejoicing'. The *Sparpaket* of the Kohl government had been reconstituted but not abandoned. The common policies of Schröder and Blair seemed more neoliberal than social-democratic. Nevertheless, specific union demands remained limited: centrally, the right to retire at 60 (rather than 65) on full pension. Though endorsed by Riester at the end of 1999, this was strongly opposed by employers – who suspected that they would be required to carry the costs – and viewed sceptically by many other union leaders. The demand was a key element in the 2000 bargaining round in engineering, which was resolved surprising rapidly in a pilot agreement in Nordrhein-Westfalen. The latter provided a relatively modest pay increase together with some compensation – though far from full – for workers taking early retirement. Within *IG Metall* itself, enthusiasm for the deal was mixed.

Since the 1998 election, history in some respects repeated itself. As under the Brandt and Schmidt governments between 1969 and 1982, most unions felt constrained by the demands of loyalty to 'their' government. Given the changed political context, the *Bündnis* itself became a cage from which it was difficult to escape. Its potential was limited by the relative narrowness of the agenda: the interaction between fiscal, monetary and employment policy was not open to discussion (Hein and Heise, 1999). Despite emphasis on the integrity of *Tarifautonomie*, the role of peak-level concertation as a tacit incomes policy seemed scarcely deniable.[25]

Conclusion: A Bermuda Triangle?

In the triangle of society-market-class, German unions today seem torn in three directions. Influential voices still urge a reconciliation of society and market. The logic of the principle of the *neue Mitte* is that the reaffirmation of their complementarity is both possible and necessary; and this is implied also by the very concept of an alliance for jobs, training and competitiveness. Yet intensified employer demands for sacrifice to defend *Standort Deutschland* make it increasingly difficult to square the circle. Are unions still struggling to function as 'intermediary organisations' (Müller-Jentsch, 1985) between economic interests which can no longer be reconciled?

Some German union leaders have been turning increasingly to the rhetoric of class in denunciations of monetarist ministers and hard-line employers: a rhetoric which, in mobilizing discontented rank-and-file activists, could assume an autonomous dynamic. It is also relevant that the institutions of workplace codetermination and the welfare state were outcomes of class struggle: 'class cooperation at enterprise level comes about as a consequence of rational, interest-led action within an economic non-zero-sum game that is in turn made possible through class confrontation at the societal level and the organizational status achieved through it' (Streeck, 1992: 61). If this is so, the retreat from at least the potential for class mobilization could be seen as one cause of the reduced effectiveness of German unions. This is consistent with the argument of Zwickel (2000) that a 'societal power struggle' is essential if unions are to resist the drift towards 'deregulation and cuts in social welfare' and achieve the goal of a 'democratic civil society'.

Yet the elements of class displayed in current union ideology seem to oscillate around principles of identity and opposition defined by Touraine (1966). There are few signs of a totalizing framework which might generate an alternative strategy to the old principles of free collective bargaining and the social market which in harsher economic conditions no longer seem able to deliver. A Bermuda triangle?

Notes

[1] For simplicity I refer merely to 'Germany' and 'German', though my focus for the period before unification in 1990 is exclusively on developments in West Germany.

[2] Much of the territory to the east became part of Poland and the USSR (which also annexed much of eastern Poland). France took over the Saarland, which returned to Germany after a plebiscite in 1956.

[3] The principle of trade union unity was largely but not totally realized. The DGB faced rivals which acted as representatives of salaried staff (the DAG) and of tenured public employees or *Beamte* (the DBB), though it claimed to outnumber both within its own ranks. There was also a tiny separatist catholic federation, the CGB.

[4] Van Kersbergen (1995: 78–9), like other commentators, sees the adoption of the Ahlen programme as reflecting a tactical manoeuvre by Adenauer to ensure the attachment of christian socialist trade unionists to his own party.

[5] German companies have a two-tier structure with a small management board (*Vorstand*) appointed by and accountable to a non-executive supervisory board (*Aufsichtsrat*).

[6] In German unions the top official is the president – or 'first president' (*erste[r] Vorsitzende[r]*), elected by the delegate conference. Böckler, himself a metal worker, was a cautious social democrat, who had been a councillor in Cologne in the 1920s when Adenauer was mayor.

[7] Under the revised arrangements the 'labour director' was no longer a union nominee, but could not be appointed without the consent of the workforce – which had the same practical effect.

[8] In this respect the DGB became analogous to the British TUC. In most other European countries the hierarchy of importance is very different; for example, Bruno Trentin, head of the CGIL metalworkers, went on to become secretary-general of the confederation.

[9] One of the leading theorists of catholic trade unionism, von Nell-Breuning, distinguished (1964: 218) between 'bargaining partnership' which he saw as characteristic of German industrial relations, and 'social partnership' which implied a much more fundamental institutionalization of cooperative relationships.

[10] By contrast, he suggests, far weaker job security in Britain encouraged a more restrictive collective orientation: rigidity in the internal labour market compensating for flexibility in the external.

[11] In this chapter I focus primarily on the policies and politics of *IG Metall*. In a brief survey this is justified by its size and leading role in collective bargaining; nevertheless it is important to stress that German trade unionism has been marked by sharp ideological cleavages. For a detailed comparison of policy developments in *IG Metall* and three other major unions see Markovits (1986).

[12] Karl Schiller, who became economics minister, was the leading Keynesian theoretician in the SPD.

[13] Most dramatic was the political violence of the 'Red Army Fraction', but there was also a far broader 'extra-parliamentary opposition'.

[14] In 1968 a new communist party, the DKP, was established in place of the outlawed former KPD. In the new political environment (which included the pursuit of less antagonistic relationships with the DDR and the Soviet bloc as a whole – the so-called *Ostpolitik*) it was not suppressed.

[15] As late as 1965, Brenner had declared that 'we have no fear of technology' (Brandt et al., 1982: 143).

[16] Previously, workers laid off as a result of a dispute in a different bargaining district were automatically entitled to unemployment benefit; this meant that a union could pursue strike action in a relatively small bargaining district, and target employers involved in supply chains which extended to other parts of the country, maximizing disruption while minimizing the cost to union funds. Article 116 provided that where the terms of an eventual agreement for the workers on strike were likely to be extended to those laid off elsewhere, unemployment benefits would no longer be payable.

[17] The title has a double meaning which is lost in translation: that workers must keep their jobs, and that work must remain compatible with human creativity and dignity.

[18] These paragraphs draw primarily on my 1996 article, which references a wide range of German sources, most of which are not cited here.

[19] Frege (1999), on the basis of research in the textile industry, has contested these arguments. Her positive assessment is in large measure shared by Turner (1998: 4–16). Wever (1995: 161) stresses the diversity of experience, which entails that 'one can find evidence … in favor of almost any proposition'.

[20] Given the existence of significant bonus payments in many western firms, this did not indeed mean equalization of total earnings. In addition, the working week remained longer in the east: 38 hours (in fact a considerable reduction from the pre-unification norm), as against the phased reduction to 35 in the west.

[21] The method of compilation in Germany shows a higher rate than in international comparative statistics; EU data show the 1997 peak as 9.9 per cent.

[22] A prominent group of intellectuals close to the trade unions wrote a commentary in the DGB's theoretical journal (Epskamp et al., 1992) with the ironical title 'Abolish the DGB!', arguing that if the member unions were unwilling to allow the DGB to take effective initiatives they would do better to use for other purposes the 12 per cent of their income contributed to the confederation.

[23] Polls indicated that only a quarter of trade unionists who voted supported the existing coalition parties, as against over 40 per cent of the voters as a whole.

[24] His call for a *neue Mitte* (new centre) mirrored Blair's enthusiasm for a 'third way'; and in June 1999 (on the eve of the elections for the European Parliament, in which both SPD and Labour suffered serious losses) both leaders endorsed a joint policy statement 'The Way Forward for Europe's Social Democrats'.

[25] In September 2000 this led *IG Medien* – the smallest DGB affiliate, and traditionally the most left-wing – to resolve to withdraw from the *Bündnis* and to argue with its partners in the new *ver.di* for a similar decision.

7

Italian Trade Unionism

Between Class and Society

The post-war reconstruction of Italian trade unionism followed a trajectory in many respects distinct from that in Germany. In part this was because the end of the war came in a very different manner. In 1943, following the allied landings in Sicily and with an invasion of the mainland imminent, Mussolini was ousted in a palace coup and the new government negotiated an armistice soon afterwards, declaring war on the Germans who now occupied much of the country and supported Mussolini's rump government in part of the north. As the allies fought their way up slowly from the south, a powerful partisan movement, in which communists played a key role, rapidly developed organization and influence in the north.

Many paradoxes ensued. First, whereas Nazi Germany surrendered unconditionally and was subject to years of allied occupation, the Italian fascist state – minus Mussolini – was able to switch from enemy to ally, and hence emerged from the war among the victors. In consequence, the allied authorities rapidly handed over control to the new Italian government, and as a corollary many political, legislative and economic institutions were carried over from the fascist regime into the post-war era.[1] Second, many of the key decisions on the shape of the post-war regime emerged through negotiation between the successor fascist-monarchist government and opposition leaders returning from exile. The economically backward, politically conservative south was the first to be freed. A militant resistance movement in the more radical industrial heartlands of the north soon won mass support and played a major role in achieving liberation; but by then the main characteristics of the new regime were already determined.[2] Third, as part of this process, a new trade union structure was imposed from above. In the 'pact of Rome' in June 1944, representatives of the former communist, socialist and catholic unions agreed to establish a single organization, the *Confederazione Generale Italiana del Lavoro* (CGIL).

This artificial unity was short-lived. The strains of the cold war were reinforced by domestic Italian divisions, linked to the dominant parliamentary position of the newly-established christian-democratic party (DC) under de Gasperi and the powerful opposition status of the communist party (PCI) after its brief period as member of the governing coalition. Within a few years, CGIL was confronted by two smaller breakaways. The splits weakened labour both politically and industrially, allowing major (as well as smaller) employers to victimize union activists and assert virtually unilateral authority in the workplace.

Much of the subsequent history involved the consolidation of distinctive and opposing identities and ideologies within the rival confederations; and their later uneasy and incomplete redefinition, particularly on the part of the dominant CGIL. Its own self-definition as a vehicle of militant class opposition was in part eroded by the 'historic compromise' embraced by the PCI in the 1970s, when it in effect assumed the responsibility to act as protector of the social and political order in the face of extremist threats. The identity as vehicle of social integration was reinforced by economic crisis in the 1980s and political crisis in the 1990s. Italian trade unionism became increasingly defined by a tension between class politics and social integration. To the extent that this has meant neglecting a role as labour market actor, however, the consequences have been discomfiting.

Unity and Division

The dynamics of Italian trade unionism were driven by a complex pattern of political identities and cleavages. One axis was the tension between the catholic church, with its traditional grip over public life and its effort to maintain this control despite economic and social modernization; and those committed to a separation between church and state, with a secular basis to key public institutions (notably the educational system). The Italian state had been constituted in the 1860s on the principle of secularization; this was modified after the turn of the century and reversed in 1929 by Mussolini's notorious 'concordat' with the Vatican, allowing privileges which were to prove politically explosive in the post-war era. Another axis was the split between socialists and communists. In Italy, however, this familiar cleavage was less radical than in most other European countries. The PSI, unique among majority socialist parties in the belligerent countries, had refused to support the 1914–18 war and shared communist aspirations for revolution in the period of post-war turmoil. Mussolini's seizure of power in 1922 came before the confrontations between communists and reformists had reached the pitch of hostility which developed elsewhere; and in 1934 a formal unity pact was agreed between PSI and PCI, providing an effective basis for common anti-fascist struggle (Kendall, 1975: 149). After the war, the PSI majority was to display a far more positive orientation towards the communists and the Soviet Union than their counterparts elsewhere in Europe, a factor which soon resulted in disunity and fragmentation.[3]

CGIL was in essence a political creation, an expression of the shared commitment of the three main political tendencies to a consensual process of post-war reconstruction. This unity, which had its parallel in the participation of socialist and communist ministers in de Gasperi's first DC-led government, could not survive the renewal of party-political cleavages.

The break-up resulted from a combination of domestic and external pressures. In the final stages of the liberation struggle in the north, the resistance movement developed into a powerful and radical insurrectionary force. Incorporating socialists and communists in the de Gasperi government was a necessary means of outflanking the rank-and-file militants, a strategy with which the PCI leadership (for reasons reflecting Stalin's own *raison d'état*) was willing to collaborate. Once order was restored de Gasperi no longer required his junior partners, and excluded them from a new government formed in May 1947. The christian democrats' political ambitions meshed closely with American foreign policy: the State Department made clear to de Gasperi that the USA would provide economic assistance to Italy, but only if the PCI was marginalized and indeed if the government adopted austerity measures which the communists could scarcely accept. Within weeks of the formation of the new government, aid was offered within the framework of the newly announced Marshall Plan (Romero, 1992: 139–41).

Splitting CGIL was the counterpart of this political project. The process ran in parallel with the breach in the World Federation of Trade Unions (WFTU) in 1948 and the formation of the International Confederation of Free Trade Unions (ICFTU) the following year. Systematic intervention by the Americans (notably involving the AFL agents Lovestone and Brown) encouraged the divisions in the Italian movement, while the embittered national elections of April 1948 provided domestic pressure to the same end. The catholic fraction, tightly organized within a notionally 'educational movement' (ACLI) founded at the same time as CGIL itself (Bedani, 1995: 18; Pasture, 1994: 73), liaised closely with the government, the Americans and the Vatican in preparing for a breakaway.[4] The pretext occurred in July 1948, soon after the DC had won a landslide election victory, when the attempted assassination of the communist leader Palmiro Togliatti precipitated a wave of spontaneous strikes which the communists, supported by socialists and radicals, endorsed the better to control (Horowitz, 1963: 215-16).[5]

ACLI's objective was to lead a broad non-communist confederation, and to this end a 'free' CGIL (LGCIL) was created in October 1948. But its putative allies rejected a precipitate break from CGIL, and their anti-clerical sentiments were at least as intense as their anti-communism, despite strong American pressure. In May 1949 republicans, social democrats and some 'autonomist' socialists finally abandoned CGIL and most of those seceding then established a new federation, FIL (Horowitz, 1963: 220–2). Early in 1950 a majority of its delegates approved a merger with LCGIL, but a significant section broke away to form UIL (*Unione Italiana del Lavoro*) in March 1950. Two months later LCGIL and the remaining elements of FIL joined to create the CISL (*Confederazione Italiana dei Sindacati Lavoratori*) (Romero, 1992: ch. 5). The name was significant: as a confederation of unions CISL emphasized the relative autonomy of its sectoral organizations, as against the greater centralization of CGIL; this in turn was meant to indicate an 'economic' rather than a 'political' orientation. CGIL remained easily the largest confederation, dominated by the communists but with a significant left-socialist minority.

In the immediate aftermath, each confederation inclined to varying degrees to one of the three 'ideal types' of trade unionism outlined in the introduction to this book. CGIL, with by far the largest membership, effectively joined the PCI in opposition and embraced an ideology of militant class struggle. Economic demands were framed more as reference points for collective mobilization than as elements in a 'realistic' bargaining agenda. CGIL was particularly suspicious of the idea of negotiations on a sectional basis which might undermine class unity.

As has been seen, the second main confederation, CISL, was closely associated with the governing party, and its leaders sympathized politically with many leading employers. Though dominated by christian democrats it was not explicitly a catholic trade union; on the contrary, it insisted on its religious neutrality and accordingly affiliated to the new ICFTU rather than to the smaller christian international (Pasture, 1994: 71).[6] As a corollary, non-catholics were accorded disproportionate weight within its governing bodies (as was also the case for non-communists within CGIL). Nevertheless, in line with catholic social doctrine, CISL identified its role as advancing workers' interests by strengthening their organized integration in society, thus encouraging social and political order. 'In the economic sphere ... it emphasized the necessity of increased productivity and production, stability of the economy, and relationship of wage movements to these factors' (Horowitz, 1963: 232). The professions of political neutrality were also tendentious: it maintained its own 'current' within the DC party, and its leader Giulio Pastore, who had been secretary-general since CISL's formation, stood down in 1958 to become a government minister (Bianchi, 1996: 58).

UIL, with far fewer members, was able to attract to its ranks important sections of republicans and social democrats who had initially joined CISL but found the dominance of ACLI uncongenial. It asserted its political autonomy and came closest to the model of business unionism – though business unionism on the American model was virtually inconceivable in the Italian context, where 'political exchange' has always been a crucial element in employment regulation. Hence the UIL statutes insisted on the need 'to intervene actively in all problems relating to economic and social policy and whenever, directly or indirectly, the future of the working class is at stake' (Bedani, 1995: 50). It attempted to distinguish itself from CGIL by an emphasis on winning immediate material gains for workers, and from CISL by its greater willingness to support militant action which might embarrass the government.

Fragmentation and the confrontation between rival confederations resulted in trade union weakness and a loss of membership, particularly from the ranks of CGIL (Ferner and Hyman, 1992: 544–6; Romagnoli, 1989: 94–5). In part this reflected high levels of unemployment and the influx into expanding industrial workplaces of migrants from conservative rural areas. It also linked as both cause and consequence to an employer offensive to win back control at the point of production after the insurgency which accompanied the end of the war. Immediately after the fall of Mussolini an agreement was reached with *Confindustria* to re-establish the workplace representative structures (*commissioni interne*) which had been abolished under fascism; but their powers were limited, and they served often as little more than vehicles for a popularity contest between the rival unions. Employers often interfered blatantly to ensure the election of candidates they considered compliant. Representatives – in stark contrast to German works councillors – lacked protection against victimization. To be a union activist was often dangerous, and particularly so for those in CGIL (Flanagan et al., 1983: 509–12).

Despite unions' weakness in conventional industrial relations terms, they possessed a significant public status deriving from their role in the post-war structures of the welfare state. The various components of the elaborate social insurance system were administered by tripartite boards at both national and local level. In the public sector – where collective bargaining was not formally permitted until the 1980s – unions also participated in a vast network of regulatory committees. In consequence, 'Italian unions enjoyed greater and more pervasive influence than standard indicators of union performance (membership figures, collective bargaining outcomes, etc.) would suggest' (Regalia and Regini, 1995: 136). This had a double implication for trade union identities. First, it encouraged a broad orientation to the interests of workers as a class: in sickness and health, in work, unemployed or retired. Hence union concerns necessarily extended beyond a narrow agenda of collective bargaining with employers. Second, it embedded unions as components of the social order, and principles of anti-capitalist resistance meshed uneasily with such integrative functions. This represented part of the background to a renegotiation of union identities in the decades which followed.

Transformations in Italian Unionism: The Hot Autumn and the Historic Compromise

In the second half of the twentieth century, trade union practice diverged in significant respects from the founding ideologies of the 1940s, compelling a painful process of redefinition of identity and purpose. Four distinct phases are discussed below: the development of pragmatic company bargaining in the 1950s and 1960s; the revival of trade union strength and the move towards common perspectives after the 'hot autumn' (*autunno caldo*) of 1969, particularly marked by the re-orientation within Italian communism; the responses, at both national and company level, to economic crisis in the late 1970s and the 1980s; and the consolidation of the three main confederations as bulwarks of social order with the collapse of the old political regime in the 1990s.

From the mid 1950s, both CGIL and CISL edged from ideological confrontation towards a more pragmatic approach to industrial relations. CISL, denounced by its larger rival as a 'yellow' union willing to underwrite any terms proposed by managements, became increasingly concerned to demonstrate its independence from employers and government. This shift was encouraged by the emergence of a new cadre of officials, schooled in American approaches to collective bargaining. The outcome was a series of company agreements, often involving elements of productivity bargaining, usually negotiated by full-time officials rather than workplace representatives. UIL was often a co-signatory, but CGIL at first condemned this approach as a betrayal of broader class interests. Yet many of the agreements brought real improvements in workers' conditions, and this could be seen as one explanation for CISL's stable membership in the 1950s[7] while CGIL lost substantial ground.

Eventually CGIL too was forced to pursue credibility as a defender of workers' immediate economic interests by embracing the approach of its rival. Its change of analysis and practice was precipitated by the loss of its majority in the 1955 elections for the *commissione interna* at Fiat, one of its traditional strongholds;[8] the shift in emphasis from a broad political agenda to workplace issues was agreed the following year (Bedani, 1995: 89–91). One interpretation (Regalia et al., 1978: 102) was that 'the Italian unions escaped from their subordination to the political situation (which had resulted from both structural unemployment and the Cold War and its consequent political isolation of the PCI) and their position came to depend increasingly on purely economic variables'. Nevertheless, any move towards 'economism' was qualified. For the Italian unions the increasing dualism between the advanced sectors of manufacturing where significant wage gains could be negotiated, and a large and backward hinterland, was itself a social and political problem; hence they were 'less willing than unions in other advanced capitalist countries to pursue a bargaining strategy which benefits only those workers in positions of strength: that is, those employed in the modern sector of the economy' (Regalia et al., 1978: 103).

A new and dramatic phase of union redefinition – indeed in many respects, the re-invention of Italian trade unionism – was linked to the escalation of industrial militancy in 1968 and (particularly) 1969. Explanations varied, but the *autunno caldo* of 1969 was widely attributed to a broad discontent with conditions under an oppressive factory regime, the intensification of work pressures which had underlain the increases in productivity (and also in wages), and the more generalized grievances of a new urban workforce unused to the cost and squalor of city living. The upsurge in many of the leading manufacturing areas was driven from below: 'the factory world [was] seething with the ferment of strikes, workers' assemblies, rallies, meetings, unionization drives, and elections of workers' representatives' (Franzosi, 1995: 263).

The official confederations had not initiated the workplace militancy, but they rode the strike wave and were its main beneficiary. Membership increased rapidly: by the late 1970s roughly half of all Italian employees were unionized. The rank-and-file committees which had provided some coordination to the struggles were institutionalized as trade union-based factory councils, displacing the old system of *commissioni interne*. This assimilation of rank-and-file structures into the unions' own organizational machinery was facilitated by the convergence of the three main confederations in 1972 to form a unitary federation.[9] As so often occurred in other countries and at other times of militant advance, the unions sought to consolidate their new strength by assuming functions of order and discipline. 'Having once reached a favourable equilibrium in the industrial relations system, the unions aimed to make the new rules of the game definitive. ... The "responsible" behaviour of the unions was designed to ensure that the forms of conflict did not go beyond the level of intensity accepted by management' (Regalia et al., 1978: 117). Their organizational gains were reinforced by the novel representational rights conveyed by the 1970 Workers' Statute (*Statuto dei diritti dei lavoratori*).

Hence the Italian unions found themselves transformed into powerful actors, in both economic and political terms. Enhanced political influence was assisted by the 'opening to the left' which had taken place nationally in the 1960s, when the PSI (which had members in all three union confederations) was admitted to the governing coalition.[10] Economic strength was reflected in the self-confident use of collective pressure in the key industrial sectors. In the 1960s the concept had been developed of 'articulated' collective bargaining: modest framework agreements at confederal level, more detailed sectoral agreements, and productivity bargaining at company level. This now gave way to 'articulated bargaining without limits': gains achieved at workplace level in militant strongholds could be generalized by negotiations at higher level. The agenda of collective bargaining was broadened: challenges to managerial discipline, excessive production speeds and the extreme fragmentation of tasks which had provided the foundations for rapid industrialization; simplified grading structures, with wage increases weighted in favour 'of the lower paid; more radically, demands for action over grievances concerning the costs of housing, public transport, electricity; and pressure for the major firms to address the sharp economic disparities between Italy's developed north and backward south by investing in the *Mezzogiorno*.

For some observers, there were uneasy parallels with the situation of 'dual power' which had developed at the height of the factory council movement half a century earlier (Hyman, 1971: 46–9). Then, capitalist control of the leading industrial enterprises was challenged by a well organized, politically advanced and self-confident rank-and-file movement; but these were islands of proletarian assertiveness within an Italy much of which was marked by backwardness and conservatism, and an alliance between industrial capital and the forces of political reaction provided the basis for the triumph of fascism. Antonio Gramsci, the leading theorist of the factory council movement and the newly formed PCI, had reflected on this experience in Mussolini's gaols. His analysis, at times ambiguous, provided scope for debate by later generations, but some arguments were clear: in the countries of western Europe, the existing social, economic and political order rested not simply on the coercive structures of state power but also on popular assent generated within the institutions of civil society. Until revolutionaries had conducted a successful ideological challenge at this level – a battle for 'hegemony', inevitably a slow and uneven process – any frontal challenge to the system would be premature and could result in disaster.

By the time of the 'hot autumn', this analysis had already regained significant influence within the PCI, the first western communist party to develop the concepts of 'Eurocommunism' as a challenge to Soviet orthodoxy. The lessons seemed reinforced by the brutal overthrow of the Allende regime in Chile in September 1973: the Chilean socialists had won control of the machinery of state but not over a polarized civil society. Leaders of the PCI expressed fears of a similar disaster in Italy. 'Dual power' in the factories disrupted production and brought a sharp rise in labour costs; in conjunction with the oil price crisis of the 1970s, this resulted in accelerated inflation and balance of payments difficulties. Politically, the post-war institutional compromise was threatened by the rise of neo-fascist groups with apparent connections in high places, and by terrorist initiatives of a militant section of the left-wing 'red brigades'.

Shaken by the Chilean coup, the PCI under Enrico Berlinguer adopted a new principle, the *compromesso storico* (historic compromise), which entailed an explicit shift from a revolutionary to a reformist programme, but was consistent with a longer-term deradicalization of the party involving the marginalization or exclusion of both its 'traditional' and its 'new' left elements (Amyot, 1981). Working-class mobilization alone could not achieve socialist transformation in a country such as Italy, but on the contrary was likely to provoke a reactionary (neo-fascist) backlash. Socialism itself was not on the agenda for the foreseeable future: all that could realistically be pursued was a process of modest and incremental reform in workers' conditions. 'The historic compromise was designed to confront both the political dangers and the opportunities that had arisen out of the hot autumn' (Golden, 1988: 61). Through offering an alliance with not only other left parties but also christian democracy (or at least its 'progressive' elements) the PCI might safeguard Italian democracy, end its own political isolation (carrying further the 'opening to the left' in national politics which had begun in the 1960s), and shift government policy towards a social programme advantageous to workers.

While the PCI never achieved its objective of formal admission to power, it gained a half-way house in 1976–79 in the period of the 'national solidarity' government. As a member of the parliamentary majority it was allowed to chair a number of parliamentary committees; more generally it became 'a daily participant in the major decisions of the national government' (Lange et al., 1982: 161). Moreover, the 'blocked democracy' whereby the second largest Italian party in terms of votes (over 34 per cent in 1976) was consigned to permanent opposition, while far smaller parties were admitted to the governing coalition, was partially compensated by the 'political exchange' which brought the trade unions, and most importantly CGIL, centrally into the formulation of public policy.

This socio-political project acquired an increasingly dominant economic dimension as the breakdown in the post-war world economic order coincided with the escalating crisis of the Italian economy (certainly aggravated by the collective bargaining achievements of the newly confident trade union movement). Inflation reached one of the highest levels in Europe, unemployment mounted, and the continued competitiveness of exports appeared threatened (Flanagan et al., 1983: 496–7). Ironically, one should note that for earlier generations of communists (and indeed for the new left of the 1960s and 1970s) such an economic crisis was regarded as a springboard for revolutionary challenge to the capitalist order. But in line with the new stance of the PCI, CGIL along with the two other confederations accepted the need for bargaining restraint, while attempting to gain compensation through influence on government fiscal and social policy. These developments are explored in more detail below.

The 1970s thus saw Italian unions radically reassessing their priorities. The notion of 'free collective bargaining' was never particularly plausible in a country where employment was extensively regulated by law, and where the government was a prominent actor in industrial relations and itself, directly or indirectly, a major employer. The radical-oppositional model – at least in the view of the majority of the PCI and CGIL leadership – no longer matched the realities of

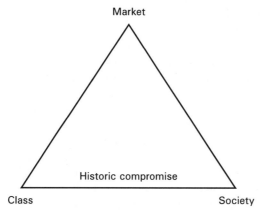

FIGURE 7.1 *Italy – between class and society*

Italian society; trade union power brought a need for responsibility, though a responsibility shaped by the distinct interests of the working class. The model of social integration adopted by CISL seemed confirmed, though with a new radical dimension. The ideology of Italian trade unionism had, in effect, developed a new synthesis on the axis between class and society (see Figure 7.1).

Reacting to Economic Crisis: From Political Exchange to Microcorporatism

Trade union redefinition and realignment involved a complex and contradictory process, reflected in recurrent tensions and occasional overt confrontations within and between the main confederations. Italian industrial relations and trade unionism were subject to a variety of mutations, the character and significance of which remain disputed. The combined effect appeared, however, to undermine the new ideological synthesis almost as it was constructed.

To some extent, Italian developments can be seen as a stark example of more general European experience of a strategic shift from class opposition to political exchange and 'social partnership'. As Crouch has argued (1993: 290–1), 'class solidarities ... that initially undermined national identity subsequently helped construct institutions that became a base for forging national cooperation. Precisely because leaders, especially of labour, were coordinating combative organizations, they were able to mobilize loyalty and obedience ... in order to secure cooperation.' In the Italian case, however, it is important to stress that the project of 'historic compromise' which initially reflected a primarily political rationale soon acquired major economic implications: in the articulation between class and society, market factors introduced new complications.

As indicated above, the shifting strategic balance between confrontation and cooperation coincided with the adverse economic circumstances which confronted trade unions in most European countries, though in a particularly heightened form: high unemployment, intensified competitive pressures in the private sector, government efforts to economize in the public sector, restructuring of employment away from traditional union strongholds, management initiatives aimed at reorganizing production and reshaping the employment relationship. An overriding problem for the unions became the character of political exchange in hard times (Baglioni, 1987). At first, a policy orientation linking class and society had seemed the basis for positive outcomes in return for bargaining restraint. For example, in 1975 the unions agreed with *Confindustria* a reform of the wage indexation system (*scala mobile*) which was intended to bring greater order to pay determination but also – in a context of rapid price inflation – guaranteed substantial increases, particularly for the lower paid, since it embodied flat-rate rises (Flanagan et al., 1983: 543–6; Negrelli and Santi, 1990: 154; Somaini, 1989: 322–5). In this first phase of social concertation, the new strategy could be presented as a novel, and constructive, development of class struggle: the thesis, for example, of Bruno Trentin (1977), one of the key figures in the hot autumn, secretary of the united metalworkers' union and later CGIL secretary-general.

Yet the implications of restraint without substantial compensating benefits were very different. As Regini commented a few years later (1984: 129), 'if the only advantages that a union gets from political exchange are in the form of power for its leaders or of organizational gains, there should be a formidable amount of opposition on the part of the rank-and-file, since self-restraint by workers would be compensated for only by gains for their representatives'. Such an unbalanced exchange was scarcely conceivable in the Italy of the early 1970s, for many of the activists and officials who had emerged after the hot autumn had won their reputations as militant protagonists of workers' immediate interests. In the powerful metalworkers' union in particular,[11] there existed a strong commitment in many of the main centres of the industry to ambitious demands and direct action (Golden, 1988: 90–1). Thus many within CGIL in particular fervently opposed the move from militancy to conciliation. 'Our objective, both today and in the future ... is that of defending the class nature of the Italian union,' declared one activist (Mershon, 1989: 218).

Thus the rationale for engagement in 'neo-corporatist' relations needed to include a claim for beneficial material consequences: 'modifying market outcomes to labour's advantage'. Regini (1984: 129–34) suggested three possible bases for such a claim. First, unions could exert greater influence on governments than on employers, and hence should rationally focus their activity on the political arena; second, and with the same strategic implication, the state alone could provide such valued benefits as social reform, a favourable tax regime, employment-generating monetary and labour market policies. It might be argued that restraint in collective wage bargaining would create a more favourable macroeconomic environment, and encourage more congenial government priorities, thus resulting in a beneficial net outcome in terms of the social wage. In the Italian case, 'the ideology of class, as opposed to sectional, interests was ... heavily used ... to reinforce workers' loyalty to the unions' policies. By presenting the content and the objectives of the political exchange under way in terms of solidaristic class interests ... the unions discouraged open dissent among a sizeable portion of their rank-and-file, namely, the more politicized.' Third, 'the national economy may be in deep crisis or highly exposed to international competition. In such situations, even a strong trade union may find it very risky to exploit to the full its organizational and market power [since] its disruption of the economy may be such as to imperil its future ability to defend its members' employment and in turn the very basis of its own power.'

While the first two arguments were consistent with a view of political exchange as a route to working-class advancement (and perhaps a component of a Gramscian struggle for hegemony), the third was clearly pessimistic and defensive: a least-worst option in hard times. Such a perspective certainly influenced the PCI, CGIL and the other confederations, and was reflected in a 1977 inter-confederal agreement to cooperate with employers in improving productivity while imposing a moratorium on company-level pay increases. The new approach was confirmed in the '*Eur*-line' agreed between the three main confederations in February 1978, which established that 'wage restraint and the flexible use of labour both within and between places of work' would be accepted in return for broader reforms in social and economic policy (Bedani, 1995: 234–5).[12]

Nevertheless, political exchange was threatened by the refusal – or inability – of the 'national solidarity' government to deliver even the intended defensive compensations for bargaining restraint. More interventionist policies to enable faster economic development in the south, a reduction in youth unemployment, reconversion of declining industrial sectors, improvements in the 'social wage' and other 'solidaristic' objectives were either not approved or were inadequately funded and implemented, and the unions became increasingly disaffected (Regini, 1984: 139–41). 'Disillusion with the EUR-Line grew as union leaders and activists began to feel that whereas they had made unilateral concessions, the state and the employers had not kept their part of the bargain' (Kreile, 1988: 59). One consequence was that in January 1979 the PCI withdrew its support for the governing coalition.

Despite the strains afflicting political exchange – by the 1980s it seemed that unions could hope at best to moderate the pace and severity of the erosion of the gains of the previous decade – the search for negotiated change continued. The central agenda item became the *scala mobile*, which had come to generate half of many employees' total income, and which under pressure from government and employers was to be incrementally restricted and eventually abolished.

As early as 1977 the unions – while insisting that the general principle of full wage indexation was sacrosanct – were willing to agree minor changes which in effect qualified this principle, in a process of 'continuous bargaining that ... had all the qualities of bazaar haggling' (Flanagan et al., 1983: 546–53). With the PCI returning to a more oppositional stance, and with disquiet within all three confederations at the adverse outcome of political exchange, the following years saw 'a long, discontinuous and fruitless negotiating effort at the central level between government, business and labour, intended to devise a hypothetical "anti-inflation pact"' (Negrelli and Santi, 1990: 164). A threat by *Confindustria* to repudiate the 1975 agreement gave new urgency to the discussions, and at the beginning of 1983 a tripartite agreement was signed covering various anti-inflationary initiatives including adjustments to the *scala mobile*.

Political exchange acquired a new dynamic after June 1983 when Bettino Craxi, a right-wing socialist who had become PSI leader a few years earlier, was appointed prime minister (in a government still dominated by the DC). A further weakening of the *scala mobile* was the subject of a protocol of agreement negotiated in February 1984; but the communist majority of the CGIL leadership, under pressure from the PCI, refused to endorse this. The CGIL-CISL-UIL unitary federation broke up in disarray when the government (probably motivated by Craxi's interest in embarrassing the PCI) enforced the new arrangements by legislation. CGIL mobilized rank-and-file protests, and the PCI initiated a referendum to abrogate the law; the challenge failed, but fairly narrowly.[13]

This did not end CGIL's participation in bipartite and tripartite negotiations over the *scala mobile* and on other proposals to control wage bargaining; the pattern continued of *Confindustria* threats to end wage indexation, followed by union concessions on its application. Finally, in July 1992, all parties agreed to abolition.[14] Meanwhile, a more general pattern had evolved after the industrial relations crisis of 1985: reflecting a recognition that any explicit social pact regulating broad social and economic issues was probably no longer on the agenda; but implicitly, there could be a trade-off across separate negotiations involving pay determination, labour market policy, taxation and social benefits.

In parallel with peak-level negotiations to resolve the Italian economic crisis there were radical changes at workplace level. The 'dual power' arising from the struggles of the hot autumn persisted in many factories even after the national switch to the pursuit of the 'historic compromise': managerial power was undermined either by militant union representatives or by an anarchic and self-confident rank and file (or both in combination). Employers became increasingly determined to win back control over production and disciplinary authority over the workforce, to rationalize work organization with concomitant job losses, and to reverse the wage equalization which had resulted from the 'solidaristic' trade union approach to collective bargaining.

The confrontation which cast a shadow across the following decade was the bitter dispute at Fiat in 1980. In the previous year, management had reasserted its grip by dismissing 61 workers for misconduct; now it issued a restructuring plan which entailed heavy redundancies. The outcome was a 35-day strike which brought some modification of the company's plans but without a settlement, and latterly 'witnessed a complete blockade of Fiat's plants, open threats of a factory occupation, and a polarization of public (and working-class) opinion that eventually resulted in a procession through the streets of Turin on the part of a self-proclaimed "silent majority" demanding an end to the dispute' (Golden, 1997: 41). This demonstration, largely involving clerical staff and middle managers, was acclaimed with some exaggeration as the 'march of the 40,000' and precipitated the collapse of the strike. Militants from the previous decade figured prominently among those selected for redundancy. Ironically, the national CGIL leaders (like those of the other main unions) had been anxious to avoid a confrontation over an issue which they felt they could not win; but the local leadership in this, the unions' symbolic stronghold insisted on militant resistance (Golden, 1988 and 1997; Locke, 1992).

Defeat at Fiat was widely expected to herald a generalized employers' offensive. Instead, it encouraged a strategic reorientation of workplace industrial relations in line with the material shift in the balance of power. While some employers, not least in engineering, relished a similar confrontation with the unions, most recognized that this should be a last resort since Italian trade unionism retained significant influence, particularly in the political arena: 'although the unions were greatly weakened, they still retained sufficient power to block, if they wished, successful adjustment to an economic environment that had become increasingly uncertain' (Regini, 1995: 111). The legal protections for employee representatives also gave companies a strong incentive to pursue workplace change through negotiation and consent, and this encouraged an approach based on 'pragmatic eclecticism' (Regini, 1992: 41). Workplace union negotiators in turn often responded pragmatically and opportunistically (Mershon, 1990).

The outcome was the development of a relationship defined by some commentators as 'microcorporatism'. A lead was provided by the large segment of the economy owned by state-controlled holding companies: the 'IRI protocol' of December 1984 provided for joint consultative committees to regulate the modernization of production systems and associated changes in employment conditions. The resulting collective determination of change was described by Negrelli (1991) as 'formalized proceduralization': the establishment of channels to negotiate consensually (though within an overall appreciation of the unequal power resources of employers and workers) issues which in the 1970s would have been determined by the interplay of unilateral management initiative and militant worker resistance (Bellardi and Bordogna, 1997).

According to Regini (1991, 1995), the 'productivism' which was a significant element in the revolutionary heritage of the vanguard of the Italian working class provided a basis for real, even if often tense, workplace accommodation. The ideology (particularly strong within CGIL) that workers possessed the right, and the capacity, to control production fed into a willingness to share with management the decision-making over policies to adapt work organization to competitive challenges in the product market. Hence 'the notable intensity and pervasiveness of formal and informal negotiations in Italian firms during the latter half of the 1980s, and often its rather consensual character' (1995: 119). A shift from Taylorist forms of division of labour and work organization towards production regimes based on new skills and increased worker discretion provided common ground for managements and workplace union representatives: 'a new and potentially positive terrain on which [Italian trade unionists were able] to continue their "contest against capital", and therefore to participate in this reorganization instead of opposing it as an unambiguous threat to their past conquests' (1995: 125). In this way, communist militants might justify ideologically a new phase of cooperation in the workplace.

Membership Decline and the Problem of Representativeness

In the 1970s and 1980s the Italian unions thus became increasingly integrated into the fabric of Italian society. In explaining this development it is necessary to consider not only the changing motivations within the unions themselves, but also the perspectives of their interlocutors in concertative relationships. In his classic analysis of 'political exchange', very much informed by Italian experience, Pizzorno (1978: 278–80) played down the conventional thesis that such relationships stemmed primarily from an attempt to contain the economic impact of organized labour. Rather, he argued, they were a response to 'a threat to social order or social consensus'. In Italy – partly because of the heritage of 'blocked democracy' – governments possessed weak legitimacy, and this to an important extent explained the growth in support for extremist movements of both right and left. Trade unions emerged from the *autunno caldo* as the most representative popular institutions in Italy, and their incorporation in the policy-making process – particularly when policies were uncomfortable in their implications – added much-needed legitimacy to the process of governance. But did such a process undermine the unions' own legitimacy? The growing attention to the question of *rappresentatività* – 'representativeness' – suggested that this was indeed a serious problem.

There were objective indicators of such a loss of legitimacy. One was the trend in membership of the three main confederations after the peak of the late 1970s. Superficially, the position appeared relatively favourable, particularly by comparison with substantial decline in many other European countries. In 1980, 9 million members were claimed; there was a slight fall in the first half of the 1980s, but then a new increase to over 10 million in 1990. However, these aggregate figures masked a sharp decline in employed membership[15] and a parallel increase in those retired, who came to comprise some 40 per cent of total membership (even higher in CGIL) (Santi, 1988: 157–9).[16] Overall density among employed workers fell by roughly ten percentage points. Much of this fall reflected structural changes in the economy: declining employment in agriculture and manufacturing, where unionization was high; whereas density fell considerably in the expanding sector of private services (Romagnoli, 1989: 98). Though the trends were less dramatic than in some other countries, it became harder for the big three unions to present themselves as authoritative representatives of Italian workers as a whole.

Concomitantly, they were faced by challenges from within the working-class constituency. To an important extent, these were linked to a revolt by many categories of skilled and professional employees, occupying secure niches in the labour market, against pay restraint and egalitarian wage strategies. As was seen above, the 1975 agreement on wage indexation established the principle of flat-rate increases. This worked to the benefit of the lower paid but disadvantaged the better off; and while those with key skills and expertise in the private sector might obtain compensation through various bonus payments, this was less easy an option in the more bureaucratically regulated public services. Hence 'perhaps the major unintended consequence of the *scala mobile* agreement of 1975 was the delegitimation of the three major union confederations in the eyes of their most highly skilled industrial workers and their public sector members' (Baccaro and Locke, 1998: 289). Against the background of pay restraint, many 'technical, professional, and even skilled workers who had once supported egalitarian policies ... defected to rival organizations' (Locke and Thelen, 1995: 355).

One expression of this challenge was the growth of 'autonomous' unions which had long had some presence in the public sector but grew significantly from the late 1970s; though reliable membership figures do not exist (Bedani, 1995: 279), during the 1980s they may have come to represent one in five or one in six of all public employees. In 1987, a range of *autonomi* demanded the right to participate in negotiations in the health service, in a confused struggle which nevertheless contributed to the 'officialization' of the oppositional organizations (Bordogna, 1989a: 50). Perhaps even more serious for the big three was the rise in the late 1980s of the *cobas* (*comitati di base* or rank-and-file committees) which coordinated highly disruptive unofficial strike action, most notably in public transport and education (Bordogna, 1994, 1989b; Fezzi, 1989). Actual numbers of strikes or days lost were not large, but the militancy seemed calculated to attract a high public profile. Commonly such disputes were explicitly intended to overturn agreements negotiated by the main confederations (Locke and Baccaro, 1996: 295). The experience prompted the first legislative regulation of industrial conflict, the June 1990 'Giugni law',[17] which imposed modest restraints on stoppages in essential services but was considered relatively effective in restraining 'wildcat' action. Its provisions were tightened in a new law of April 2000.

The issue of representativity can be seen as expressing the dilemmas of a trade union orientation bridging class politics and societal integration, particularly under adverse economic circumstances. Whatever their egalitarian professions, unions in most countries have typically found their core constituencies among the relatively advantaged – the more skilled categories in manufacturing, public-sector employees with high job security – and have in practice tended to address the distinctive interests of such groups even if in the guise of broader class interests. Certainly in the years of trade union weakness in Italy in the 1950s and 1960s, their cadres were disproportionately drawn from the skilled minority. Yet if such traditional activists provided some of the initial impetus towards the hot autumn, the vanguard role was soon assumed by the semi-skilled 'mass worker' whose interests underlay the egalitarian commitments of the main unions in the 1970s. The subsequent challenges showed that strategic minorities whose distinctive interests were neglected could inspire a potent challenge to the trade union politics of historic compromise. As Bordogna summarized the experience (1989a: 56–7), what was at issue was an 'objective contrast between two logics of representation'. The main confederations claimed to articulate 'general interests connected to those of the whole of employed labour, if not the whole economy, ... a logic of representation which is sensitive to the overall equilibrium requirements of the system'; whereas their opponents 'share an interest in the defence of the individual category and its removal from any coordination with more general demands'. What must be added, though, is that the appeal of such 'sectionalist' movements was significantly reinforced by their ability to express themes of class militancy which had formed one of the core traditions of Italian trade unionism before the historic compromise. As in Britain, class rhetoric and market preoccupations could seemingly coincide.

The Earthquake of Italian Politics and the Challenges for Trade Unionism

For most of the post-war era, Italian politics displayed a remarkable combination of stability and instability. The latter was notoriously demonstrated by the 50-plus national governments; but with few exceptions, the changes simply reshuffled ministers within coalitions dominated by the DC – often expressing shifts between right and left within a party which embraced a remarkable range of political tendencies – and with minor changes in its junior partners. In terms of party loyalties, what was striking was continuity: a shift of a few percentage points in support for any of the major parties was typically regarded as a landslide. But in the 1990s, everything changed; and the trade unions were caught up in the transformation, forced to act as reference points within a landscape of chaos.

Three factors drove the collapse of the old political structure: an escalating succession of corruption scandals, the separatist challenge in northern Italy, and the impact on the PCI of the fall of communism in eastern Europe. From small beginnings, investigations into financial corruption in local and national politics soon encompassed much of the traditional political elite, and in particular key DC and PSI figures[18] who had dominated national government and had monopolized control in many of the major Italian cities; both parties suffered badly in the 1992 elections – midway through the anti-corruption purge – and subsequently disintegrated almost totally.[19] In northern Italy, a right-wing populist movement had emerged in the late 1970s, denouncing both the self-serving representatives of the traditional parties and the transfer of resources from the richer north to the poorer south; it became a significant force in 1987, and soon afterwards the various 'leagues' established in the northern provinces came together in an umbrella *Lega Nord*. Other beneficiaries of the collapse of christian democracy were the neo-fascist MSI (later *Alleanza nazionale*, AN) in the south, and *Forza Italia* (a name representing a football slogan rather than a political position) established by media magnate Silvio Berlusconi. Meanwhile the PCI, the one main party virtually untouched by corruption allegations, faced a crisis of identity with the collapse of the Soviet Union (from which it had, however, long distanced itself) and completed its transition to social democracy in 1991 by adopting the title *Partito democratico della sinistra* (Democratic Left Party, PDS, later abbreviated to DS). The explicit move to post-communism was made at the cost of bitter internal conflict, resulting in a minority breaking away to form a new party, *Rifondazione comunista* (Refoundation of Communism, RC).

These changes entailed that in the 1990s Italian politics displayed extreme unpredictability. Following the stalemate of the 1992 elections, the socialist Giuliano Amato became premier but his government soon collapsed and was replaced in April 1993 by a 'technocratic' cabinet (consisting of ministers who were not party politicians) under the former governor of the central bank, Carlo Ciampi. A new election in 1994 completed the eclipse of the old political elite, and a right-wing coalition led by Berlusconi took office. But its basis was from the outset precarious: Berlusconi's party favoured a neo-liberal agenda, AN sought increased government support for development in the south, the *Lega* demanded that the north should have greater command over its own resources. By the end of the year the Berlusconi government had collapsed and a new 'techno-cratic' government under Lamberto Dini acted as caretaker. New elections in 1996 brought a narrow victory for a centre-left coalition (*ulivo*, or olive tree) led by Romano Prodi (later president of the European Commission) with the PDS the largest party. This was also unstable, depending on parliamentary support from the RC party which was resistant to austerity measures (and ultimately split over continued support for the *ulivo* government). In late 1998 Prodi was forced to resign, and was succeeded by Massimo D'Alema: the first (ex-)communist to head an Italian government. He was in turn obliged to stand down in early 2000 and Amato again became premier, though the prospects of the government surviving its full term seemed slim.

One consequence of the earthquake in the party system was that the tradi-tional linkages of all three major confederations either disintegrated or were transformed. The process of *incompatibilità* initiated after the hot autumn in the cause of confederal unity, which precluded any individual holding leadership positions in both a union confederation and a political party, was completed by default. UIL, which of all the big three had traditionally had the weakest party attachments, became perforce autonomous with the collapse of the PSI and the social democrats. Almost overnight, CISL lost a firm point of political reference as christian democracy disintegrated. CGIL, in the course of the shift to post-communism, had also reinforced its distance from its associated party. In 1990 the communist fraction, the main channel of party discipline and control since the union's creation, was dissolved, formally establishing a new era of pluralist poli-tics in the union. In 1991 a national congress centred on the theme 'strategy of rights, ethic of solidarity' (CGIL, 1991) adopted a post-communist identity, embracing the view (in the words of one of the advocates of reform) 'that the trade unions have an opportunity, by actively co-operating with the management, [to] contribute to the process of restructuring and thereby to foster a trend towards democratization in the workplace' (Sabbatini, 1992: 21).

Such ambitions were not on the immediate agenda. In the 1990s, the main pri-ority for all confederations was again defensive: as in the 1970s, the Italian demo-cratic settlement seemed in question, even more seriously than before. The northern separatists, neo-fascists and mass-media populists all challenged a socio-economic order based on workers' rights and social partnership. The attacks which formerly had come from an insurrectionary fringe were now the product of a powerful new component of the political establishment. The precarious political circumstances coincided with continuing economic difficulties, culminating in a drastic devaluation of the lira in September 1992. The problems of economic stabilization were accentuated by the decision to participate in European economic and monetary union despite a record of inflation, public expenditure and public debt far from compatible with the Maastricht convergence criteria (Brunetta and Tronti, 1995). All main unions thus perceived irresistible pressures: procedurally, to return to formal tripartite concertation as a basis for political stabilization; sub-stantively, to endorse austerity measures and institutional reforms which would align the Italian economy more closely with EU norms.

Across the decade of the 1990s there was an intense, and at times highly conflictual revival of political exchange which confirmed the main confederations as forces of order. The process began with the abolition of the *scala mobile*: there were protest mobilizations by all three unions in May 1992 against the unilateral decision of the employers to pay no further increments, but a government-brokered deal to end wage indexation was accepted two months later.[20] This was followed by a year-long set of negotiations, often conflictual – in April 1993 the three confederations called a demonstrative general strike to support their demands for employment-creating policies – but culminating in the first formal tripartite pact for a decade, the July 1993 accord. This was largely drafted by Giugni, who became minister of labour in the first 'technocratic' government. All parties agreed that incomes policy should become a permanent feature of Italian industrial relations (Regini, 1997: 263). Henceforth, wage determination was to be guided by the predicted rate of inflation, with scope for compensation if the forecast rate was exceeded: in effect, a much more flexible variant of the *scala*. The scope for multi-level pay bargaining was considerably constrained, and the restraints were in general respected by the unions: for example, the 1994 settlement in the pace-setting engineering industry followed the principle of moderation. The government for its part promised a series of active labour market measures to stimulate employment.

A second key issue of the 1990s was the pension system. Though public welfare expenditure in Italy, as a proportion of GDP, was below the EU average, in the case of pensions the position was reversed (Regalia and Regini, 1998: 493). In part this reflected a minimum retirement age of 60 for men and only 55 for women, but also the generous provisions in the extensive public sector (in some cases, enabling retirement after 20 years of continuous employment) and the more general principle of 'seniority pensions' available after 35 years of service. Contribution income did not match expenditure from the pension fund, which added to the general public deficit. In the July 1992 protocol the government announced its intention to raise the retirement age by stages and make other alterations, and implemented some of the provisions by decree; but more radical reform faced significant obstacles. As noted above, in the 1980s the largest sections of membership in all three confederations were pensioners; by 1993, half the membership in CGIL was retired. Negotiations were thus highly sensitive and progress was slow; and in 1994 the Berlusconi government attempted to impose reforms unilaterally. Though its plans differed little from the principles already agreed, there were mass protests and a general strike, and the government backed down. Pensions reform then became one of the priorities of the technocratic Dini government formed in January 1995, and a compromise agreement was achieved in May which was ratified in an elaborate ballot of all union members and then introduced into law.[21] The main feature was the abolition of seniority pensions over an extended period, so that workers close to possible retirement suffered only minor losses.[22] The issue of pensions returned to the top of the political agenda in late 1997, when the government – determined to meet the Maastricht requirements in time for the launch of the euro – announced a budget involving a sharp reduction in public expenditure, including further economies on pensions to be negotiated with the unions. The latter reached an agreement on the details in November, but *Rifondazione comunista* refused to support the package, resulting in a government crisis and the resignation of prime minister Prodi. A political compromise was eventually agreed, trading off pensions reform against a law imposing a maximum 35-hour working week from 2001 – an initiative bitterly criticised by the unions as well as by *Confindustria*, as an encroachment on free collective bargaining.

A third important issue was the reform of workplace representation. The 1970 *Statuto* had introduced the notion of a workplace trade union representative structure (*rappresentanza sindacale aziendale* or RSA) with an array of legal rights, but without defining the nature or composition of the new mechanisms. The flexibility was in some respects seen by the unions as an advantage, but for two reasons they came to perceive a need for a closer definition of the union-RSA relationship. The first was that, particularly in hard times, factory councils required external union support: a study in the early 1980s (Regalia, 1984) described workplace delegates as 'elected and abandoned'. But second, the RSAs could form a focus of oppositional militancy, and could pose an explicit challenge to trade union moderation. Part of the July 1993 accord was that a more formal structure should be introduced, and at the end of the year the three confederations agreed with the employers the framework for a new body, the *rappresentanza sindacale unitaria* (RSU) within which they would obtain a built-in advantage: two-thirds of the members would be directly elected by the workforce, but the other third would be nominated, in effect, by the main confederations.[23] These provisions were overturned by a 1995 referendum, which rejected a privileged status for narrowly defined 'most representative' unions.[24] The procedure was then revised with the reserved third to be nominated by those unions which were signatories to the national agreement in the sector. In the event, this formula was unnecessary, for the confederations won massive majorities in the subsequent elections.

There were, however, many challenges to the confederations' 'representativeness' which imposed constraints on moderation throughout the 1990s and may well have encouraged them in organizing episodic mass demonstrations, protest mobilizations and even general strikes. In the 'post-communist' transformation of CGIL, an important faction, *essere sindacato* ('to be a union') contested the new moderate line; partly because of the tactical skills of secretary-general Trentin its challenge was effectively contained, and there was no breakaway to parallel that within the ex-PCI. But the July 1992 agreement on abolition of the *scala* provoked substantial opposition from the left of the union, and was also reflected in the emergence of a new rank-and-file movement, the *autoconvocati* (approximate meaning: 'spontaneous assemblies') which organized a new 'hot autumn' in 1992 and backed the 1995 referendum initiative (Guarriello, 1996: 92–3).

A new phase of political exchange evolved in the late 1990s. An evaluation of the July 1993 pact by a special committee, chaired by Giugni, concluded that it had been in general very successful and had helped bring Italy within the Maastricht convergence targets, though the success of the predominant anti-inflation objectives entailed the need and possibility of a return to greater decentralization. However, the employment-creation objectives of the 1993 agreement had been largely a failure. Moreover, the 'employment pact' agreed in September 1996 had been a damp squib, mainly resulting in a liberalization of temporary work and doing little to redress regional imbalances in the labour market. A more substantial measure was the 'Treu package' of July 1997: an agreement initiated by the Prodi government and its minister of labour Tiziano Treu (like his predecessor Giugni, in real life an industrial relations professor) which introduced annualized working hours and adjusted social security contributions to discourage excessive working time. This was followed in December 1998 by a new tripartite 'social pact for development and employment' which covered a range of issues: reduced indirect employment costs; new measures for development in the *Mezzogiorno*; and increased training provision. The agreement confirmed the importance of trade union (and employer) involvement in the determination of economic and social policy, at both national and local level; but (partly because of CGIL opposition) did not approve government proposals for further changes to the collective bargaining system.[25]

By the end of the century, the main confederations had firmly embraced the function of seemingly indispensable (even if at times conflictual) 'social partners'. This role was not without its contradictions. As has been seen, moderation evoked opposition from outside and from below, in particular in the case of CGIL. To some extent this was counteracted by a more systematic effort than in previous decades to win rank-and-file assent: notably the membership ballots to ratify the abolition of the *scala* in 1992 and to endorse pensions reform in 1995. And as seen above, elections to the new RSUs demonstrated a continuing high level of support for the main federations.

Nevertheless, the dilemmas of representativeness persisted and in some respects intensified. Some argued that the substantial decentralization of collective bargaining in the 1980s weakened the ability of unions nationally to provide organizational coordination or ideological leadership (Locke, 1992): a judgment perhaps premature, but probably correct as a longer-term prediction. This should be seen in the context of a practice of 'negotiated legislation' and 'regulated deregulation' which emerged as distinctive features of Italian industrial relations in recent times. Relaxation of the complex and restrictive accumulation of employment law typically followed, and was generally regarded as conditional on the agreement of employers' organizations and the 'most representative' unions; and normally the legal constraints were not unconditionally abolished but rather became subject to derogation or variation by collective agreement. In both respects the main unions could be considered legally privileged collective actors, a status increasingly questioned during the 1990s.[26]

More Triangulation: It takes Three to Compromise ...

The 'historic compromise' of the 1970s involved two intersecting sets of triangular relationships. One encompassed government, employers and unions in the process of political exchange; the other, the new accommodations between the confederations themselves. The creation of the unitary federation and the adoption of the principle of 'incompatibility' signalled an effort to overcome old ideological identities, fashion a new and distinctively trade union role, and ultimately repair the organizational fractures of the late 1940s. As has been seen, the tensions inherent in the first project ultimately aborted the second. How far did history repeat itself in the 1990s?

Interconfederal triangulation acquired a new dynamic in the 1990s. As noted above, the traditional points of ideological reference dissolved with the collapse of the old political order, the revival of peak-level concertation over economic and social policy and the challenges from the *cobas* and autonomous unions. A formal proposal for unification was outlined by CISL secretary-general D'Antoni at the union's conference in July 1993, coinciding with the tripartite agreement on incomes policy and bargaining reform; the leaders of the other two confederations, who were present, responded positively if cautiously. Efforts were made to develop a common position, but the unity process ran into the ground. The process was revived by CGIL in May 1997, with a suggestion that a new confederation might be formed by 2000; CISL endorsed the idea at its conference later in the month, as also did UIL. But again the process stalled amid acrimony before the target date was reached.

After each breakdown, CISL accused the other confederations of foot-dragging, an indication that they were not really serious about unity; CGIL and UIL retorted that any notion of rapid unification was unrealistic, and that CISL was posturing. To build a new union would involve abandoning many former cherished organizational principles and conceptions of trade union identity, declared Trentin (1993: 6) in response to the original initiative, 'and this is not a painless process'. A year later his successor Cofferati reiterated the belief that 'unity is an indispensable process for Italian workers, but not an easy process' (Stelluti et al., 1995: 101). And indeed alternative conceptions of procedure were at issue: CISL was keen that the structures and principles of the new union should be negotiated from above, then endorsed by the membership; CGIL, that there should be an active (and presumably lengthy) involvement of the rank and file in shaping the new venture. Behind this difference were perhaps questions of simple arithmetic: in construction from above, each confederation could expect equal weight; with evolution from below, the greater numbers in CGIL would carry more weight. Each organization was serious about unity, but on its own terms. 'It would be hasty and incorrect, naturally, to draw a demarcation line between those for and against unity. The debate is more subtle, and concerns the content of a process by its nature complex and difficult' (Lauzi, 1998: 303).[27]

There were also important questions of substance and identity which created recurrent tensions. One was the CGIL vision of trade unionism as a social movement with a broad understanding of its constituency and their common interests; the other, shared by CISL and UIL, put more emphasis on bargaining for the particular employment interests of the membership (Giugni, 1995: 9, 14). This linked to major differences over decentralization of collective bargaining and acceptance of more flexible forms of employment contract, extremely contentious issues at the end of the 1990s. Another key confrontation was between CISL support for employee share-ownership, rejected by CGIL which, however, endorsed employee participation as involvement (possibly conflictual) in job control.[28] The meaning of political autonomy was also part of the terrain of debate. CGIL leaders insisted that they shared a commitment to independence, but critics argued that they were over-supportive of the *ulivo* government (though in fact CGIL was the most resistant of the three to some of its labour market proposals). There was also a marked ambivalence within CISL: in some respects a reversal of the original explicit commitment to a non-confessional identity. D'Antoni had aspirations to make CISL a social substitute for the vanished DC party, in the process asserting the importance of catholic values. Asked in September 1994 whether he was more attracted by trade union unity or unity of the political centre (in effect, re-inventing the old DC) he replied: 'trade union unity, if we achieve it within two years' (Stelluti et al., 1995: 110). In May 1998, having endorsed the new unity moves a year before, D'Antoni virtually ensured their failure by calling for what was quickly dubbed a 'grand CISL', building links between the confederation and catholic social and cooperative organizations.[29] This was calculated to embarrass CGIL and to outrage UIL, with its long commitment to laicism. CISL went on to organize a unilateral demonstration in November 1999 against the D'Alema government's economic and social policies, an affront to the other confederations.

In the second arena of triangulation, the process of political exchange, many of the problems identified by Regini (1984) in the experience of the 1970s clearly recurred. From the outset, the central issue was one of crisis management, and the unions' role was in effect concession bargaining at the level of the state. The positive benefit they could claim was that the burdens of restructuring the labour market and the welfare state were more equitably distributed than might otherwise have been the case, and that the impact of the more disruptive changes was cushioned. This was a precarious basis to appeal for support within their own constituency, and may well have contributed to the continuing decline of unionization among the employed workforce. By the end of the 1990s, total membership claimed by the three confederations was 11 million; but only just over half were dependent employees (out of a total employed workforce of 20 million). Every other member was now retired: if the German unions were accused of pursuing an 'alliance for pensions', their Italian counterparts were unquestionably an alliance of pensioners.[30]

If the achievements of the unions from concertation in hard times were too limited or too negative for some within their core constituency, the constraints of tripartite exchange were too great for those interlocutors who were anxious for more rapid and more radical change. Sections of employers voiced growing frustration during the 1990s at the failure to achieve the far-reaching elimination of labour market regulation and the sharp reduction in social spending and hence taxation to which they aspired. This hard-line tendency captured control of *Confindustria* with the election in March 2000 of a new president, against the preference of most larger companies but reflecting the views of smaller firms (where unionization is typically weak) and of aggressive entrepreneurs such as Berlusconi. The new leadership team declared that concertation would be sustained only if it contributed to more rapid economic liberalization, abandoning any commitment of principle to social partnership.

The collapse of the old political order brought new complexities to the re-invention of political exchange. In one respect, the elimination of old political reference points forced governments to turn to the unions as sources of legitimation and order. Yet the severity of economic difficulties, and the rise of a new, authoritarian right made concertation precarious. The policies of retrenchment of the Berlusconi government provoked two general strikes in 1994; the government collapsed before it became clear whether the right-wing government wanted, and could achieve, a more stable relationship with the unions. A new, and perhaps more cohesive, government of the right – which at the time of writing seems all too likely – would possibly oblige Italian unions to return to a more explicit politics of opposition and mobilization. It is unclear how far a strategy of class compromise can persist in the new environment of Italian politics.

Conclusion: To be a Union; but How?

Essere sindacato: the slogan presupposes that it is clear what it means to be a trade union. But the whole theme of this book is that the meaning of trade unionism has historically been bitterly contested, and today – not least in Italy[31] – is a subject of doubt and disputation. Is a trade union a bargaining agent, a social partner, a mobilizer of discontent, or all of these at one and the same time?

In Italy, in recent years, there have been many attempts to dissolve the disagreements with bland formulae. Seeking to define the distinctive philosophies of the three main confederations today, Accornero (1992: 37) identified CGIL with the defence of workers' rights, CISL with the pursuit of social solidarity, UIL with the representation of workers as citizens. These were scarcely substantial differences, and in the 1990s it appeared the formal self-images of the confederations were increasingly converging while the internal controversies over union identity had become the more substantial basis of contention.

The ideological edge of Italian trade unionism was clearly blunted by its encounter with the hard realities of the 1980s and 1990s. If the dialectic of class and society has become more contradictory, the pressures of the market have also increased. In the 1970s, the ideologies of both class militancy and societal integration challenged the force of market principles in employment; but market forces have now become a point of reference for all major unions. Privatization, though commencing later in Italy than in many other European countries, proceeded rapidly in the 1990s, considerably reducing the umbrella of the state. Competitiveness in external product markets has for two decades put major pressures on large, previously sheltered private domestic producers, transforming the role of union representation. Neo-liberal efforts to expose the employment relationship to increased market forces have caused disorientation, as have the efforts of strongly placed employee groups to pursue particularistic rather than general interests. If in future both employers and governments see less need to integrate the unions within a concerted process of social and economic change, it is unclear whether *sindacalismo* still possesses the ideological resources to mobilize resistance.

To some extent, the concept of solidarity offered a basis for a more concrete understanding of *sindacalismo*. In the socialist and communist traditions, solidarity was a rallying cry for working-class unity in response to a common fate and in a struggle for common interests. In the catholic tradition, it was an appeal for the stronger and more advantaged to accept an obligation to support the cause of the weak and disadvantaged. With the accommodation of class and society as points of reference, a synthesis of the two conceptions became possible, shared – albeit with differences of emphasis – by all three confederations.[32] If Italian unions are to remain powerful actors in the new century, the meaning of solidarity must once more be clarified and given strategic content in response to the new challenges of the market.

Notes

[1] Among continuities were much of the corpus of fascist labour law, the state holding companies which dominated some of the most modern sectors of Italian industry, and the main employers' confederation *Confindustria*.

[2] One exception was that the decision to retain the discredited monarchy was overturned.

[3] One symbolic indicator of the unclear demarcation between socialists and communists in Italy was the widespread use of the hammer and sickle as an emblem of parties of the left. A more practical expression of political convergence was that until the Hungarian crisis of 1956 the PCI and PSI campaigned on a common platform in national elections.

[4] There is strong evidence that the christian democrats had decided on a split during 1947, before the height of the cold war, and were merely awaiting an appropriate moment (Bedani, 1995: 38).

[5] The catholic members of the CGIL executive did not initially oppose this decision but rapidly changed their position.

[6] Nevertheless ACLI, while not formally a trade union itself, *did* affiliate to the christian IFCTU.

[7] Its reported membership showed year-to-year fluctuations but stability over the decade as a whole.

[8] The victory by CISL was soon to prove an embarrassment; three years later, in 1958, when it had become clear that the majority of its workplace delegates were acting as adjuncts of management, the decision was taken to expel over a hundred of them from the union. Those expelled set up a new company union and won the subsequent CI elections.

[9] This accommodation – which was followed by the support of CISL and UIL for the admission of CGIL to the new European Trade Union Confederation – was intensely (if for the most part surreptitiously) resisted by the Americans; see Gumbrell-McCormick 2000: 365.

[10] This had provoked a new split within the party, with a left-wing section (including many of those affiliated to CGIL) objecting to participation in a DC-led government and breaking away to form PSIUP (Italian Socialist Party of Proletarian Unity).

[11] The metalworkers' organizations were the largest single section in each of the three federations, and most strongly radicalized by the hot autumn. Even beforehand, the CISL metalworkers had embraced an explicit 'class and conflict perspective', challenging the moderate confederal leadership (Bianchi, 1996: 64). In this sector the unification project was taken a stage further than in the parent confederations, with the three federations uniting to form a single body, FLM.

[12] Eur was a suburb of Rome where the meeting took place.

[13] In the referendum, held in June 1985, 45.6 per cent supported the challenge to the legislation.

[14] The CGIL leader, Trentin, having signed the agreement despite the opposition of the now ex-communist party PDS (see below), offered his resignation; this was not accepted (Bedani, 1995: 272; Locke and Baccaro, 1999: 246–7).

[15] The fall over the decade was roughly 20 per cent in both CGIL and CISL, while numbers in UIL held firm.

[16] The rapid growth in pensioner membership was made possible by the provisions in the 1970 Statute allowing the check-off for union subscriptions, with direct deductions either from wages or from pensions (Chiarini, 1999: 581–3).

[17] Named after Gino Giugni, the socialist senator and labour law professor who initiated the legislation.

[18] In particular Craxi, who – even after the end of his years as premier – had remained a major power behind the throne, in close alliance with important factional leaders within the DC. This had assisted the PSI in obtaining rich pickings from the spoils system.

[19] One outcome was the re-invention by a substantial section of christian democrats of the pre-Mussolini 'popular party' (PPI); but the remnants of DC split in two directions as Italy became polarized between centre-left and centre-right multi-party coalitions.

[20] Technically, the July 1992 'protocol' was not an agreement but a statement of government policy, endorsed by unions and employers (Locke and Baccaro, 1996: 298).

[21] The pensioners' federations played an important part in the negotiations and their members participated in the ballot – though with the weight of their votes reduced to reflect the fact that they paid lower subscriptions than those in work (Chiarini, 1999: 583–4).

[22] For this reason, *Confindustria* – which had demanded far more radical economies – refused to sign the agreement.

[23] This formula was proposed by *Confindustria*, then anxious to bolster the position of its interlocutors.

[24] On 11 June 1995 a package of 12 issues was subject to popular referendum, an important constitutional procedure in Italy. Of these, one was to repeal statutory backing for check-off arrangements, two concerned restrictions on eligibility for representation on RSUs and one challenged the privileges of the 'most representative' confederations in the public sector. Of the other plebiscites, by far the most important was one restricting concentration of ownership of television channels in the hands of a single company. Berlusconi, the clear target of this proposal, mobilized participation on the right; the unions, preoccupied with the debate over pensions reform, did not intervene to a similar degree. The result was a victory for Berlusconi and a political defeat for the unions.

[25] One outcome of the pact was a series of active labour market measures introduced in April 2000.

[26] For example, there was an important referendum challenge to trade union status in 1999, initiated by the Radical party. Its proposals covered a wide range of political issues (including electoral reform); in the field of industrial relations they sought the unconditional abolition of a number of labour market regulations, removal of public funding for trade union advice centres, further-reaching changes to the pension system than those already approved, abolition of the direct payment of trade union membership dues through the social security institutions, and the removal of the option of a reinstatement order in cases of unfair dismissal. The constitutional court ruled all but the last two proposals inadmissible. The outcome, in May 2000, was ambiguous: the first proposal obtained a majority, the second did not, but the whole exercise failed because of a low turn-out. The participation rate of only just over 30 per cent was widely viewed as a victory for the right-wing parties, which had called for abstention. However, the unions were also divided: while CGIL and UIL campaigned for a 'no' vote, CISL regarded abstention as the better tactic.

[27] Larizza, leader of UIL, had made a similar point in 1994 (Stelluti et al., 1995: 111).

[28] This conception of conflictual participation is well illustrated by Meardi's study of CGIL activists at Fiat: 'a class perspective on work organization remains the strongest feature of their discourse' (1996: 292).

[29] In October 2000 he announced his resignation from the union leadership in order to establish a political foundation intended to form the embryo of a new christian-democratic party. It was unclear whether or not his departure would ease relations with the other two confederations.

[30] By 1999 they comprised 55 per cent of membership in CGIL, 50 per cent in CISL, 'only' 25 per cent in UIL.

[31] In Italy, a particular problem is that the term *sindacato* can denote an individual sectoral union, a single confederation, or the trade union movement as a whole. To add to potential confusion, the term is also applied to employers' organizations.

[32] It is perhaps possible to detect parallels with the Webbs' revised definition of a trade union: a combination of people 'for the purpose of maintaining or improving the conditions of their working lives'.

8

Challenges and Changes

The Variable Geometry of Trade Unionism

'Arguments about convergence and divergence have tended to dominate comparative industrial relations writing in Europe in the past few years' (Smith, 1999: 16). Do the three national movements examined in the previous chapters provide evidence of a convergence in ideologies and identities? To a degree, certainly. All trade union movements have faced challenges in some respects similar: the declining importance of traditional core occupational and industrial constituencies; the weakening of the ties between work and other social identities; often, a less supportive political context; and the dilemmas associated with a harsher, more internationally competitive economic environment. To this catalogue may be added the fact that, on the defensive, union policy-makers are increasingly sensitive to initiatives by their counterparts in other countries from which lessons may be derived.

Yet convergence should not be exaggerated. First, 'globalization' is by no means a homogeneous and uncontradictory process. 'The global economy emerging from informational-based production and competition is characterized by its *interdependence*, its *asymmetry*, its *regionalization*, its *selective inclusiveness*, its *exclusionary segmentation*, and, as a result of all these features, an extraordinarily *variable geometry* that tends to dissolve historical, economic geography' (Castells, 1996: 106). One consequence is an uneven distribution of losers and (far fewer) winners, between (and also of course within) countries. Second, as Locke and Thelen (1995) have clearly demonstrated, developments which constitute major challenges for unions in some countries occasion little disquiet in others. Specific historic achievements can acquire almost iconic status and can be abandoned only at immense cost: the *scala mobile* in Italy is an obvious example. If 'European trade unions are under siege' (Ross and Martin, 1999: 368), they are under very different types of siege. Third, even when union movements face comparable imperatives for action, their responses are shaped by their different starting points and can involve a dynamic which is path-dependent. And fourth, and by no means least, objective constraints, however coercive, offer alternatives for strategic choice. What should have emerged clearly from the previous examination of national movements is that union action is not simply determined externally but is also the outcome of internal discussion, debate and often conflict.

Solidarity and the Construction of Labour Movements

How do unions unite workers who are differentiated? We are shaped by our direct experiences, immediate *milieux*, specific patterns of social relations. Broader identities and affiliations are founded on the direct, immediate and specific, through intersubjectivities which link these to the external and encompassing. Solidarity implies the perception of commonalities of interest and purpose which extend, but do not abolish, consciousness of distinct and particularistic circumstances.

Trade unions reflect these processes. The earliest unions typically emerged as organizations of distinct occupational communities of interest within local labour markets. The development of multi-occupational unionism with a broader geographical compass normally required either the external intervention of a politically driven class project, or the gradual experience of the limited efficacy of too narrow a representational base. The 'one big union' of syndicalist aspirations remained a dream.

The boundaries of union inclusion are also frontiers of exclusion. The perceived common interests of the members of a particular union (or confederation) are defined in part in contradistinction to those of workers outside. In compartmentalizing workers, unions traditionally have compartmentalized solidarity.

'Interests can only be met to the extent that they are partly redefined' (Offe and Wiesenthal, 1985: 184). It is a sociological truism that the elusive notion of interests has both objective and subjective dimensions, and that the relationship between the two is never fixed. Through their own internal processes of communication, discussion and debate – the 'mobilization of bias' – unions can help shape workers' own definitions of their individual and collective interests. Cumulatively, the outcomes compose the patterns of commonality and conflict among the interests of different groups and hence contribute to the dynamics of sectionalism and solidarity within labour movements.

Borrowing from Durkheim – though applying his concepts in an idiosyncratic manner, indeed – one may define one classic form of interest definition and representation as 'mechanical solidarity'. Durkheim attributed order and stability in traditional society to the repressive imposition of standardized rules and values on members whose circumstances were relatively homogeneous. Traditional trade unionism in many countries displayed some similarities. The aggregation of interests which is essential for any coherent collective action involves establishing priorities among a variety of competing grievances and aspirations. One reason why many employers, and also governments, came to perceive the value (to themselves) of the existence of a recognized vehicle of employee 'voice' was that unions filtered out (or perhaps suppressed) certain demands and discontents while highlighting others. Another was that unions could be induced to share responsibility for disruptive initiatives and uncomfortable changes.

Often the type of solidarity underlying twentieth-century trade unionism reflected and replicated on the one hand the discipline and standardization imposed by 'Fordist' mass production, on the other the patterns of differentiation within the working class between those who were central to this production process and those who were more marginal. To reiterate an argument made much earlier in this book: within companies and sectors, collective bargaining priorities were normally set by 'core' employees (male, white, with a stable place in the internal labour market); within national labour movements, priorities were imposed by the large unions of manual workers such as miners and engineers.

Associated with this form of solidarity was clearly an implicit bias in terms of *whose* interests counted for most. But also affected was the conception of *which* interests were relevant for union representation and bargaining policy. A specific conception of the relationship between 'work' and 'life' can be seen in retrospect to have informed working-class organization; one which in particular counter-posed a full-time (male) wage-worker in mine, mill or factory and a full-time (female) domestic worker in the home. That reality was always more complex than this did not prevent the model from shaping firmly the conceptions of which issues were union-relevant and which were not.

These characteristics were most clearly linked to market-oriented trade union-ism. The 'higgling of the market' was a game most readily played by those with advantages in terms of the quality of their labour power. This bias was often counteracted, at least rhetorically, where class or society were more salient reference points. Here, the rise and consolidation of national labour movements tended to involve clear egalitarian commitments: to a narrowing of income dif-ferentials, progressive taxation policy, and universal entitlement to social benefits and services. In many ways, one of the most impressive testimonies to the strength of solidaristic principles was the degree to which working-class organi-zations, drawing their cadres of activists and leaders from the better educated, higher paid and more secure categories of the labour force, nevertheless espoused policies of particular benefit to the less advantaged. Sectional interests were per-ceived as best pursued through a more general commitment to social justice. The post-war consolidation of the Keynesian welfare state – whether through the political victory of labour or the acceptance by conservative regimes of the need to reform and humanize capitalism – represented the apparent victory of these principles.

Paradoxically, the form of this victory contained the seeds of its own defeat. The egalitarian project in most European countries was a type of 'socialism within one class' (and more often than not, within one gender). The central achievement of most welfare states was to redistribute income within the work-ing population across the life-cycle (a process which came to generate increasing tensions with a change in demographic structure). Egalitarian wage policy pri-marily involved the narrowing of differentials within bargaining groups, to the particular advantage of manual workers classified as lower-skilled. In itself this helped reduce gender differentials; but to the extent that employment tended to be demarcated between (higher-paid) primarily male sectors and (lower-paid) primarily female sectors, in those countries where the most important level of collective bargaining was the industry or sector then inequalities tended to remain large.

In most countries the post-war decades saw some narrowing of income differentials between manual workers and white-collar employees. Yet to the extent that these categories were separately represented for purposes of pay determination, levelling was often greater *within* each group; the result, as occurred in Sweden, might be that the lower range of white-collar salaries became higher than the top manual wages. As technological change blurred the (always to some extent artificial) boundary between the two categories, consciousness of inequity was inevitable: with higher-skilled manual workers either escaping through reclassification to staff status or demanding a widening of pay differentials (Kjellberg, 1992). Sweden is also a clear example of the erosion of the previously hegemonic role of manual worker unionism, with the share of LO in total union membership falling from 80 per cent in 1950 to roughly 50 per cent today. Both trends shifted the balance of power towards the better off.

In part, then, the retreat from egalitarianism involved a revolt of the (relatively) advantaged against the particular manifestations (rising taxes, narrowing differentials) of the specific character of the egalitarian project. Such a revolt might take the form (as in Italy) of sectional industrial militancy, or (as in Britain in the 1980s) of support for tax-cutting political policies. But the retreat also reflected the erosion of the classic ideological foundations of this project.

The exhaustion of western communism, and the post-1989 collapse of the Soviet bloc, eliminated one point of reference for traditional notions of solidarity. Rather, the majorities in most communist parties embraced social democracy as an alternative perspective justifying policies which had already been pragmatically adapted over the years or even decades. In one sense, post-communism put the formal seal to an evolution which, though by very different routes and in very different historical contexts, marked the redefinition of mainstream trade unionism across western Europe in the second half of the twentieth century. In the three countries examined in detail in this book, each union movement adopted as its dominant ideology a version of social democracy: a process, as suggested in a previous chapter, which can be identified across post-war western Europe more generally. Yet post-war social democracy depended on the existence – or the vision – of the Keynesian welfare state. Its viability was put increasingly in question, for reasons both domestic and external.

Domestically, most European social-democratic parties identified a causal link between declining electoral success and the dwindling of their traditional manual working-class base; the typical conclusion was the need to appeal to the expanding 'new middle class' by diluting or abandoning former policy commitments to generous and universal social welfare funded by high and progressive taxation and to forms of labour market intervention which offset the inegalitarian dynamics of the market. Externally, as was argued in an earlier chapter, intensified transnational competition seemed to spell the end of 'Keynesianism in one country' (Pontusson, 1992: 33). As the French discovered at the beginning of the 1980s, and the Swedes at the end of the decade, speculative fluctuations of currency markets punished national governments whose defence of the Keynesian welfare state stood out against the general adoption of neo-liberal principles of fiscal rectitude. The pressures of regime competition – which underlay the German

Standort debate of the 1990s – were intensified by European monetary union. Having endorsed the Maastricht project, European social-democratic parties and mainstream union movements alike were weakly placed to propagate a programmatic alternative to the neo-liberalism at its core. Political economism, as an overarching trade union project, had reached the end of the road.

The End of Ideology? Beyond National Identities

The discussion in this book has used three national cases to address the interface between 'moral economy' and 'political economy'. All three trade union movements have suffered intense ideological disorientation. The axes of identification established in the post-war decades have become unstable; unions seem increasingly adrift within a sea of variable geometry. One reason is that the conceptions of market, class and society which have traditionally informed trade union action have been bounded by parochial (and often idiosyncratic) national parameters. The geometry of trade union ideology and identity – the underlying *project* which gives movements their life and mission – has hitherto been cast within national political and intellectual traditions and has followed the dynamics of national industrial relations systems. Such confines intensify the current ideological *impasse*. Free collective bargaining, historic compromise, social market: none of these traditional axes of union policy retains much credibility within individual national boundaries. So demarcated, trade unions seem condemned to act as mediators of transnational economic forces, negotiating the erosion of previous achievements in the fields of social welfare and employment regulation (Mahnkopf and Altvater, 1995). Is there an alternative?

There are no easy solutions, and academic observers possess no privileged insights. Yet there are two possible elements of an answer. The ideal of social Europe – rescued from current evasive obfuscations and given concrete, intelligible meaning – could be one starting point. If national regulatory capacity, though by no means eclipsed, is increasingly constrained, the search for supranational regulation must be a major part of the trade union agenda. Though the European Union is far from constituting a supranational state, or indeed a supranational industrial relations arena, there are emergent elements of a possible industrial relations regime, if unions cross-nationally can fashion a common project and pursue it against powerful resistance from those who benefit from labour's disarray.

Second, it seems clear that part of the problem is an erosion of credible mobilizing rhetorics, of visions of a better future, of *utopias*. Building collective solidarity is in part a question of organizational capacity, but just as fundamentally it is part of a battle of ideas. The crisis of traditional trade unionism is reflected not only in the more obvious indicators of loss of strength and efficacy, but also in the exhaustion of a traditional discourse and a failure to respond to new ideological challenges. It is those whose projects are hostile to what unions stand for who have set the agenda of the past decades. Unions have to recapture the ideological initiative. To remain significant agents of social and economic mobilization, unions need new utopias, and these are unlikely to have much purchase if their focus is solely at national level.

In a world – and a Europe – marked both by differentiation and by interdependence, there is a need for a trade unionism which reflects Durkheim's alternative concept of 'organic solidarity', what has been called 'a kind of unionism that replaces organizational conformity with coordinated diversity' (Heckscher, 1988: 177). Any project aiming to create such a model must recognize and respect differentiations of circumstances and interests: within the constituencies of individual trade unions, between unions within national labour movements, between workers in different countries. The alignment and integration of diverse interests is a complex and difficult task which requires continuous processes of negotiation; real solidarity cannot be imposed by administrative fiat, or even by majority vote.

This links to the issues of strategic leadership and democratic activism. It is easy to recognize that an urgent current need is for new models of transnational solidarity and for enhanced capacity for transnational intervention. But neither can be manufactured from above. The dual challenge is to formulate more effective processes of strategic direction while sustaining and enhancing the scope for initiative and mobilization at the base, to develop *both* stronger centralized structures *and* the mechanisms for more vigorous grassroots participation: which entails new kinds of *articulation* between the various levels of union organization, representation and action.

Within the European Union, one of the more fatuous of recent rhetorical devices is the idea of 'social dialogue'. Much time and energy are spent by representatives of European labour in discussion with their counterparts on the employer side. Very exceptionally indeed this results in an agreement, couched in such general terms and with such limited content as to contain little of practical significance. Rather more frequently, discussions result in a 'joint opinion'. It may indeed be comforting (or perhaps not!) to know that union representatives can at times align their opinions with those of employers; but the effect in the real world is imperceptible. But *within* and *between* trade unions themselves, the pursuit of dialogue and the search for common opinion are vital requirements. Hence the task of European trade unions today may be encapsulated in the slogan: *develop the internal social dialogue!* Enhanced organizational capacity and solidarity demand a high level of multi-directional discussion, communication and understanding. To be effective at international level, above all else, trade unionism must draw on the experience at national level of efforts to reconstitute unions as bodies which foster interactive internal relationships and serve more as networks than as hierarchies.[1]

One problem for those seeking to create a European industrial relations system (a possible translation of that elusive term, *espace social*) is an implausible specification of the objective. Typically, a European industrial relations system is seen essentially as a transnational version of national systems. But there is little prospect of creating direct analogues of national collective bargaining and 'political exchange' cross-nationally since – as already argued – the EU is in key respects *not* a supranational state, and nor are the European 'social partners' authoritative national trade unions and employers' organizations writ large. The risk is that much energy and many resources are invested in the pursuit of elaborate form with minimal substance.

The underlying flaw in the pursuit of European-level regulation by supranational equivalents of collective bargaining or legal enactment is that such processes and the resulting instruments lack the support of the more diffuse shared perspectives and normative commitments which give them much of their effectiveness at national level. The search for a European industrial relations system has in the main been an élite project, bureaucratically conducted. Without engaging with popular concerns and aspirations, the whole elaborate repertoire of Commission communications, joint opinions, drafts and redrafts of directives and the rest is little more than a side-show with minimal relevance for the real world of work and employment. What is lacking is a moral economy at European level – beyond the traditional abstract commitment to a 'social market' on the part of both social and christian democrats, a commitment which (as seen earlier) was always ambiguous and has been increasingly undermined by the marketizing pressures of the last decades.

The goal of effective European regulation must remain a chimera unless popular commitment can be mobilized in its support. Yet to the extent that there is a dominant 'public opinion' in most European countries it is suspicious of, if not downright antagonistic to, the idea of European integration. 'Widespread citizen hostility to the process of unification is reinforced by the discourse of most political leaders presenting the European Union as the necessary adaptation to globalization, with the corollary of economic adjustment, flexibility of labor markets, and shrinkage of the welfare state' (Castells, 1998: 326). All too often, the representatives of European labour have embraced too uncritically the process of unification as marketization, unwittingly fuelling disenchantment with their own representative status.

This might be reversed if it were possible to formulate, and propagate, unambiguous standards of moral economy with an appeal across countries and languages which could inspire enthusiasm in place of alienation. How could a meaningful European moral economy be constructed? Ideas, ideals and identities typically emerge through contestation and struggle; sometimes they represent accommodations between conflicting interests, but often also the points of reference whereby oppressed majorities can challenge imperious minorities. They are both the product and the foundation of civil society, in the sense defined earlier as a sphere of social relations distinct from both state power and market dominance. At national level, unions in many countries have long derived their influence in large measure from their status as key actors within civil society; or more recently have recognized that they can sustain or recapture a significant role only by forging effective links with the other components of civil society. By contrast, the weakness of a European civil society is a major obstacle to the creation of a genuine European system of industrial relations.

Notionally, a European civil society already exists. The European Commission has declared its desire to foster a European 'civil dialogue', and provides material support for a wide variety of NGOs which can function as interlocutors (just as it subsidizes employee representation within the longer-established routines of social dialogue). But this is window-dressing. Organizations licensed from above cannot realistically be regarded as thereby representatives of popular will. Without widespread consciousness of European citizenship it is fatuous to speak of European civil society.

Yet real intimations of a European civil society are not altogether absent. To take one obvious example, the struggle from the 1960s for women's rights created a climate of opinion which formed the basis for the innovative decisions of the European Court of Justice and the interventionist policies of the Commission in the field of equal opportunities. Another instance is the outrage caused by Renault's closure of its Vilvoorde plant, reinforcing demands for an effective European employment policy. The consolidation of this emergent European civil society should be seen as an important task for trade unions and for other supporters of effective social regulation in employment. One problem is that the concept of civil society has itself been appropriated and devalued by enthusiasts of a deeply ambiguous 'third way', often to give a human face to neoliberal policy; to recapture a progressive meaning it is necessary to embrace Standing's argument (1999: 387) that 'a *network* of citizenship associations is needed to give voice to *all* those faced by insecurity'.

If trade unions are to reassert their relevance as representatives of labour and as actors at European level, there has to be a radical shift of emphasis which embraces such a concept. While engaged with the process of European integration, they must become far more vocal and forceful as opponents of the dehumanizing advance of market forces. It will be a difficult struggle, but the goal must be to construct a new embeddedness of market processes at European level and hence a new defence for the status of employees – and particularly of those most vulnerably placed within the emerging peripheral labour market. Concerned scholars have a duty to assist such a struggle, which should be at the heart of a conflict of perspectives on the meaning and future of Europe.

Note

[1] In several respects, modern information technologies offer the potential for labour movements to break out of the iron cage which for so long has trapped them in organizational structures which mimic those of capital. Intelligent use of new modes of information and communication can assist in the work of consciousness-building and representation. The invention of the networked trade union at international level has a credibility in the era of e-mail, the web page and the electronic discussion group which was inconceivable a few brief years ago. With imagination, unions may transform themselves and build an emancipatory potential for labour in the new millennium. In the 'virtual trade union' of the future, the dialectic of market, class and society may perhaps be realigned to dissolve old constraints and engender new opportunities. For a valuable discussion see Waterman, 1998.

References

Accornero, A. (1992) *La parabola del sindacato: ascesa e declino di una cultura.* Bologna: il Mulino.

Adenauer, K. (1975) *Reden 1917–1967: Eine Auswahl.* Stuttgart: Deutsche Verlagsanstalt.

Adler, A. (ed.) (1983) *Theses, Resolutions and Manifestos of the First Four Congresses of the Third International.* London: Pluto.

Allen, V.L. (1957) *Trade Union Leadership.* London: Longman.

Altvater, E. (1995) 'Economic Policy and the Role of the State: The Invisible, the Visible and the Third Hand' in M. Walzer (ed.), *Toward a Global Civil Society*, pp. 149–58. Providence: Berghahn.

Amyot, G. (1981) *The Italian Communist Party.* London: Croom Helm.

Arlt, H.-J. and Hemmer, H.O. (1993) 'Der Fall des Kollegen Franz', *Gewerkschaftliche Monatshefte,* 6'93: 330–5.

Arlt, H.-J. and Nehls, S. (eds) (1999) *Bündnis für Arbeit: Konstruktion, Kritik, Karriere.* Opladen: Westdeutscher Verlag.

Arnot, R.P. (1949) *The Miners.* London: Allen and Unwin.

Baccaro, L. and Locke, R.M. (1998) 'The End of Solidarity? The Decline of Egalitarian Wage Policies in Italy and Sweden', *European Journal of Industrial Relations*, 4 (3): 283–308.

Bagehot, W. (1963) *The English Constitution* [originally published 1867]. London: Fontana.

Baglioni, G. (1987) 'Constants and Variants in Political Exchange', *Labour*, 1: 57–94.

Bagwell, P. (1971) 'The Triple Industrial Alliance, 1913–1922' in A. Briggs and J. Saville (eds), *Essays in Labour History 1886–1923*, pp. 96–128. London: Macmillan.

Bahnmüller, R. and Bispinck, R. (1999) 'Deutschland: Ende der Bescheidenheit in Euroland?' in T. Schulten and R. Bispinck (eds), *Tarifpolitik unter dem EURO*, pp. 71–98. Hamburg: VSA-Verlag.

Bassett, P. and Cave, A. (1993) *All for One: the Future of the Unions.* London: Fabian Society.

Bealey, F. and Pelling, H. (1958) *Labour and Politics 1900–1906.* London: Macmillan.

Beck, U. (2000) 'Mehr Zivilcourage bitte', *Die Welt*, 25 May: 11.

Bedani, G. (1995) *Politics and Ideology in the Italian Workers' Movement.* Oxford: Berg.

Beetham, D. (1997) 'Market Economy and Democratic Polity', *Democratization*, 4 (1): 76–93.

Bellardi, L. and Bordogna, L. (eds) (1997) *Relazioni industriali i contrattazione aziendale.* Milan: FrancoAngeli.

Bergmann, J., Jacobi, O. and Müller-Jentsch, W. (1975) *Gewerkschaften in der Bundesrepublik.* Frankfurt: EVA.

Bernstein, E. (1961) *Evolutionary Socialism.* New York: Schocken. (Published 1899 as *Die Voraussetzungen des Sozialismus und die Aufgaben der Sozialdemokratie.* First English edition 1909.)

Bevan, A. (1952) *In Place of Fear.* London: Heinemann.

Bevin, E. (1940) Foreword to J. Price, *Labour in the War.* Harmondsworth: Penguin.

Bianchi, G. (1996) 'Between Identity and Pragmatism: Italian Trade Unionism on its Way to Europe' in P. Pasture, J. Verberckmoes and H. De Witte (eds), *The Lost*

Perspective, Vol. 1: Ideological Persistence in National Traditions, pp. 52–90. Aldershot: Avebury.

Bispinck, R. (1997) 'The Chequered History of the Alliance for Jobs' in G. Fajertag and P. Pochet (eds), *Social Pacts in Europe*, pp. 63–78. Brussels: ETUI.

Bispinck, R. (1998) 'Wage-Setting System' in R. Hoffmann, O. Jacobi, B. Keller and M. Weiss (eds), *The German Model of Industrial Relations between Adaptation and Erosion*, pp. 9–26. Düsseldorf: Hans-Böckler-Stiftung.

BMA (Bundesministerium für Arbeit und Sozialordnung) (2000) *Statistisches Taschenbuch 1999: Arbeits- und Sozialstatistik*. http://www.bma.de/download/stat1999

Booth, A.L. (1995) *The Economics of the Trade Union*. Cambridge: Cambridge UP.

Bordogna, L. (1989a) 'The COBAS Fragmentation of Trade-Union Representation' in R. Leonardi and P. Corbetta (eds), *Italian Politics: A Review, Vol. 3*, pp. 50–64.

Bordogna, L. (1989b) 'Il pubblico impiego alimenta i Cobas', *Lavoro 80*, 8: 69–73.

Bordogna, L. (1994) *Pluralismo senza mercato: Rappresentanza e conflitto nel settore publico*. Milan: Aisri/FrancoAngeli.

Borsdorf, U. (1975) 'Hans Böckler: Repräsentant eines Jahrhunderts gewerkschaftlicher Politik' in H.O. Vetter (ed.), *Vom Sozialistengesetz zur Mitbestimmung*, pp. 15–58. Cologne: Bund.

Borsdorf, U. (1982) *Hans Böckler: Arbeit und Leben eines Gewerkschafters von 1875 bis 1945*. Cologne: Bund.

Bosch, G. (1994) 'Federal Republic of Germany' in G. Bosch, P. Dawkings and F. Michon (eds), *Times Are Changing: Working Time in 14 Industrialised Countries*, pp. 127–52. Geneva: ILO.

Boyer, R. (1996) 'State and Market: A New Engagement for the Twenty-First Century?' in R. Boyer and D. Drache (eds), *States Against Markets: The Limits of Globalization*, pp. 84–114. London: Routledge.

Brandt, G., Jacobi, O. and Müller-Jentsch, W. (1982) *Anpassung an der Krise: Gewerkschaften in den siebziger Jahren*. Frankfurt: Campus.

Braunthal, J. (1967) *History of the International, 1914–1943*. London: Nelson.

Brody, D. (1991) 'Labor's Crisis in Historical Perspective' in G. Strauss, D.G. Gallagher and J. Fiorito (eds), *The State of the Unions*, pp. 277–311. Madison: IIRA.

Brose, E.D. (1985) *Christian Labor and the Politics of Frustration in Imperial Germany*. Washington: Catholic University of America Press.

Brunetta, R. and Tronti, L. (1995) 'Italy: The Social Consequences of Economic and Monetary Union', *Labour 9* (IIRA issue): S149–201.

Bullock, A. (1967) *The Life and Times of Ernest Bevin, Vol. 2: Minister of Labour*. London: Heinemann.

Burawoy, M. (1979) *Manufacturing Consent*. Chicago: University of Chicago Press.

Burgess, K. (1975) *The Origins of British Industrial Relations*. London: Croom Helm.

Byrne, P. (1997) *Social Movements in Britain*. London: Routledge.

Castells, M. (1996) *The Rise of the Network Society*. Oxford: Blackwell.

Castells, M. (1998) *End of Millennium*. Oxford: Blackwell.

Charles, R. (1973) *The Development of Industrial Relations in Britain, 1911–1939*. London: Hutchinson.

Chiarini, B. (1999) 'The Composition of Union Membership: The Role of Pensioners in Italy', *British Journal of Industrial Relations*, 37 (4): 577–600.

Citrine, W. (1939) *The ABC of Chairmanship*. London: Co-operative Printing Society.

Citrine, W. (Lord) (1964) *Men and Work*. London: Hutchinson.

Clegg, H.A. (1951) *Industrial Democracy and Nationalization*. Oxford: Blackwell.

Clegg, H.A. (1962) 'The Webbs as Historians of Trade Unionism', *Bulletin of the Society for the Study of Labour History*, 4: 8–9.

Clegg, H.A. (1979) *The Changing System of Industrial Relations in Great Britain*. Oxford: Blackwell.

Clegg, H.A. (1985) *A History of British Trade Unions Since 1889, Vol. II: 1911–1933*. Oxford: Clarendon Press.

Clegg, H.A., Fox, A. and Thompson, A.F. (1964) *A History of British Trade Unions Since 1889, Vol. I: 1889–1910*. Oxford: Clarendon Press.

Coates, K. and Topham, T. (1980) *Trade Unions in Britain*. Nottingham: Spokesman.

Coates, D. (1975) *The Labour Party and the Struggle for Socialism*. Cambridge: Cambridge UP.

Coates, R.D. (1980) *Labour in Power?* London: Longman.

Cohen, J. and Arato, A. (1992) *Civil Society and Political Theory*. Cambridge: MIT Press.

Cole, G.D.H. (1913) *The World of Labour*. London: Bell.

Cole, G.D.H. (1923) *Workshop Organization*. Oxford: Clarendon Press.

Commons, J.R. (1924) *Legal Foundations of Capitalism*. New York: Macmillan.

Courtois, F. (1991) 'The Origins of the Trade Union Question in the Communist World' in M. Waller, S. Courtois and M. Lazar (eds), *Comrades and Brothers: Communism and Trade Unions in Europe*, pp. 7–17. London: Cass.

Cox, R.W. (1987) *Production, Power and World Order*. New York: Columbia UP.

Cronin, J.E. (1984) *Labour and Society in Britain 1918–1979*. London: Batsford.

Crouch, C. (1977) *Class Conflict and the Industrial Relations Crisis*. London: Heinemann.

Crouch, C. (1993) *Industrial Relations and European State Traditions*. Oxford: Clarendon Press.

Crouch, C. and Pizzorno, A. (eds) (1978) *The Resurgence of Class Conflict in Western Europe Since 1968* (2 Volumes). London: Macmillan.

Crouch, C. and Streeck, W. (eds) (1997) *Political Economy of Modern Capitalism*. London: Sage.

Croucher, R. (1982) *Engineers at War 1939–1945*. London: Merlin.

Cully, M., Woodland, S., O'Reilly, A. and Dix, G. (1999) *Britain at Work*. London: Routledge.

Dahrendorf, R. (1965) *Gesellschaft und Demokratie in Deutschland*. Munich: Piper.

Dörre, K. (1998) 'Auf dem Weg zum desorganisierten Kapitalismus?' in B. Cattero (ed.), *Modell Deutschland – Modell Europa*, pp. 119–38. Opladen: Leske + Budrich.

Drucker, H.M. (1979) *Doctrine and Ethos in the Labour Party*. London: Allen and Unwin.

Dufour, C. (1992) 'Introduction' in IRES, *Syndicalismes: dynamique des relations professionnelles*, pp. 9–32. Paris: Dunod.

Dunlop, J.T. (1944) *Wage Determination under Trade Unions*. New York: Kelley.

Durand, C. (1971) *Conscience ouvrière et action syndicale*. Paris: Mouton.

Durkheim, E. (1933) *The Division of Labor in Society*. New York: Macmillan.

EC (European Commission) (2000) *Employment in Europe 1999*. Luxembourg: OOPEC.

Eley, G. (1990) 'Edward Thompson, Social History and Political Culture' in H.J. Kaye and K. McClelland (eds), *E.P. Thompson: Critical Perspectives*, pp. 12–49. Cambridge: Polity.

Epskamp, H., Hoffmann, J., Jacobi, O., Mückenberger, U., Oetjen, H., Schmidt, E. and Zoll, R. (1992) '"Schafft den DGB ab!"', *Gewerkschaftliche Monatshefte*, 1'92: 63–80.

Erbès-Seguin, S. (1999) 'Le contrat du travail: une relation hybride' in S. Erbès-Seguin (ed.), *Le contrat: Usages et abus d'une notion*, pp. 217–31. Paris: Desclée de Brouwer.

Fajertag, G. and Pochet, P. (eds) (1997) *Social Pacts in Europe*. Brussels: European Trade Union Institute and Observatoire social européen.

Feldman, G.D. (1975) 'Die Freien Gewerkschaften und die Zentralarbeitsgemeinschaft 1918–1924' in H.O. Vetter (ed.), *Vom Sozialistengesetz zur Mitbestimmung*, pp. 229–52. Cologne: Bund.

Ferner, A. and Hyman, R. (eds) (1992) *Industrial Relations in the New Europe*. Oxford: Blackwell.

Fezzi, M. (ed.) (1989) 'Dopo i Cobas: questioni sulla rappresentatività sindacale', *Lavoro 80*, 8.

Fichter, M. (1997) 'Trade Union Members: A Vanishing Species in Post-Unification Germany?', *German Studies Review*, 20 (1): 83–104.

Fishman, N. (1995) *The British Communist Party and the Trade Unions 1933–45*. Aldershot: Scolar.

Flanagan, R.J., Soskice, D.W. and Ulman, U. (1983) *Unionism, Economic Stabilization and Incomes Policies: European Experience*. Washington: Brookings.

Flanders, A. (1954) 'Collective Bargaining' in A. Flanders and H.A. Clegg (eds), *The System of Industrial Relations in Great Britain*, pp. 252–322. Oxford: Blackwell.

Flanders, A. (1970) *Management and Unions*. London: Faber.

Flanders, A. (1974) 'The Tradition of Voluntarism', *British Journal of Industrial Relations*, 12 (3): 352–70.

Flecker, J. and Schulten, T. (1999) 'The End of Institutional Stability: What Future for the "German Model"?', *Economic and Industrial Democracy*, 20 (1): 81–115.

Fogarty, M.P. (1957) *Christian Democracy in Western Europe 1820–1953*. London: Routledge.

Foster, J. (1974) *Class Struggle and the Industrial Revolution*. London: Weidenfeld and Nicholson.

Fox, A. (1974) *Beyond Contract: Work, Power and Trust Relations*. London: Faber.

Fox, A. (1975) 'Collective Bargaining, Flanders and the Webbs', *British Journal of Industrial Relations*, 13: 151–74.

Fox, A. (1985) *History and Heritage*. London: Allen and Unwin.

Francis, H. and Smith, D. (1980) *The Fed: A History of the South Wales Miners in the Twentieth Century*. London: Lawrence and Wishart.

Franzosi, R. (1995) *The Puzzle of Strikes: Class and State Strategies in Postwar Italy*. Cambridge: Cambridge UP.

Fraser, W.H. (1974) *Trade Unions and Society: The Struggle for Acceptance, 1850–1880*. London: Allen and Unwin.

Freeman, R.B. and Medoff, J.L. (1984) *What Do Unions Do?* New York: Basic Books.

Frege, C.M. (1999) *Social Partnership at Work: Workplace Relations in Post-Unification Germany*. London: Routledge.

Freyssinet, J. (1993) 'Syndicalismes en Europe', *Le mouvement social*, 162: 3–16.

Friot, B. (1999) 'Les enjeux actuels d'une définition contractuelle de l'emploi' in S. Erbès-Seguin (ed.), *Le contrat: Usages et abus d'une notion*, pp. 195–215. Paris: Desclée de Brouwer.

Fulcher, J. (1988) 'Labour Movements, Employers and the State in Britain and Sweden', *British Journal of Industrial Relations*, 26: 246–74.

Fulcher, J. (1991) *Labour Movements, Employers and the State*. Oxford: Clarendon.

Fürstenberg, F. (1985) 'Sozialkulturelle Aspekte der Sozialpartnerschaft' in P. Gehrlich, E. Grande and W.C. Müller (eds), *Sozialpartnerschaft in der Krise: Leistungen und Grenzen des Neokorporatismus in Österreich*, pp. 29–39. Vienna: Böhlau.

Gaugler, E. (1993) 'Sozialpartnerschaft' in G. Enderle, K. Homann, M. Honecker, W. Kerber and H. Steinmann (eds), *Lexikon der Wirtschaftsethik*, pp. 991–4. Freiburg: Herder.

Geary, D. (1981) *European Labour Protest, 1848–1939*. London: Methuen.

Geary, D. (1991) *European Labour Politics from 1900 to the Depression*. London: Macmillan.

Gellner, E. (1995) 'The Importance of Being Modular' in J.A. Hall (ed.), *Civil Society: Theory, History, Comparison*, pp. 32–55. Cambridge: Polity.

Giddens, A. (1973) *The Class Structure of the Advanced Societies*. London: Hutchinson.

Giddens, A. (1979) *Central Problems in Social Theory*. London: Macmillan.

Giddens, A. (1989) *Sociology*. Cambridge: Polity.

Giner, S. (1995) 'Civil Society and its Future' in J.A. Hall (ed.), *Civil Society: Theory, History, Comparison*, pp. 301–25. Cambridge: Polity.

Gitelman, H.M. (1965) 'Adolph Strasser and the Origins of Pure and Simple Unionism', *Labor History*, 6: 71–83.

Giugni, G. (1995) 'La caduta delle ragioni di divisione nell'esperienza sindacale e italiane', *Prospettiva sindacale*, 87: 7–19.

Golden, M. (1988) *Labor Divided: Austerity and Working-Class Politics in Contemporary Italy*. Ithaca: Cornell UP.

Golden, M. (1997) *Heroic Defeats*. Cambridge: Cambridge UP.

Goldthorpe, J. (ed.) (1984) *Order and Conflict in Contemporary Capitalism*. Oxford: Clarendon.

Gonin, M. (ed.) (1971) *La CFDT*. Paris: Seuil.

Gourevitch, P., Martin, A., Ross, G., Allen, C., Bornstein, S. and Markovits, A. (1984) *Unions and Economic Crisis: Britain, West Germany and Sweden*. London: Allen and Unwin.

Gramsci, A. (1971) *Selections from the Prison Notebooks*. London: Lawrence and Wishart.

Gramsci, A. (1977) *Selections from Political Writings 1910–20*. London: Lawrence and Wishart.

Granovetter, M. (1985) 'Economic Action and Social Structure: The Problem of Embeddedness', *American Journal of Sociology*, 91: 481–510.

Gray, J. (1998) *False Dawn: The Delusions of Global Capitalism*. London: Granta.

Gray, R. (1981) *The Aristocracy of Labour in Nineteenth-Century Britain*. London: Macmillan.

Grebing, H. (1970) *Geschichte der deutschen Arbeiterbewegung*. Munich: dtv.

Gregory, R. (1968) *The Miners and British Politics, 1906–1914*. Oxford: Oxford UP.

Groux, G. and Mouriaux, R. (1989) *La CFDT*. Paris: Economica.

Guarriello, F. (1996) 'Participation in Italian Industrial Relations' in G. Kester and H. Pinaud (eds), *Trade Unions and Democratic Participation in Europe*, pp. 87–94. Aldershot: Avebury.

Gumbrell-McCormick, R. (2000) 'Facing New Challenges: The International Confederation of Free Trade Unions (1972–1990s)' in A. Carew, M. Dreyfus, G. Van Goethem, R. Gumbrell-McCormick and M. van der Linden, *The International Confederation of Free Trade Unions*, pp. 341–517. Bern: Peter Lang.

Hall, J.A. (1995) 'In Search of Civil Society' in J.A. Hall (ed.), *Civil Society: Theory, History, Comparison*, pp. 1–31. Cambridge: Polity.

Hall, J.R. (1997) 'Introduction: The Reworking of Class Analysis' in J.R. Hall (ed.), *Reworking Class*, pp. 1–37. Ithaca: Cornell UP.

Hammerschmied, G., Jacobi, O. and Verzetnisch, F. (1997) 'Sozialpartnerschaft: Auf dem Weg zu einem sozialen Europa' in M. Juch and S. Rosenberger (eds), *Global Change: Europa – Eine Antwort auf die Globalisierung*, pp. 8–31. Vienna: Zukunfts- und Kulturwerkstätte.

Hann, C. (1996) 'Introduction: Political Society and Civil Anthropology' in C. Hann and E. Dunn (eds), *Civil Society: Challenging Western Models*, pp. 1–26. London: Routledge.

Hardman, J.B.S. (1928) *American Labor Dynamics*. New York: Harcourt, Brace.

Harrison, R. (1965) *Before the Socialists*. London: Routledge.

Hassel, A. (1999) 'The Erosion of the German System of Industrial Relations', *British Journal of Industrial Relations*, 37 (3): 483–505.

Heckscher, C.C. (1988) *The New Unionism*. New York: Basic Books.

Heery, E. (1998a) 'Campaigning for Part-Time Workers', *Work, Employment and Society*, 12 (2): 351–66.

Heery, E. (1998b) 'The Relaunch of the Trades Union Congress', *British Journal of Industrial Relations*, 36 (3): 339–60.

Hein, E. and Heise, A. (1999) 'Beschäftigungspolitische Möglichkeiten und Beschränkungen des Bündnisses für Arbeit: der fehlende "Makro-Dialog"', *WSI-Mitteilungen*, 12/1999: 825–38.

Herberg, W. (1968) 'Bureaucracy and Democracy in Labor Unions' in R.L. Rowan and H.R. Northrup (eds), *Readings in Labor Economics and Labor Relations*, pp. 237–45. Homewood: Irwin. [Originally published in *Antioch Review*, 1943.]

Hicks, J.R. (1933) *The Theory of Wages*. London: Macmillan.

Hinton, J. (1973) *The First Shop Stewards' Movement*. London: Allen and Unwin.

Hinton, J. and Hyman, R. (1975) *Trade Unions and Revolution: The Industrial Politics of the Early British Communist Party*. London: Pluto.

Hirst, P. and Thompson, G. (1996) *Globalization in Question*. Cambridge: Polity.

Hobsbawm, E.J. (1949) 'General Labour Unions in Britain, 1889–1914', *Economic History Review*, 1: 123–42.

Hobsbawm, E.J. (1964) *Labouring Men*. London: Weidenfeld and Nicholson.

Hobsbawm, E.J. (1984) *Worlds of Labour*. London: Weidenfeld and Nicholson.

Hoffmann, J., Hoffmann, R., Mückenberger, U. and Lange, D. (eds) (1990) *Jenseits der Beschlußlage: Gewerkschaft als Zukunftwerkstatt*. Düsseldorf: Hans-Böckler-Stiftung.

Homann, W. (1955) 'Die Entwicklung der Sozialpartnerschaft, dargestellt an den Wandlungen der Gewinnbeteiligung seit der Mitte des 19. Jahrhunderts'. Doctoral dissertation, Freie Universität Berlin.

Hook, S. (1961) 'Introduction' in E. Bernstein, *Evolutionary Socialism*, pp. vii–xx. New York: Schocken.

Horowitz, D.L. (1963) *The Italian Labor Movement*. Cambridge: Harvard UP.

Howell, C. (1992) *Regulating Labor: The State and Industrial Relations Reform in Postwar France*. Princeton: Princeton UP.

Hoxie, R.F. (1923) *Trade Unionism in the United States* (2nd edn). New York: Appleton.

Humphrey, A.W. (1912) *A History of Labour Representation*. London: Constable.

Hyman, R. (1971) *Marxism and the Sociology of Trade Unionism*. London: Pluto.

Hyman, R. (1985) 'Mass Organization and Militancy in Britain' in W.J. Mommsen and H.-G. Husung (eds), *The Development of Trade Unionism in Great Britain and Germany*, pp. 250–65. London: Allen and Unwin.

Hyman, R. (1987) 'Rank-and-File Movements and Workplace Organization, 1914–1939' in C. Wrigley (ed.), *A History of British Industrial Relations 1914–1939*, pp. 129–58. Brighton: Harvester.

Hyman, R. (1992) 'Trade Unions and the Disaggregation of the Working Class' in M. Regini (ed.), *The Future of Labour Movements*, pp. 150–68. London: Sage.

Hyman, R. (1993) 'Praetorians and Proletarians: Unions and Industrial Relations' in J. Fyrth (ed.), *Labour's High Noon: The Government and the Economy 1945–51*, pp. 165–94. London: Lawrence and Wishart.

Hyman, R. (1994) 'Changing Trade Union Identities and Strategies' in R. Hyman and A. Ferner (eds), *New Frontiers in European Industrial Relations*, pp. 108–39. Oxford: Blackwell.

Hyman, R. (1995) 'Changing Union Identities in Europe' in P. Leisink, J. van Leemput and J. Vilrokx (eds), *Innovation or Adaptation: Trade Unions and Industrial Relations in a Changing Europe*, pp. 53–73. Aldershot: Edward Elgar.

Hyman, R. (1996a) 'Union Identities and Ideologies in Europe' in P. Pasture, J. Verberckmoes and H. De Witte (eds), *The Lost Perspective, Vol. 2: Significance of Ideology in European Trade Unionism*, pp. 60–89. Aldershot: Avebury.

Hyman, R. (1996b) 'Institutional Transfer: Industrial Relations in Eastern Germany', *Work, Employment and Society*, 10 (4): 601–39.

Hyman, R. (1999) 'National Industrial Relations Systems and Transnational Challenges', *European Journal of Industrial Relations*, 5 (1): 89–110.

Hyman, R. and Brough, I. (1975) *Social Values and Industrial Relations*. Oxford: Blackwell.

IG Metall (1984) *Aktionsprogramm: Arbeit und Technik – 'Der Mensch muß bleiben'*. Frankfurt: IGM.

IG Metall (1991) *Tarifreform 2000: Ein Gestaltungsrahmen für die Industriearbeit der Zukunft*. Frankfurt: IGM.

Jacobi, O. (1995) 'Collective Bargaining Autonomy: The Future of Industrial Relations in Germany' in R. Hoffmann, O. Jacobi, B. Keller and M. Weiss (eds), *German Industrial Relations under the Impact of Structural Change, Unification and European Integration*, pp. 38–52. Düsseldorf: Hans-Böckler-Stiftung.

Jacobi, O., Keller, B. and Müller-Jentsch, W. (1992) 'Germany: Codetermining the Future?' in A. Ferner and R. Hyman (eds), *Industrial Relations in the New Europe*, pp. 218–69. Oxford: Blackwell.

Jacobi, O., Keller, B. and Müller-Jentsch, W. (1998) 'Germany: Facing New Challenges' in A. Ferner and R. Hyman (eds), *Changing Industrial Relations in Europe*, pp. 190–238. Oxford: Blackwell.

Jacobi, O., Schmidt, E. and Müller-Jentsch, W. (1978) 'Vorbemerkung' in O. Jacobi, E. Schmidt and W. Müller-Jentsch (eds), *Arbeiterinteressen gegen Sozialpartnerschaft: Kritisches Gewerkschaftsjahrbuch 1978/79*, pp. 7–9. Berlin: Rotbuch.

Jefferys, J.B. (ed.) (1948) *Labour's Formative Years 1848–1879*. London: Lawrence and Wishart.

Jefferys, S. (1997) 'The Exceptional Centenary of the *Confédération générale du travail*, 1895–1995', *Historical Studies in Industrial Relations*, 3: 123–41.

Jones, B. (1996) 'The Social Constitution of Labour Markets: Why Skills Cannot Be Commodities' in R. Crompton, D. Gallie and K. Purcell (eds), *Changing Forms of Employment*, pp. 109–32. London: Routledge.

Jones, J.L. (1982) 'Review of Croucher', *Marxism Today*, November: 43–4.

Kaiser, J.H. (1956) *Die Repräsentation organisierter Interessen*. Berlin: Duncker and Humblot.

Katzenstein, P.J. (1984) *Corporatism and Change*. Ithaca: Cornell UP.

Katzenstein, P.J. (1985) *Small States in World Markets*. Ithaca: Cornell UP.

Keane, J. (1988) *Civil Society and the State*. London: Verso.

Kelly, J. (1988) *Trade Unions and Socialist Politics*. London: Verso.

Kelly, J. (1998) *Rethinking Industrial Relations: Mobilization, Collectivism and Long Waves*. London: Routledge.

Kelly, J.E. and Heery, E. (1994) *Working for the Union: British Trade Union Officers*. Cambridge: Cambridge UP.

Kendall, W. (1975) *The Labour Movement in Europe*. London: Allen Lane.

Kerr, C. (1952) 'Collective Bargaining in Postwar Germany', *Industrial and Labor Relations Review*, 5: 323–42.

Kessler, S. and Bayliss, F. (1995) *Contemporary British Industrial Relations*. London: Macmillan.

Kirchlechner, B. (1978) 'New Demands or the Demands of New Groups? Three Case Studies' in C. Crouch and A. Pizzorno (eds), *The Resurgence of Class Conflict in Western Europe Since 1968, Vol. 2*, pp. 161–76. London: Macmillan.

Kjellberg, A. (1992) 'Sweden: Can the Model Survive?' in A. Ferner and R. Hyman (eds), *Industrial Relations in the New Europe*, pp. 88–142. Oxford: Blackwell.

Klein, A., Legrand, H.-J. and Leif, T. (1993) 'Die Blockademacht partikularer Interessen: Die Diskussion zur Gewerkschaftsreform stellt die Organisations- und Politikfähigkeit des DGB auf den Prüfstand' in T. Leif, A. Klein and H.-J. Legrand (eds), *Reform des DGB*, pp. 11–28. Cologne: Bund.

Korpi, W. (1978) *The Working Class in Welfare Capitalism*. London: Routledge.

Korpi, W. (1983) *The Democratic Class Struggle*. London: Routledge.

Korpi, W. and Shalev, M. (1979) 'Strikes, Industrial Relations and Class Conflict in Capitalist Societies', *British Journal of Sociology*, 30: 164–87.

Kotthoff, H. (1994) *Betriebsräte und Bürgerstatus*. Munich: Hampp.

Kowol, K. (1981) '"Neue Beweglichkeit": Für eine Ausbau dieser neuen Kampfform' in O. Jacobi, E. Schmidt and W. Müller-Jentsch (eds), *Starker Arm am kurzen Hebel: Kritisches Gewerkschaftsjahrbuch 1981/82*, pp. 150–3. Berlin: Rotbuch.

Kravaritou, Y. (1994) *European Employment and Industrial Relations Glossary: Greece*. London: Sweet and Maxwell.

Kreile, M. (1988) 'The Crisis of Italian Trade Unionism in the 1980s', *West European Politics*, 11 (1): 54–67.

Krips, G. (1958) 'Der Wandel des Verhältnisses der Sozialpartner zueinander in der Weimarer Republik und in der Gegenwart'. Doctoral dissertation, Universität Köln.

Lachs, T. (1976) *Wirtschaftspartnerschaft in Österreich*. Vienna: ÖGB.

Lang, K. (1992) 'A Drop or a Change in the Nature of Level of Mobilisation?' in K. Pumberger and W. Stützel (eds), *Strike and Structural Change: The Future of the Trade Unions' Mobilisation Capacity in Europe*, pp. 21–9. Brussels: ETUI.

Lange, P., Ross, G. and Vannicelli, M. (1982) *Unions, Change and Crisis: French and Italian Union Strategy and the Political Economy, 1945–80*. London: Allen and Unwin.

Lauzi, G. (1998) 'I sindacati confederali' in G. Baglioni, S. Negrelli and D. Paparella (eds), *Le relazioni sindacali in Italia: Rapporto 1996–97*, pp. 301–10. Rome: Edizioni Lavoro.

Leif, T., Klein, A. and Legrand, H.-J. (1993) *Reform des DGB*. Cologne: Bund.

Lenin, V.I. (1961) *Collected Works, Vol. 1*. Moscow: Foreign Languages Publishing House.

Leo XIII, Pope (1891) *Rerum Novarum*. Reprinted in S. Larson and B. Nissen (eds), *Theories of the Labor Movement*, 1987, pp. 258–68. Detroit: Wayne State UP.

Limmer, H. (1966) *Die deutsche Gewerkschaftsbewegung*. Munich: Olzog.

Locke, R.M. (1992) 'The Demise of the National Union in Italy: Lessons for Comparative Industrial Relations Theory', *Industrial and Labor Relations Review*, 45: 229–49.

Locke, R.M. and Baccaro, L. (1996) 'Learning from Past Mistakes? Recent Reforms in Italian Industrial Relations', *Industrial Relations Journal*, 27 (4): 289–303.

Locke, R.M. and Baccaro, L. (1999) 'The Resurgence of Italian Unions?' in A. Martin and G. Ross (eds), *The Brave New World of European Labor: European Trade Unions at the Millennium*, pp. 217–68. New York: Berghahn.

Locke, R.M. and Thelen, K. (1995) 'Apples and Oranges Revisited: Contextualized Comparisons and the Study of Comparative Labor Politics', *Politics and Society*, 23 (3): 337–67.

Lorwin, L.L. (1929) *Labor and Internationalism*. London: Allen and Unwin.

Lovell, J. (1977) *British Trade Unions, 1875–1933*. London: Macmillan.

Lowe, R. (1983) 'Corporate Bias: Fact or Fiction', *SSRC Newsletter*, 50: 17–18.

McAdam, D., McCarthy, J.D. and Zald, M.N. (1996) 'Introduction' in D. McAdam, J.D. McCarthy and M.N. Zald (eds), *Comparative Perspectives on Social Movements*, pp. 1–22. Cambridge: Cambridge UP.

McIlroy, J. (1995) *Trade Unions in Britain Today* (2nd edn). Manchester: Manchester UP.

McIlroy, J. (1998) 'The Enduring Alliance? Trade Unions and the Making of New Labour, 1994–1997', *British Journal of Industrial Relations*, 36 (4): 537–64.

MacShane, D. (1992) *International Labour and the Origins of the Cold War*. Oxford: Clarendon.

Mahnkopf, B. and Altvater, E. (1995) 'Trade Unions as Mediators of Transnational Economic Pressures?', *European Journal of Industrial Relations*, 1 (1): 101–17.

Mann, M. (1973) *Consciousness and Action among the Western Working Class*. London: Macmillan.

Marin, B. (1985) 'Austria – The Paradigm Case of Liberal Corporatism' in W. Grant (ed.), *The Political Economy of Corporatism*, pp. 89–125. London: Macmillan.

Markovits, A.S. (1986) *The Politics of the West German Trade Unions*. Cambridge: Cambridge UP.

Marsden, D. (1999) *A Theory of Employment Systems*. Oxford: Oxford UP.

Martin, R. (1980) *TUC: Growth of a Pressure Group*. Oxford: Clarendon.

Martínez Lucio, M. (1992) 'Spain: Constructing Institutions and Actors in a Context of Change' in A. Ferner and R. Hyman (eds), *Industrial Relations in the New Europe*, pp. 482–523. Oxford: Blackwell.

Marx, K. and Engels, F. (1975–) *Karl Marx/Frederick Engels Collected Works* (50 Volumes). London: Lawrence and Wishart. [Referenced in text as MECW with Volume number.]

Meacham, S. (1977) *A Life Apart: The English Working Class 1890–1914*. London: Thames and Hudson.

Meardi, G. (1996) 'Trade Union Consciousness, East and West: A Comparison of Fiat Factories in Poland and Italy', *European Journal of Industrial Relations*, 2 (3): 275–302.

Mershon, C.A. (1989) 'Between Workers and Union: Factory Councils in Italy', *Comparative Politics*, 21: 215–35.

Mershon, C.A. (1990) 'Relationships Among Union Actors after the Hot Autumn', *Labour*, 4: 35–58.

Metcalf, D. (1999) 'The British National Minimum Wage', *British Journal of Industrial Relations*, 37 (2): 171–201.

Middlemas, K. (1979) *Politics in Industrial Society*. London: André Deutsch.

Middlemas, K. (1980) *Power and the Party: Changing Faces of Communism in Western Europe*. London: André Deutsch.

Miliband, R. (1961) *Parliamentary Socialism*. London: Allen and Unwin.

Miller, D. (1982) 'Social Partnership and the Determinants of Workplace Independence in West Germany', *British Journal of Industrial Relations*, 20 (1): 44–66.

Miller, S. and Potthoff, H. (1986) *A History of German Social Democracy*. Oxford: Berg.

Mills, C.W. (1948) *The New Men of Power: America's Labor Leaders*. New York: Harcourt, Brace.

Milne-Bailey, W. (1934) *Trade Unions and the State*. London: Allen and Unwin.

Minkin, L. (1978) *The Labour Party Conference*. Manchester: Manchester UP.

Minkin, L. (1991) *The Contentious Alliance: Trade Unions and the Labour Party*. Edinburgh: Edinburgh UP.

Mommsen, H. (1985) 'The Free Trade Unions and Social Democracy in Imperial Germany' in W. Mommsen and H.-G. Husung (eds), *The Development of Trade Unionism in Great Britain and Germany, 1880–1914*, pp. 371–89. London: Allen and Unwin.

Moore, B. (1978) *Injustice: The Social Bases of Obedience and Revolt*. London: Macmillan.

Moorhouse, H.F. (1978) 'The Marxist Theory of the Labour Aristocracy', *Social History*, 3 (1): 61–82.

Mortimer, J. (1993) 'The Changing Mood of Working People' in J. Fyrth (ed.), *Labour's High Noon: The Government and the Economy 1945–51*, pp. 243–54. London: Lawrence and Wishart.

Moses, J.A. (1982) *Trade Unionism in Germany from Bismarck to Hitler, 1869–1933*. London: Prior.

Moses, J.A. (1990) *Trade Union Theory from Marx to Walesa*. New York: Berg.

Mouriaux, R. (1983) *Les syndicats dans la société française*. Paris: Presses de la Fondation Nationale des Sciences Politiques.

Mouriaux, R. (1985) *Syndicalisme et Politique*. Paris: éditions ouvrières.

Mühlbradt, W. and Lutz, E. (1969) *Der Zwang zur Sozialpartnerschaft*. Neuwied: Luchterhand.

Müller-Jentsch, W. (1975) 'Betriebsratwahlen 1975' in O. Jacobi, W. Müller-Jentsch and E. Schmidt (eds), *Gewerkschaften und Klassenkampf: Kritisches Jahrbuch '75*, pp. 47–50. Frankfurt: Fischer.

Müller-Jentsch, W. (1985) 'Trade Unions as Intermediary Organizations', *Economic and Industrial Democracy*, 6: 3–33.

Müller-Jentsch, W. and Sperling, H.-J. (1978) 'Economic Development, Labour Conflicts and the Industrial Relations System in West Germany' in C. Crouch and A. Pizzorno (eds), *The Resurgence of Class Conflict in Western Europe Since 1968, Vol. 1*, pp. 256–306. London: Macmillan.

Müller-Jentsch, W. and Sperling, H.-J. (1995) 'Towards a Flexible Triple System?' in R. Hoffmann, O. Jacobi, B. Keller and M. Weiss (eds), *German Industrial Relations under the Impact of Structural Change, Unification and European Integration*, pp. 9–29. Düsseldorf: Hans-Böckler-Stiftung.

Müller-Jentsch, W. and Sperling, H.-J. (1998) 'The Reorganization of Work as a Challenge for Works Councils and Trade Unions' in R. Hoffmann, O. Jacobi, B. Keller and M. Weiss (eds), *The German Model of Industrial Relations between Adaptation and Erosion*, pp. 75–95. Düsseldorf: Hans-Böckler-Stiftung.

Musson, A.E. (1955) *The Congress of 1868*. London: TUC.

Musson, A.E. (1972) *British Trade Unions, 1800–1875*. London: Macmillan.

Negrelli, S. (1991) *La società dentro l'empresa*. Milan: FrancoAngeli.

Negrelli, S. and Santi, E. (1990) 'Industrial Relations in Italy' in G. Baglioni and C. Crouch (eds), *European Industrial Relations*, pp. 154–98. London: Sage.

Nicholson, M. (1986) *The TUC Overseas: The Roots of Policy*. London: Allen and Unwin.

Nielsen, K. (1995) 'Reconceptualising Civil Society for Now: Some Somewhat Gramscian Turnings' in M. Walzer (ed.), *Toward a Global Civil Society*, pp. 41–67. Providence: Berghahn.

Niethammer, L. (1975) 'Strukturreform und Wachstumspakt' in H.O. Vetter (ed.), *Vom Sozialistengesetz zur Mitbestimmung*, pp. 303–58. Cologne: Bund.

O'Higgins, P. (1997) '"Labour Is Not a Commodity": An Irish Contribution to International Labour Law', *Industrial Law Journal*, 26: 225–34.

O'Neill, J. (1998) *The Market: Ethics, Knowledge and Politics*. London: Routledge.

Offe, C. and Wiesenthal, H. (1985) 'Two Logics of Collective Action' in C. Offe, *Disorganized Capitalism*, pp. 170–220. Cambridge: Polity.

Otto, B. (1975) *Gewerkschaftsbewegung in Deutschland*. Cologne: Bund.

Panitch, L. (1980) 'Recent Theorizations of Corporatism', *British Journal of Sociology*, 31: 161–87.

Pasture, P. (1994) *Christian Trade Unionism in Europe since 1968*. Aldershot: Avebury.

Patch, W.L. (1985) *Christian Trade Unions in the Weimar Republic, 1918–1933*. New Haven: Yale UP.

Pelling, H. (1954) *The Origins of the Labour Party*. London: Macmillan.

Pelling, H. (1961) *A Short History of the Labour Party*. London: Macmillan.

Pelling, H. (1963) *A History of British Trade Unionism*. Harmondsworth: Penguin.

Pelling, H. (1968) *Popular Politics and Society in Late Victorian England*. London: Macmillan.

Pérez-Díaz, V. (1995) 'The Possibility of Civil Society: Traditions, Character and Challenges' in J.A. Hall (ed.), *Civil Society: Theory, History, Comparison*, pp. 80–109. Cambridge: Polity.

Perlman, S. (1928) *The Theory of the Labor Movement*. New York: Macmillan.

Phelps Brown, E.H. (1965) *The Growth of British Industrial Relations*. London: Macmillan.

Pirker, T. (1960) *Die Blinde Macht: Die Gewerkschaftsbewegung in Westdeutschland*. Munich: Mercator.

Pizzorno, A. (1978) 'Political Exchange and Collective Identity' in C. Crouch and A. Pizzorno (eds) *The Resurgence of Class Conflict in Western Europe Since 1968, Vol. 2*, pp. 277–98. London: Macmillan.

Plumb, J.H. (1969) *The Death of the Past*. London: Macmillan.

Polanyi, K. (1957) *The Great Transformation*. Boston: Beacon.

Pontusson, J. (1992) 'Introduction: Organizational and Political-Economic Perspectives on Union Politics' in M. Golden and J. Pontusson (eds), *Bargaining for Change*, pp. 1–41. Ithaca: Cornell UP.

Potter, B. (1891) *The Co-operative Movement in Great Britain*. London: George Allen.

Price, J. (1940) *Labour in the War*. Harmondsworth: Penguin.

Price, R. (1980) *Masters, Unions and Men*. Cambridge: Cambridge UP.

Price, R. (1986) *Labour in British Society*. London: Croom Helm.

Ram, M. (1994) *Managing to Survive: Working Lives in Small Firms*. Oxford: Blackwell.

Regalia, I. (1984) *Eletti e abbandonati*. Bologna: il Mulino.

Regalia, I. and Regini, M. (1995) 'Between Voluntarism and Industrialization: Industrial Relations and Human Resource Practices in Italy' in R. Locke, T. Kochan and M. Piore (eds), *Employment Relations in a Changing World Economy*, pp. 131–64. Cambridge: MIT Press.

Regalia, I. and Regini, M. (1998) 'Italy: The Dual Character of Industrial Relations' in A. Ferner and R. Hyman (eds), *Changing Industrial Relations in Europe*, pp. 459–503. Oxford: Blackwell.

Regalia, I., Regini, M. and Reyneri, E. (1978) 'Labour Conflicts and Industrial Relations in Italy' in C. Crouch and A. Pizzorno (eds), *The Resurgence of Class Conflict in Western Europe Since 1968, Vol. I*, pp. 101–58. London: Macmillan.

Regini, M. (1984) 'The Conditions for Political Exchange' in J. Goldthorpe (ed.), *Order and Conflict in Contemporary Capitalism*, pp. 124–42. Oxford: Clarendon.

Regini, M. (1991) *Confini mobili*. Bologna: il Mulino.

Regini, M. (1992) 'Employers' Reactions to the Productivity Drive: The Search for Labour Consensus', *Labour*, 6: 31–47.

Regini, M. (1995) *Uncertain Boundaries*. Cambridge: Cambridge UP.

Regini, M. (1997) 'Still Engaging in Corporatism? Recent Italian Experience in Comparative Perspective', *European Journal of Industrial Relations*, 3 (3): 259–78.

Reid, A. (1978) 'Politics and Economics in the Formation of the British Working Class', *Social History*, 3 (3): 347–61.

Reynaud, J.-D. (1975) *Les syndicats en France*. Paris: Seuil.

Ridley, F.F. (1970) *Revolutionary Syndicalism in France*. Cambridge: Cambridge UP.

Roberts, B.C. (1958) *The Trades Union Congress*. London: Allen and Unwin.

Rogers, J. (1995) 'A Strategy for Labour', *Industrial Relations*, 34 (3): 367–81.

Romagnoli, G. (1989) 'Il sindacato' in G.P. Cella and T. Treu (eds), *Relazioni industriali*, pp. 85–134. Bologna: il Mulino.

Romero, F. (1992) *The United States and the European Trade Union Movement, 1944–1951*. Chapel Hill: University of North Carolina Press.

Ross, G. and Martin, A. (1999) 'Through a Glass Darkly' in A. Martin and G. Ross (eds), *The Brave New World of European Labor: European Trade Unions at the Millennium*, pp. 368–99. New York: Berghahn.

Rothstein, B. (1990) 'Marxism, Institutional Analysis and Working-Class Power', *Politics and Society*, 18: 317–45.

Sabbatini, C. (1992) 'The Strike: Its Changing Functions against an Evolving Background' in K. Pumberger and W. Stützel (eds), *Strike and Structural Change: The Future of the Trade Unions' Mobilisation Capacity in Europe*, pp. 17–22. Brussels: ETUI.

Santi, E. (1988) 'Ten Years of Unionization in Italy (1977–1986)', *Labour*, 2 (1): 153–82.

Savage, M. and Miles, A. (1994) *The Remaking of the British Working Class 1840–1940*. London: Routledge.

Saville, J. (1960) 'Unions and Free Labour' in A. Briggs and J. Saville (eds), *Essays in Labour History*, pp. 317–50. London: Macmillan.

Saville, J. (1973) 'The Ideology of Labourism' in R. Benewick, R.N. Berki and B. Parekh, *Knowledge and Belief in Politics*, pp. 213–26. London: Allen and Unwin.

Saville, J. (1988) *The Labour Movement in Britain*. London: Faber.

Sayer, A. (1995) *Radical Political Economy: A Critique*. Oxford: Blackwell.

Sayer, A. and Walker, R. (1992) *The New Social Economy: Reworking the Division of Labour*. Oxford: Blackwell.

Schauer, H. (1994) 'Die Industriegewerkschaft und was dann?' in K. Benz-Overhage, W. Jüttner and H. Peter (eds), *Zwischen Rätesozialismus und Reformprojekt*, pp. 117–27. Cologne: spw-Verlag.

Schauer, H., Dabrowski, H., Neumann, U. and Sperling, H.-J. (1984) *Tarifvertrag zur Verbesserung industrieller Arbeitsbedingungen: Arbeitspolitik am Beispiel des Lohnrahmentarifvertrags II*. Frankfurt: Campus.

Schmidt, E. (1971) *Ordnungsfaktor oder Gegenmacht: Die politische Rolle der Gewerkschaften*. Frankfurt: Suhrkamp.

Schmidt, E. (1973) 'Betriebsratwahlen 1972' in O. Jacobi, W. Müller-Jentsch and E. Schmidt (eds), *Gewerkschaften und Klassenkampf: Kritisches Jahrbuch '73*, pp. 43–5. Frankfurt: Fischer.

Schmidt, R. (1998) 'The Transformation of Industrial Relations in Eastern Germany' in R. Hoffmann, O. Jacobi, B. Keller and M. Weiss (eds), *The German Model of Industrial Relations between Adaptation and Erosion*, pp. 51–60. Düsseldorf: Hans-Böckler-Stiftung.

Schmidt, W. (1985) *Sozialer Frieden und Sozialpartnerschaft*. Frankfurt: Lang.

Schneider, M. (1985) 'The Christian Trade Unions and Strike Activity' in W.J. Mommsen and H.-G. Husung (eds), *The Development of Trade Unionism in Great Britain and Germany*, pp. 283–301. London: Allen and Unwin.

Schneider, M. (1989) *Kleine Geschichte der Gewerkschaften*. Bonn: Dietz.

Schumann, M. (1971) *Am Beispiel der Septemberstreiks: Anfang der Rekonstruktionsperiode der Arbeiterklasse?* Frankfurt: EVA.

Schuster, D. (1974) *Die deutschen Gewerkschaften seit 1945*. Stuttgart: Kohlhammer.

Scott, A. (1990) *Ideology and the New Social Movements*. London: Routledge.

Shaw, M. (1994) 'Civil Society and Global Politics', *Millennium*, 23 (3): 647–67.

Silvia, S.J. (1999) 'Every Which Way but Loose: German Industrial Relations Since 1980' in A. Martin and G. Ross (eds), *The Brave New World of European Labor: European Trade Unions at the Millennium*, pp. 75–124. New York: Berghahn.

Sinzheimer, H. (1916) *Ein Arbeitstarifgesetz. Die Idee der sozialen Selbstbestimmung im Recht*. Munich: Duncker und Humblot.

Skrzypczak, H. (1975) 'Zur Strategie der Freien Gewerkschaften in der Weimarer Republik' in H.O. Vetter (ed.), *Vom Sozialistengesetz zur Mitbestimmung*, pp. 201–27. Cologne: Bund.

Smith, M. (1999) 'The Convergence/Divergence Debate in Comparative Industrial Relations' in M. Rigby, R. Smith and T. Lawlor (eds), *European Trade Unions: Change and Response*, pp. 1–17. London: Routledge.

Smith, M.P. (1998) 'Facing the Market: Institutions, Strategies and the Fate of Organized Labor in Germany and Britain', *Politics and Society*, 26 (1): 35–67.

Somaini, E. (1989) 'Politica salariale e politica economica' in G.P. Cella and T. Treu (eds), *Relazioni industriali*, pp. 307–44. Bologna: il Mulino.

Spiro, H.J. (1958) *The Politics of German Codetermination*. Cambridge: Harvard UP.

Standing, G. (1997) 'Globalization, Labour Flexibility and Insecurity', *European Journal of Industrial Relations*, 3 (1): 5–37.

Standing, G. (1999) *Global Labour Flexibility: Seeking Distributive Justice*. London: Macmillan.

Stedman Jones, G. (1983) *Languages of Class*. Cambridge: Cambridge UP.

Steenson, G.P. (1991) *After Marx, Before Lenin*. Pittsburgh: University of Pittsburgh Press.

Stelluti, C., De Bortoli, F., Cofferati, S., D'Antoni, S., Larizza, P. and Fassino, P. (1995) 'Tavola rotonda', *Prospettiva sindacale*, 87: 95–130.

Stourzh, G. (1986) 'Zur Institutionengeschichte der Arbeitsbeziehungen und der sozialen Sicherung' in G. Stourzh and M. Grandner (eds), *Historische Wurzeln der Sozialpartnerschaft*, pp. 13–37. Munich: Oldenbourg.

Streeck, W. (1984a) 'Guaranteed Employment, Flexible Manpower Use, and Cooperative Manpower Management' in T. Shigeyoshi and J. Bergmann (eds), *Industrial Relations in Transition*, pp. 81–116. Tokyo: Tokyo UP.

Streeck, W. (1984b) 'Neo-Corporatist Industrial Relations and the Economic Crisis in West Germany' in J.H. Goldthorpe (ed.), *Order and Conflict in Contemporary Capitalism*, pp. 291–314. Oxford: Clarendon.

Streeck, W. (1988) 'Industrial Relations in West Germany, 1980–1987', *Labour*, 2 (3): 3–44.

Streeck, W. (1991) 'More Uncertainties: German Unions Facing 1992', *Industrial Relations*, 30 (3): 317–49.

Streeck, W. (1992) *Social Institutions and Economic Performance*. London: Sage.

Streeck, W. (1994) 'Pay Restraint Without Incomes Policy: Institutionalized Monetarism and Industrial Unionism in Germany' in R. Dore (ed.), *Return to Incomes Policy?*, pp. 118–40. London: Pinter.

Streeck, W. (1997) 'German Capitalism: Does It Exist? Can It Survive?' in C. Crouch and W. Streeck (eds), *Political Economy of Modern Capitalism*, pp. 33–54. London: Sage.

Streeck, W. and Heinze, R.G. (1999) 'Runderneuerung des deutschen Modells: Aufbruch für mehr Jobs' in H.-J. Arlt and S. Nehls (eds), *Bündnis für Arbeit: Konstruktion, Kritik, Karriere*, pp. 147–66. Opladen: Westdeutscher Verlag.

Streeck, W. and Visser, J. (1997) 'The Rise of the Conglomerate Union', *European Journal of Industrial Relations*, 3 (3): 305–32.

Sturmthal, A. (1964) *Workers' Councils*. Cambridge: Harvard UP.

Swenson, P. (1989) *Fair Shares: Unions, Pay and Politics in Sweden and West Germany*. Ithaca: Cornell UP.

Tálos, E. (1982) 'Sozialpartnerschaft und Neokorporatismustheorien', *Österreichische Zeitschrift für Politikwissenschaft und Neokorporatismustheorie*, 11 (3): 263–87.

Tálos, E. (1985) 'Sozialpartnerschaft: Zur Entwicklung und Entwicklungsdynamik kooperativ-konzertieter Politik in Österreich' in P. Gehrlich, E. Grande and W.C. Müller (eds), *Sozialpartnerschaft in der Krise: Leistungen und Grenzen des Neokorporatismus in Österreich*, pp. 41–83. Vienna: Böhlau.

Tálos, E. (1993) 'Entwicklung, Kontinuität und Wandel der Sozialpartnerschaft' in E. Tálos (ed.), *Sozialpartnerschaft*, pp. 11–34. Vienna: Verlag für Gesellschaftskritik.

Tarrow, S. (1998) *Power in Movement* (2nd edn). Cambridge: Cambridge UP.

Tawney, R.H. (1921) *The Acquisitive Society*. London: Bell.

Taylor, R. (1978) *The Fifth Estate: Britain's Unions in the Seventies*. London: Routledge.

Thelen, K.A. (1991) *Union of Parts: Labor Politics in Postwar Germany*. Ithaca: Cornell UP.

Therborn, G. (1992) 'Lessons from "Corporatist" Theorizations' in J. Pekkarinen, M. Pohjola and B. Rowthorn (eds), *Social Corporatism: A Superior Economic System?*, pp. 24–43. Oxford: Clarendon Press.

Thompson, E.P. (1965) 'The Peculiarities of the English', *Socialist Register, 1965*, 311–62.

Thompson, E.P. (1968) *The Making of the English Working Class*. Harmondsworth: Penguin.

Thompson, E.P. (1971) 'The Moral Economy of the English Crowd in the Eighteenth Century', *Past and Present*, 50: 76–136.

Thompson, E.P. (1978) *The Poverty of Theory and Other Essays*. London: Merlin.

Thomson, A.W.J. (1979) 'Trade Unions and the Corporate State in Britain', *Industrial and Labor Relations Review*, 33 (1): 36–54.

Touraine, A. (1966) *La conscience ouvrière*. Paris: Seuil.

Touraine, A. (1977a) *La société invisible*. Paris: Seuil.

Touraine, A. (1977b) *The Self-Production of Society*. Chicago: University of Chicago Press.

Touraine, A., Wieviorka, M. and Dubet, F. (1987) *The Workers' Movement*. Cambridge: Cambridge UP.

Traxler, F. (1982) *Evolution gewerkschaftlicher Interessenvertretung*. Vienna: Braumüller.

Traxler, F. (1992) 'Austria: Still the Country of Corporatism' in A. Ferner and R. Hyman (eds), *Industrial Relations in the New Europe*, pp. 270–97. Oxford: Blackwell.

Trentin, B. (1977) 'Sindacato, organizzazione e conscienza di classe' in A. Accornero, A. Pizzorno, B. Trentin and M. Tronti (eds), *Movimento sindacale e società italiana*, pp. 213–36. Milan: Feltrinelli.

Trentin, B. (1993) 'Unità e credibilità', *Nuova rassegna sindacale*, 26: 4–6.

TUC (1994) *Representation at Work*. London: TUC.

TUC (1995) *Your Voice at Work*. London: TUC.

TUC (1997) *Partners for Progress*. London: TUC.

Tuchtfeldt, E. (1992) 'Sozialpartnerschaft' in E. Gaugler and W. Weber (eds), *Handwörterbuch des Personalwesens*, pp. 2080–9. Stuttgart: Poeschel.

Turner, H.A. (1962) *Trade Union Growth, Structure and Policy*. London: Allen and Unwin.

Turner, H.A., Clack, G. and Roberts, G. (1967) *Labour Relations in the Motor Industry*. London: Allen and Unwin.

Turner, L. (1991) *Democracy at Work*. Ithaca: Cornell UP.

Turner, L. (1998) *Fighting for Partnership*. Ithaca: Cornell UP.

Turner, L. (1999) 'Review of Kelly', *British Journal of Industrial Relations*, 37 (3): 507–9.

Undy, R., Ellis, V., McCarthy, W.E.J. and Halmos, A.M. (1981) *Change in Trade Unions*. London: Hutchinson.

van Kersbergen, K. (1995) *Social Capitalism: A Study of Christian Democracy and the Welfare State*. London: Routledge.

von Nell-Breuning, O. (1964) 'Partnerschaft' in H. Thyen and W. Scheuten (eds), *Handwörterbuch der Sozialwissenschaften, Vol. 8*, pp. 216–23. Stuttgart: Fischer.

Waddington, J. and Whitston, C. (1997) 'Why Do People Join Unions in a Period of Membership Decline?', *British Journal of Industrial Relations*, 35 (4): 515–46.

Wallich, H.C. (1955) *Mainsprings of the German Revival*. New Haven: Yale UP.

Wallraff (1975) 'Die Belastung einer Gewerkschaft durch ideologische Differenzen: Spannungen innerhalb der christlichen Gewerkschaftsbewegungen in den Jahren 1900–1914' in H.O. Vetter (ed.), *Vom Sozialistengesetz zur Mitbestimmung*, pp. 135–52. Cologne: Bund.

Walzer, M. (1995) 'The Civil Society Argument' in R. Beiner (ed.), *Theorizing Citizenship*, pp. 153–73. Albany: SUNY Press.

Waterman, P. (1998) *Globalization, Social Movements and the New Internationalisms*. London: Mansell.

Webb, S. and Webb, B. (1894) *The History of Trade Unionism*. London: Longman.

Webb, S. and Webb, B. (1897) *Industrial Democracy*. London: Longman.

Webber, D. (1997) 'The Second Coming of the Bonn Republic' in L. Turner (ed.), *Negotiating the New Germany*, pp. 227–53. Ithaca: ILR Press.

Weber, M. (1968) *Economy and Society*. New York: Bedminster.

Weekes, B., Mellish, M., Dickens, L. and Lloyd, J. (1975) *Industrial Relations and the Limits of Law*. Oxford: Blackwell.

Weiler, P. (1993) *Ernest Bevin*. Manchester: Manchester UP.

Wever, K.S. (1995) *Negotiating Competitiveness: Employment Relations and Organizational Innovation in Germany and the United States*. Boston: Harvard Business School Press.

White, J.L. (1978) *The Limits of Trade Union Militancy*. Westport: Greenwood.

Windolf, P. (1989) 'Productivity Coalitions and the Future of European Corporatism', *Industrial Relations*, 28: 1–20.

Wright, E.O. (1997) 'Rethinking, Once Again, the Concept of Class Structure' in J.R. Hall (ed.), *Reworking Class*, pp. 41–72. Ithaca: Cornell UP.

Zoll, R. (1976) *Der Doppelcharakter der Gewerkschaften*. Frankfurt: Suhrkamp.

Zweig, F. (1952) *The British Worker*. Harmondsworth: Penguin.

Zwickel, K. (1993) 'Den Bund erneuern', *Gewerkschaftliche Monatshefte*, 12'93: 726–39.

Zwickel, K. (1999) 'Ein Jahr Rot-Grün: Kein Grund zum Jubel', *Metall*, 51 (9): 6.

Zwickel, K. (2000) 'Machtfragen', *Mitbestimmung*, 1 + 2/2000: 31–3.

Index